IMPEACHMENT

WHAT EVERYONE NEEDS TO KNOW®

IMPEACHMENT

WHAT EVERYONE NEEDS TO KNOW®

MICHAEL J. GERHARDT

OXFORD
UNIVERSITY PRESS

OXFORD
UNIVERSITY PRESS

Oxford University Press is a department of the University of Oxford. It furthers
the University's objective of excellence in research, scholarship, and education
by publishing worldwide. Oxford is a registered trade mark of Oxford University
Press in the UK and certain other countries.

"What Everyone Needs to Know" is a registered trademark of Oxford
University Press.

Published in the United States of America by Oxford University Press
198 Madison Avenue, New York, NY 10016, United States of America.

© Oxford University Press 2018

Library of Congress Cataloging-in-Publication Data
Names: Gerhardt, Michael J., 1956–, author.
Title: Impeachment : what everyone needs to know / Michael J. Gerhardt.
Description: New York : Oxford University Press, 2018. |
Series: What Everyone Needs to Know |
Includes bibliographical references and index.
Identifiers: LCCN 2018013560 (print) | LCCN 2018013641 (ebook) |
ISBN 9780190903671 (updf) | ISBN 9780190903688 (epub) |
ISBN 9780190903657 (pbk. : alk. paper) |
ISBN 9780190903664 (hardback : alk. paper)
Subjects: LCSH: Impeachments—United States | Presidents—United States.
Classification: LCC KF5075 (ebook) | LCC KF5075 .G47 2018 (print) |
DDC 342.73/068—dc23
LC record available at https://lccn.loc.gov/2018013560

1 3 5 7 9 8 6 4 2
Paperback printed by LSC Communications, United States of America
Hardback printed by Bridgeport National Bindery, Inc., United States of America

*To my beautiful family, who make every moment
of the journey wonderful*

CONTENTS

4. Defining Impeachable Offenses   59

5. Explaining the Procedures in Impeachment   73

7. Impeachment in the States and around the World   125

8. Will Donald Trump Be Impeached?   145

ACKNOWLEDGMENTS

I owe the idea of this book to Nancy Toff at Oxford University Press. Without her determination, interest, and confidence, this book never would have happened. I appreciate her encouragement and support throughout the writing and preparation of this book. Elizabeth Vaziri at Oxford University Press was instrumental and indispensable in bringing this book to fruition. I am grateful to Alphonsa James and her team for their help throughout the production. And I cannot thank Haily Wren Klabo, Class of 2019 at the University of North Carolina Law School, enough for her indefatigable research assistance.

This book draws on my study, research, writing, and advising regarding impeachment for more than thirty years, beginning with my article "The Constitutional Limits to Impeachment and Its Alternatives," 68 Texas Law Review 1 (1989), and including my book, *The Federal Impeachment Process: A Constitutional and Historical Analysis* (University of Chicago Press, 3rd edition, 2018). Portions of the material in *The Federal Impeachment Process: A Constitutional and Historical Analysis* have been reproduced with the permission of the University of Chicago Press.

IMPEACHMENT

WHAT EVERYONE NEEDS TO KNOW®

INTRODUCTION

Donald Trump's presidency has brought the nation back to familiar constitutional territory: talk of impeachment, this time based on a wide range of alleged misconduct, including possible financial conflicts of interest,[1] his presidential campaign's possible collusion with the Russian government to influence the 2016 presidential election,[2] obstruction of justice,[3] threatening freedom of the press,[4] encouraging the harassment or prosecution of political enemies,[5] and degrading the presidency,[6] just to name a few of the charges made against him. It is tempting to write this talk off as simply partisan hyperbole, and, to be sure, much of it is. But talk of presidential impeachment is not new; the threat of impeachment has been leveled against many presidents, and now, as has often been the case in the past, conversations about impeachment largely reflect misunderstandings of how the Constitution works in this area.[7]

The first, and perhaps most important, thing that everyone needs to know about impeachment is that there is a lot to learn. The purpose of this book is to provide that education. My hope is that this book will be a sound, thorough explication of the subject of impeachment. This book is not a how-to manual for getting rid of President Trump—or any other president one may dislike. It is not a brief for those already hell-bent on using impeachment to undo the results of a presidential election that did not go their way. Rather, this book is for those who are genuinely interested in learning the fundamental aspects of impeachment and the ongoing challenges in its usage as a principal mechanism for checking the misconduct of presidents, judges, cabinet officers, and certain other high-ranking officials.

The framers of the Constitution anticipated that efforts to impeach might be driven by partisan rage. So, the framers created a carefully calibrated process that has several built-in safeguards against the intemperate urge to abuse the only constitutional mechanism that they had devised for cutting a president's or Supreme Court justice's tenure short. Impeachment is a last resort for holding high-ranking officials accountable for serious misconduct when other mechanisms fail or are not available. The leaders who are subject to impeachment may be held accountable in many other ways: elections in the case of presidents; dismissals in the case of cabinet officials or other high-ranking political appointees; forced resignations, particularly for political appointees, in the case of embarrassing mistakes; congressional oversight; or, in the worst case imaginable for political retribution, assassination. History is replete with examples of these different mechanisms.

For instance, President Andrew Jackson was threatened with impeachment more than once[8] and the Senate eventually censured him for illegally removing funds from the National Bank in an effort to destroy it,[9] a censure that Jackson was later able to get the Senate to expunge.[10] President John Tyler faced threats of impeachment in the House; none was successful, but they all challenged his assertions of presidential prerogatives such as the veto. Andrew Johnson was the first president to be formally impeached—for his refusal to abide by or adhere to Congress's Reconstruction policy—and he fell a single vote short of being convicted and removed from office for that defiance.[11] In the modern era, the forced resignation of Richard Nixon in 1974 was the beginning of a national obsession with impeachment.[12] Soon after Nixon's resignation, President Gerald R. Ford was threatened with retaliation for his pardon of Nixon;[13] President Reagan faced calls for impeachment due to the so-called Iran-Contra affair;[14] Bill Clinton faced impeachment threats throughout most of his presidency,[15] culminating in his actual impeachment by the House of Representatives for obstruction of justice and perjury;[16] George W. Bush was threatened with impeachment based on his misstatements about the presence of weapons of mass destruction in Iran justifying the invasion of that country in a preemptive strike;[17] President Obama faced repeated objections to his alleged lawlessness in office;[18] and impeachment threats began against President Donald Trump well before his election in 2016 and inauguration the following January.[19] Some charges against President Trump are unusual if not unique, given his extensive business ties, which have not (yet) been disclosed fully to the American people or Congress;[20] however, many claims against the president attempt to liken his alleged misconduct to that of Richard Nixon.[21] Yet, many Democrats appear all too eager to find fault with him while many Republicans appear all too eager to dismiss charges of possible misconduct for the sake of pursuing other business.[22]

Consider this book, not just for the present, but for any other time in our future, as the deep breath, the really deep breath, that we all need when there is persistent talk of impeachment and the partisan rage risks getting the best of us. We need an authoritative, evenhanded effort to explain the law of impeachment, and I hope that this book will fulfill that ambitious objective. Its purpose is to provide a firm understanding of the unique federal process set forth in the US Constitution for impeaching and removing not just a president of the United States but also the vice president and "all Civil Officers of the United States," including Supreme Court justices and all other federal judges.

Impeachment is serious business. In his landmark study of the American Constitution, Lord James Bryce observed that impeachment is "like a hundred-ton gun which needs complex machinery to bring it into position; an enormous charge of powder to fire it; and a large mark to aim at."[23] The observation remains apt, and impeachment is complicated by its relationship to many other features of our constitutional system. For example, presidential impeachment is directed at serious misconduct in office, but impeachment is not an appropriate mechanism to deploy for misconduct that falls short of the constitutional standard for impeachment or for physical or mental deterioration that disables presidents from doing their jobs. The Twenty-fifth Amendment is designed to deal with presidential incapacity. Members of Congress, scholars, and pundits disagree about the extent to which mechanisms other than impeachment, such as a censure resolution approved by the House of Representatives or the Senate criticizing the president or allowing sitting presidents to be criminally prosecuted, are constitutionally permissible.

People can disagree, however, about fundamental aspects of the impeachment process. For example, they can disagree about whether impeachment actually keeps presidents in check. Some people consider the fact that the only two presidents who have had to go through the entire process were not removed from office (both Presidents Johnson and Clinton were acquitted) as demonstrating that the system worked precisely as desired, with the arduous requirements for conviction and removal moderating against the partisan rage against each of them. In their view, the system worked again when Nixon resigned after he was confronted with the credible threat of impeachment, conviction, and removal. Yet, there are others who might argue that the system failed in the cases of Johnson and Clinton and that Nixon's resignation might merely show how forcing a president to resign is more effective as a strategy than making recourse to the cumbersome process of impeachment.

Another basic question has to do with the differences in presidents' and judges' tenure and duties. This has come up because the only officials who have actually been convicted and removed from office are federal judges. This pattern leads many members of Congress and scholars to ask whether the impeachment trials and the Senate's convictions and removals of those judges are pertinent to presidential impeachments—that is, how relevant are those precedents to the impeachments of presidents? As this book will show, this is a deceptively difficult question to answer.

For one thing, judges and presidents have vastly different duties, and therefore they can abuse their powers in different ways. Moreover, the attributes needed to do their respective jobs are different; integrity and temperament are indispensable for judges to do their jobs, but are they indispensable for presidents? Some people might think they are not; they may think that other strengths may overcome deficiencies in these areas. Their tenures are also different, with judges appointed for life (as a way to protect them from political retaliation) and presidents elected for one or two terms. Presidents might be selected in spite of the public's awareness of their weaknesses, or the public might ratify their past misconduct, whereas certain weaknesses (e.g., performing poorly in law school or repeatedly failing the bar) or misconduct (e.g., having a criminal record) might be more disqualifying for judges than presidents. Understanding these differences will be helpful for understanding impeachment more generally.

In its effort to be comprehensive, the book deals with these and many other perennially challenging questions about impeachment.

It delves deeply into the history and practice of impeachment, not just at the federal level but also at the state level in this country and in other nations around the world.

The book begins with the basic procedures set forth for impeachment in the Constitution, followed by a close examination of the basic terms and concepts employed in the application and analysis of impeachment, the origins of impeachment in this country, how Congress has exercised this authority over the years, and a thorough examination of the many questions that have arisen over the course of the American experience with impeachment. While the material might sometimes seem technical, it will illuminate impeachment in all its complexity.

Making sense of impeachment requires constitutional interpretation. The Constitution is rarely self-defining. Interpreting the Constitution requires coordinating several different sources of constitutional meaning. These include the plain meaning of the text, the original meaning of the disputed language or terms, how the Congress has understood and exercised its powers in this area (known as historical practices), the likely consequences of different constructions of the Constitution, the basic design or structure of the Constitution, moral reasoning, and the distinctiveness of national identity. As with everything else in constitutional law, the answer to the big questions that come up in this field, such as what grounds people may be impeached for, turns on which sources people consult and how they construe or coordinate them.

Usually, we expect courts to do the hard work of constitutional interpretation. But, in the context of impeachment, the critical decision-making is done by members of Congress, not by courts, and therefore by political authorities whose command of constitutional law and commitment to principled construction of the Constitution are perennially questioned. Indeed, public approval of, if not confidence in, Congress is often poor, though that might not matter much if the public's approval of, or confidence in, a president is even lower. Faithful readers will have to consider whether Congress is up to the task that the framers gave it.

Chapter 1

THE BASIC TERMS

What does the term "impeachment" mean?

At least as a concept, if not in practice, impeachment has been around for a long time. The word itself derives from a Latin root used to refer to being caught or entrapped.[1] The dictionary definition is that impeachment is the process by which a legislative body formally charges a high-ranking official with misconduct.

The term is also used to refer, as a shorthand, to the overall process set forth in the Constitution for handling the misconduct of certain high-ranking officials, including the president. Sometimes, commentators or members of Congress might use the phrase "the impeachment process" or "the removal process" instead of "impeachment" to refer to the general scheme set forth in the Constitution for Congress to address the misconduct of certain officials. More often than not, when people employ the term "impeachment," they are referring to this general usage.

But there is another meaning of the term "impeachment." This is the technical meaning of the term. Impeachment could refer, depending on the context, to the particular power that the House of Representatives has to formally charge certain federal officials, including presidents, with the kind of misconduct for which they could be ultimately convicted in the Senate and removed from office.[2] It is always important to pay attention to the context to ascertain which of these meanings the speaker or writer might be intending to express.

What does the Constitution explicitly say about the impeachment process?

The Constitution has five provisions that explicitly set forth the phases and grounds for impeachment and the range of officials who may be subject to the impeachment process. These provisions are sometimes referred to as the impeachment clauses.[3]

First, Article I provides in pertinent part that "The House of Representatives shall . . . have the sole power of Impeachment."[4] While this provision clearly vests the House with the authority to impeach, the term "impeachment" is not defined in the Constitution. Moreover, this provision says nothing about how the House should conceive of its role in exercising this power. Nor does this clause say anything about the procedures, burden of proof, or rules of evidence that should apply in the House's impeachment proceedings.

Article I further provides that "The Senate shall have the sole Power to try all Impeachments. When sitting for that purpose, they shall be on Oath or Affirmation. When the President of the United States is tried, the Chief Justice shall preside: And no Person shall be convicted without the Concurrence of two thirds of the members present."[5]

The Constitution does not define the word "try" (indeed, it comes without a glossary or framer-approved annotation), leaving many people to wonder what the Senate must do, if anything, when it sets about to "try" an impeachment.[6] For example, they wonder whether it must provide a trial similar or perhaps identical to the kind employed in civil or criminal proceedings. Moreover, this clause does not specify what precisely happens upon conviction, leaving some scholars to wonder whether the sanctions that follow upon conviction—removal and disqualification—immediately go into effect or whether another vote must be taken prior to imposing one or both of them.[7]

In the very next clause of Article I, Section 3, the Constitution provides that "Judgment in Cases of Impeachment shall not extend further than to removal from Office, and disqualification to hold and enjoy any Office of honor, Trust or Profit under the United States: but the Party convicted shall nevertheless be liable and subject to Indictment, Trial, Judgment and Punishment, according to Law."[8]

This clause raises some serious questions. While it specifies that "removal" and "disqualification" are sanctions following upon conviction, it does not specify whether these sanctions automatically apply upon a conviction or whether separate votes must be taken in the Senate on one or both sanctions (and, if so, whether a simple majority or a supermajority of at least two-thirds is required for approval of one or both sanctions). In suggesting that the "Judgment" in an impeachment trial "shall not extend further than" to either of the specific sanctions mentioned, this clause raises the possible inference that the Senate might be able to impose a sanction that falls short of either of these. Moreover, this clause makes clear that impeachment does not preclude subsequent punishment in a court of law. It is less clear, however, whether it allows or requires impeachment to precede a criminal or civil trial for the same underlying misconduct, or whether the clause is merely clarifying that impeachment and legal proceedings are not mutually exclusive.

In yet another constitutional provision pertaining to impeachment, Article II expressly provides, among other things, that the President "shall have Power to grant Reprieves and Pardons for Offenses against the United States, except in cases of Impeachment."[9] This clause obviously makes clear that the pardon power does not extend to the impeachment process. Yet it does not clarify whether a president may pardon himself or whether such a pardon might provide a basis for impeachment, conviction, and removal.

What does the Constitution implicitly say about impeachment?

There are several constitutional provisions that relate to impeachment implicitly or indirectly. There have been ongoing disagreements about how or in what ways these various clauses relate, if at all, to the impeachment process. For example, Article III of the Constitution provides that "Judges, both of the supreme and Inferior Courts shall hold their Offices during good Behavior, and, shall, at stated Times, receive for their services a Compensation, which shall not be diminished during their Continuance in Office."[10] Although it is plainly the purpose of this clause to set out the terms governing the tenure of Article III judges, the clause is not self-defining. It does not make clear whether "during good Behavior" merely defines the tenure for judges or further provides a basis for any form of discipline for misconduct in office other than, or in addition to, impeachment. Put differently, there is uncertainty about what defines the bad "behavior" for which a federal judge may lose his position. Is it solely the grounds set forth in the Constitution for impeachment and removal, namely, "Treason, Bribery, or other high Crimes and Misdemeanors"? Or does it also include misbehavior falling short of those misdeeds but which, nonetheless, deviates from the "good behavior" that Article III judges must have to retain their positions? And, if there is bad behavior for which judges may be removed from office, by what procedures may those judges be dismissed from office? In addition, it is unclear whether the tenure for Article III judges may be subject to congressional regulation, that is, whether Congress may enact a statute that defines the "good Behavior" required for tenure as a federal judge, or establishes other conditions on judicial tenure, such as age limit or years of service.

The Fifth Amendment mandates to the federal government that no one shall "be deprived of life, liberty, or property without due process of law."[11] This language raises the question of whether impeachment proceedings (including trials) must comply with "due process of law." But, whether this clause applies to the impeachment process depends in part on whether an impeachable official's position qualifies as "property" or "liberty" for purposes of the due process clause. If an impeachable official's office does not count as a protected "liberty" or "property" interest that is presumably protected by that clause, then the clause's applicability to the impeachment context is settled. That question would also be settled if it turns out that the original meaning of the Fifth Amendment does not support its application to the impeachment process. But, if the original meaning does support applying the Fifth Amendment due process clause to impeachment or if an impeachable official's position qualifies as a "liberty" or "property" interest for purposes of the due process clause, then the next question is, what "process of law" is due in an impeachment proceeding?

To begin with, it would seem the answer is "none" with respect to an impeachment proceeding in the House. Given that an impeachment by the House does not actually take anything away from the people who are impeached (i.e., it does not "deprive" them of any protected interest, to use one of the key terms in the clause), then it would seem to follow that the Fifth Amendment due process clause does not oblige the House to do anything in an impeachment proceeding.

But there is another possible way to read the clause: could it require nothing more than merely fulfilling each phase of an impeachment—namely, that the House is satisfied that there is a basis for impeachment and the Senate goes through the motions of an impeachment trial before voting to convict and remove someone from office? If something more is required in the House prior to impeachment or in the Senate prior to voting to convict and remove, what precisely is it? Perhaps it could be argued that "due process of law" makes no sense in the impeachment context because impeachment is a unique constitutional proceeding and not a legal proceeding or one governed by the usual requirements of due process. In any event, if all due process requires is notice and a hearing, it seems that is easily satisfied by the House in announcing, formulating, and approving charges of impeachment and by the Senate's merely making its members aware of what the House did, provide some kind of process, and voting on the impeachment articles. It is also intriguing to think that perhaps the due process required in the impeachment process is satisfied by the House and the Senate each simply discharging their respective authorities over impeachment and removal.

What are the emoluments clauses?

There are three clauses in the Constitution that constrain or condition the receipt of "emoluments" by federal officials, who all appear to be subject to impeachment, though none of these clauses defines the term "emolument" or explains the relationship between impeachment and the inappropriate receipt of "emoluments." Article I, Section 6, provides that "No Senator or Representative shall, during the Time for which he was elected, be appointed to any civil Office under the Authority of the United States, which shall have been created, or the Emoluments whereof shall have been increased during such time . . ."[12] Article I, Section 9, provides that "No Title of Nobility shall be granted by the United States: And no Person holding any Office of Profit or Trust under them, shall, without the Consent of the Congress, accept of any present, Emolument, Office or Title, of any kind whatever, from any King, Prince, or foreign State."[13] And Article II provides in pertinent part that "The President shall, at stated Times, receive for his Services, a Compensation, which shall neither be increased nor diminished during the Period for which he will have been elected, and he shall not receive within that Period any other Emolument from the United States, or any of them."[14]

None of these clauses defines the term "emolument." Nor does any of them specify a sanction for their violations, though Article 1, Section 9 (commonly called the foreign emoluments clause) vests Congress with the authority to approve emoluments from foreign states or officials. These clauses leave open the question as to whether impeachment is the appropriate or at least a legitimate response to a violation of the clause.

What are the origins of impeachment?

The practice of impeachment derives principally from two sources, both of which were familiar to Americans at the time of the nation's founding, particularly to the delegates attending the constitutional and ratification conventions. The first source is England. The framers of the Constitution knew the history of impeachment in England,[15] where the Parliament had that power for centuries before the Constitutional Convention held in 1787.[16] In England, any person, whether an official or not, could be impeached by the Parliament for anything,[17] with the House of Commons having the authority to charge someone with misconduct and the House of Lords having the power to hold a trial and impose sanctions for that misconduct.[18] There was no limit to the punishments that could be imposed, even death.[19]

The English regarded impeachment as a political proceeding rather than a legal one, and they understood impeachable offenses as political crimes.[20] For example, the constitutional scholar Raoul Berger, in an influential study of the impeachment process published in 1974, suggested that the English practice treated "high crimes and misdemeanors" as "a category of political crimes against the state."[21] In England, an impeachable offense was any wrongdoing that injured the state.[22] The eminent legal historian William Blackstone, whose commentaries on the laws of England the framers considered as authoritative,[23] traced this understanding of "high crimes and misdemeanors" to the ancient or classical law of treason. That law distinguished "high" treason, which was disloyalty to a superior, from "petit" treason, which was disloyalty to an inferior.[24]

The second source from which the framers drew in designing the federal impeachment process was the states. From the time that people began emigrating from England to America until the break from England, the colonies did not have laws vesting them expressly with the power of impeachment. The power to hold public officials accountable for their misconduct was generally manifested in the form of an indictment (usually by the lower house) for misconduct, or an address, which was an appeal to the governor to initiate some action to redress the wrongdoing alleged.[25] Nonetheless, Americans adapted the English procedures and precedents, as best they could, to their circumstances.[26] Between 1776 and 1787, the states adopted mechanisms for impeachment (or addressing official misconduct) in their constitutions, which generally narrowed the bases and application of impeachment to officeholders.[27] In doing so, the states created a uniquely American system of impeachment, with the framers, as Peter Hoffer and N. E. H. Hull state, "fitting it to American needs, making it republican [because its objective was to protect the common good of the society], defining its limits, experimenting with constitutional formulations, and prosecuting individual cases."[28]

The states' impeachment mechanisms significantly effected the design of the Constitution's impeachment process.[29] As Hoffer and Hull suggest further in their study of early impeachment history in the United States, the constitutional delegates all "agreed to ground rules on impeachment which mirrored state provisions—only officers could be impeached for crimes done in office, with removal and disqualification the only punishments—rather than English precedent."[30]

What were the specific controversies regarding official misconduct that the Constitutional Convention addressed?

In settling on the impeachment mechanism that we have today, the framers addressed several major questions about the scope of impeachable offenses, the officials subject to impeachment, presidential and judicial selection and tenure, the proper forum for impeachment trials, and the nature of judicial tenure and means for disciplining or removing judges. These issues arose as the framers considered four major proposals for a new constitution during the convention held from May 27 to September 17, 1787.

What were the plans that the framers debated before settling on the version of the impeachment process set forth in the Constitution?

Edmund Randolph of Virginia made the first significant proposal regarding the proper forum for impeachment trials.[31] It was included as part of the Virginia Plan, which he introduced at the convention. Early in the proceedings, Randolph suggested, with James Madison in agreement, the need to establish a national judiciary, which would hold office during "good behavior" and which would have the power to impeach "any national officers."[32] Immediately after Randolph had proposed the Virginia Plan, Charles Pinckney proposed the South Carolina Plan, which he never wrote down but left for Madison to sketch in his notes. (Given Madison's antipathy toward Pinckney, this arrangement worked to the disadvantage of Pinckney, whose presence was barely acknowledged later in Madison's notes.) A major element of the South Carolina plan appeared to be its proposal for a confederation among the states, with a bicameral legislature composed of a Senate and a House of Delegates.

The South Carolina Plan apparently fizzled almost immediately and was overshadowed by the introduction of the New Jersey Plan, which William Paterson proposed as an alternative to the Virginia Plan. The New Jersey Plan vested the national judiciary with "the authority to hear and determine in the first instance on all impeachments of federal officers."[33] It further provided that Congress could remove the chief executive upon the application of a majority of the state governors.[34] James Wilson of Pennsylvania took the floor to contrast how the two plans handled impeachment.[35] He noted that the Virginia Plan provided for removal of officers upon impeachment and conviction by the federal judiciary, whereas the New Jersey Plan provided for removal only through the application of a majority of state governors.[36]

On June 18, Alexander Hamilton of New York, in one of the few times that he spoke at the constitutional convention, proposed an entirely different plan, which he modeled on the English system.[37] Under his plan, the chief executive, senators, and federal judges were all to serve during "good behavior."[38] His plan further provided that the "Governors, Senators, and all officers of the United States were to be liable to impeachment for maladministration and corrupt conduct; and upon conviction to be removed from office, and disqualified for holding any place of trust or profit—all impeachments to be tried by a Court to consist of the Chief or Judge of the Superior Court of Law of each state, provided such judge shall hold his place during good behavior and have a permanent salary."[39]

What happened next?

In late July, the Committee of Detail, which was responsible for putting all resolutions and suggestions into proper form, considered a compromise solution to allow impeachment trials "before the Senate and the judges of the federal judicial Court."[40] But on August 6, the Committee of Detail released its official report proposing that the House of Representatives "shall have the sole power of impeachment" and that the president "shall be removed from his office on impeachment by the House of Representatives, and conviction in the Supreme Court. . . ."[41] The Committee of Detail further suggested that the Supreme Court should be vested with the original jurisdiction of "the trial of impeachments."[42] In other words, Hamilton's plan would have made the Supreme Court the one and only venue for an impeachment trial.

Three weeks later, at the suggestion of New York's Gouverneur Morris, the constitutional convention postponed consideration of the proposal to hold impeachment trials in the Supreme Court.[43] John Dickinson of Delaware made a motion to provide that judges serve "during good behavior" but "may be removed by the Executive on the application [of] the Senate and the House of Representatives."[44] Elbridge Gerry of Massachusetts agreed and seconded the motion,[45] but Morris argued against Dickinson's proposal on the ground that it was contradictory "to say that the Judges should hold their offices during good behavior, and yet be removable without a trial."[46]

Roger Sherman of Connecticut disagreed, noting that the English system included a similar mechanism.[47] Wilson argued that such a provision was less dangerous in England because it was unlikely the House of Lords and the House of Commons would ever agree on a matter of judicial removal.[48] "[T]he Judges would be in a bad situation," he said, "if made to depend on every gust of faction which might prevail in the two branches of [the American] government."[49] Randolph and John Rutledge of South Carolina agreed with Wilson and opposed Dickinson's motion.[50] By the time the motion came to a vote, only the representatives from Connecticut favored it, while seven states opposed it.[51]

On September 4, with most delegates anxious to complete their task, the Committee of Eleven, which was responsible for reporting on those provisions of the Constitution not yet considered, urged all the delegates to accept the proposal that the "Senate of the United States shall have the power to try all impeachments."[52] The Committee of Eleven approved having the president chosen by a college of electors rather than the Senate.[53]

In the ensuing debate, Madison objected to designating the Senate as the forum for trying impeachments because, he argued, it would have made the president "improperly dependent" on the Senate "for any act which might be called a misdmeasnor [sic]."[54] Madison proposed, instead, that the Supreme Court, acting alone or in concert with another body, would be the more appropriate forum.[55]

Some constitutional delegates worried that some justices might have a conflict of interest in trying the president who appointed them. Pennsylvania's Morris favored the Senate as the forum for impeachment trials because "there could be no danger that the Senate would say untruly on their oaths that the President was guilty of crimes."[56] Morris worried that the Supreme Court "might be warped or corrupted," because the justices of the Supreme Court "were too few in number." Pinckney agreed with Madison that empowering the Senate to try impeachments would make the president too dependent on the national legislature.[57] Hugh Williamson of North Carolina faulted the Senate, too, for being too lenient in presidential impeachment trials because it shared various powers with the president,[58] while Roger Sherman of Connecticut opposed the Supreme Court as the venue for trying impeachments because the president appointed its members, some of whom might overlook his transgressions because of the loyalty they might feel toward him.[59]

Eventually, the delegates at the Constitutional Convention agreed that the Senate posed the fewest problems of the proposed forums. When the full convention voted to invest the Senate with the authority to try impeachments, only two states—Pennsylvania and Virginia—objected.[60]

Another major controversy relating to impeachment that was discussed at some length at the constitutional convention involved the president's impeachability. Even though almost all state constitutions had provided that governors may be impeached, there was an extended debate in the middle of July on the propriety of subjecting presidents to impeachment.[61] Pinckney agreed with Morris that impeachment would make the president too dependent on those who had the power to impeach him.[62] But George Mason of Virginia, Wilson, Gerry, William Davie of North Carolina, and Benjamin Franklin of Pennsylvania all agreed on the necessity for including presidential impeachment in the Constitution.[63] Davie described it as "an essential security for the good behaviour of the Executive."[64] Franklin suggested it was preferable to the alternative—"the practice before this in cases where the chief Magistrate rendered himself obnoxious" and was subject to "assassination in [which] he was not only deprived of his life but of the opportunity of vindicating his character."[65] Franklin believed that it was "the best way therefore to provide . . . for the regular punishment of the Executive when his misconduct should deserve it, and for his honorable acquittal when he should be unjustly accused."[66]

Madison declared that presidential impeachment was "indispensable" to provide a check against a president who "might pervert his administration into a scheme of peculation and oppression. He might betray his trust to foreign powers."[67] His fellow Virginian, Randolph, agreed that "tumults and insurrections" would inevitably result if the Constitution provided no mechanism for punishing presidential abuse of power.[68] As the debate neared its conclusion, Morris acknowledged that the debate had changed his mind.[69] The delegates tentatively agreed to a clause providing for the president's removal for "malpractice or neglect of duty."[70] On July 26, the committee reaffirmed the provision that the president shall be "removable on impeachment and conviction of malpractice or neglect of duty."[71] At the end of the convention, only South Carolina and Massachusetts opposed making the president impeachable.[72]

But, a related controversy during the convention concerned the scope of impeachable offenses. Throughout the early convention discussions on this question, every speaker agreed that certain high-ranking officials should not be immune from prosecution for common-law crimes, such as treason and murder. Many delegates appeared to envision a body of offenses for which certain federal officials may be impeached and removed from office. Several delegates favored restricting the grounds for impeachment to include "maladministration,"[73] "corrupt administration,"[74] "neglect of duty,"[75] and "misconduct in office"[76] and leaving common-law crimes such as treason and murder to be heard only in courts of law. But several other delegates, including Paterson, Randolph, Wilson, and Mason, argued that the impeachment process should be used only to sanction misuse of power in accordance with how their state constitutions dealt with such misconduct. By late August, the Committee of Detail suggested that federal officials "shall be liable to impeachment and removal from office for neglect of duty, malversation, or corruption."[77]

Yet on September 8, 1787, the Committee of Eleven came up with a different proposal.[78] It suggested that the grounds for impeachment and removal should be limited to "treason or bribery."[79] A fierce debate arose over the proposal, with Mason and Gerry arguing for broader grounds for impeachment and Madison opposing Mason's favored term of "maladministration," arguing that it was so "vague a term [that it would be] equivalent to a tenure during pleasure of the Senate."[80] Mason agreed with Madison's proposal to broaden the grounds for impeachment to extend to "bribery and other high crimes and misdemeanors," which Mason seemed to apprehend as including maladministration.[81] With no further discussion, the motion carried.[82]

A final dispute over impeachment at the convention had to do with the required threshold for the numbers of votes to convict and remove an impeached official from office. The debate turned, in part, on how the delegates viewed the Senate. They considered the House to be more subject to factions and to hasty, intemperate action than the Senate, which they had designed—with six-year terms, election by state legislatures and not popular majorities, and an older minimum-age requirement than for those who would serve in the lower chamber—to function with greater caution, deliberation, and wisdom than the House.[83]

The debate turned as well on how high the threshold had to be for conviction and removal. The delegates settled on the two-thirds requirement for conviction and removal as a way to "republicanize" the impeachment process, that is, to ensure that the senators were guided by the noblest possible concerns about the welfare of the country and the Constitution. This feature, too, emphasized the extent to which the entire process differed from the English system, in which Parliament could impeach someone for anything, only a majority vote was required, and Parliament could impose any punishment it saw fit to impose, including death.

What do the basic terms in the impeachment clauses mean?

Some constitutional terms pertaining to the impeachment process are straightforward and easy to define, whereas some are not. First, the easy ones. The Constitution's explicit mention of specific officials as subject to impeachment—the president and the vice president, for example—clearly makes those officials subject to impeachment.[84] The Constitution also declares that the chief justice of the United States presides over presidential impeachment trials.[85] We also know from the language of the Constitution that during such trials senators must be on "oath or affirmation," meaning in all likelihood that they must all take some kind of oath at some point during the trial, presumably at the beginning.[86]

Moreover, the Constitution defines the term "Treason" as "consist[ing] only in Levying War against [the United States,] or in adhering to their Enemies, giving them Aid and Comfort."[87] "Bribery" also has a clear meaning, since Congress has codified it as a serious federal crime since 1790. [88] If you want to know the definition of bribery, all you have to do is read the federal criminal code.

This leaves at least three phrases pertaining to the scope of impeachable offenses whose meaning are contested: "other high crimes and misdemeanors," "during good Behavior," and "due process of law." The delegates' different proposals regarding impeachment considered during the constitutional convention sheds some light on the meanings of "during good behavior," which we know defines the tenure of federal judges, and "other high crimes and misdemeanors," which refers to the scope of impeachable offenses beyond "treason" and "bribery."

While books can be and indeed have been written[89] on the meanings of each of these three grand phrases, some basic understandings of them are widely shared. To begin with, we can figure out from the phrase "Treason, Bribery, and other High crimes and misdemeanors" that, whatever "other High crimes and misdemeanors" means, those words refer to misconduct on the same order of magnitude or seriousness as "Treason and Bribery." Further, the word "high" modifies both the terms "crimes" and "misdemeanors." It also follows that some kinds of misconduct must fall short of an impeachable offense, or why bother, as the framers did, to reject the English example of allowing impeachment to be based on anything, choosing instead to narrow the range of misconduct for which people could be impeached and convicted? These steps allow us at the outset to rule some things out as impeachable offenses because they are minor misdeeds—say, jaywalking—and therefore not serious enough to rise to the level of qualifying as impeachable offenses.

Besides the fact that the constitutional convention debates further inform our understanding of the scope of impeachable offenses, a recurrent point made during the ratification conventions and early years of the Republic was that the meaning of "other high crimes and misdemeanors" had to be worked out over time. The practice of impeachment, in other words, has enriched our understanding of the meaning of the constitutional language "other high crimes and misdemeanors."

The next phrase of concern to the impeachment process, "during good behavior," is commonly regarded by scholars, judges, and members of Congress as referring to "life tenure,"[90] in contrast to the tenure of elected officials. The latter is defined in the Constitution as limited by a term of years for particular offices, while life tenure is the unique tenure enjoyed by federal judges. The trickier part is determining whether this special tenure of judges means that they may serve as judges unless or until they die, resign, or are impeached and removed from office, or whether judges may lose their tenure due to bad behavior, which might include but is not limited to "Treason, Bribery, and other High crimes and misdemeanors." In general, widening the grounds for disciplining judges beyond the specific grounds for impeachment set forth in the Constitution has concerned many scholars, members of Congress, and judges. They worry that any such broadening would threaten judicial independence—that is, it would make it easier to remove judges and possibly increase the likelihood that they could face political reprisal for their decisions.[91] They believe that the Constitution grants federal judges special tenure that guarantees them the freedom to make difficult decisions without worrying about whether they could be punished for those decisions. Consequently, there has been general consensus in favor of narrowing, rather than broadening, the grounds for which federal judges could be disciplined. At the same time, they also understand that judges, perhaps more than any other officials in our constitutional order, symbolize integrity; they must be beyond reproach in how they conduct themselves.[92] This means, as a practical matter, judges must take great care to protect their reputations and comply with the law that they are expected to apply to others.

Is impeachment a legal or political issue?

Impeachment has elements of both legal and political proceedings. As a result, it is a unique process. Several delegates made that point during the constitutional and ratifying conventions,[93] and the sanctions that may result from a conviction are unique. The Constitution provides that someone convicted and removed from office "nevertheless shall be liable and subject to Indictment, Trial, Judgment, and Punishment. . . ." The Constitution further provides that the pardon power may not be used in cases of impeachment.[94] In the constitutional conventions, the delegates talked about—and seemed to have assumed—that impeachment was a political proceeding. As Justice Joseph Story explained in his influential commentaries on the Constitution, "The jurisdiction [with respect to impeachment] is to be exercised over offences, which are committed by public men in violation of their public trust and duties."[95] "Those duties," he explained further, "are in many cases political. . . . Strictly speaking, then, the power partakes of a political character, as it respects injuries to the society in its political character."[96]

As the eminent constitutional scholar Charles Black suggested in his superb treatise on the subject of impeachment, impeachment is a hybrid of the two kinds of proceedings—it has elements of both.[97] On the one hand, impeachment is a legal proceeding insofar as it is authorized by the Constitution, the supreme law of the land (according to Article VI of the Constitution), and it has some legal ramifications, namely, that someone who is convicted and removed is barred by the law of the land from further occupying the office from which he or she has been removed.

On the other hand, impeachment is political in the sense that the principal decision makers are all political officials whose judgment on the matter of impeachment or removal is considered final. Because members of Congress are disposed to take political considerations into account whenever they decide matters, the framers presumed that politics or political factors, even partisanship, might drive or creep into the process. The sanctions themselves, of course, have political consequences. For example, it might thrust into the presidency a vice president who has different political support or popularity than the ousted president had, while members of Congress might find themselves rewarded or punished in the electoral support for their votes in impeachment proceedings.

Indeed, the English system, which served as a model for the federal impeachment process, considered it to be a political, not a legal, proceeding.[98] In the American system, impeachment was considered to be a political process, because political figures were among its principal subjects; the sanctions resulting from an impeachment could come only from impeachment, not from any legal proceeding; the decision makers were politically accountable; and the consequences of impeachment were political—political careers could end or produce a shock to the political system.[99]

The impeachment process is political in another, important sense. It is an example of a process that calls upon members of Congress to engage in what scholars have called "constitutional politics."[100] Constitutional politics is not the same as partisan or electoral politics—it involves engaging in a higher and more ennobling form of political activity, which has to do with the big questions pertaining to the Constitution and to the institutions and actors constrained by the Constitution.[101] When we speak of members of Congress having to rise to the challenge of an impeachment inquiry, we are implicitly suggesting that we expect them to rise above petty partisan politics and consider the big questions that have an impact on our polity and understanding of the Constitution.

How useful is impeachment?

The framers purposefully made impeachment difficult to achieve. In order to impeach, convict, and remove someone from office, the government has to go through several hoops. Getting through all these successfully is hard. Other than the impeachment of a president, vice president, or Supreme Court justice, an impeachment is unlikely to generate much interest among the public and therefore little motivation in the members of Congress to put aside other business for the sake of participating in impeachment proceedings. The likelihood that impeachment diverts members from work is more likely to be pertinent to their re-election, and the fact that impeachment is cumbersome has made impeachment quite uncommon as a recourse for handling the misconduct of certain public officials. It has been surprisingly rare in our history: the House has impeached only nineteen people;[102] and of those, only eight were convicted and removed from office.[103] Of the people convicted in an impeachment trial by the Senate, all have been lower-court federal judges,[104] three of whom were not only removed from office, but also disqualified from ever holding another federal office or receiving any federal pensions for their federal service.[105]

Is impeachment the only mechanism for addressing the serious misconduct of the president, the vice president, and other officials subject to impeachment?

There is no simple answer to this question. There are other mechanisms, such as censure, the Twenty-fifth Amendment, congressional oversight, electoral accountability, and civil or criminal lawsuits that might be available to address misconduct. Censure refers to a resolution approved by one or both chambers of Congress condemning a public official for some reason. The Twenty-fifth Amendment addresses presidents' incapacity to perform their duties. Congressional oversight usually involves a committee in the House of Representatives or Senate overseeing the activities of the executive branch, including but not limited to reviewing or monitoring federal agencies and other federal officials' programs, activities, and implementation of the laws that the Congress has enacted. The relationship between impeachment and each of these other mechanisms is explored throughout this book.

Chapter 2

THE HISTORY OF THE FEDERAL IMPEACHMENT PROCESS

How many people have been impeached, and why?

Over the course of American history, the House of Representatives has formally impeached nineteen individuals.[1] Most of these people have been lower-court federal judges, and the Senate has convicted only eight of the nineteen people whom the House has impeached. The impeached officials were:

- William Blount, a US senator, in 1797, for conspiring to assist Great Britain's attempts to seize Spanish-controlled territories in Florida and Louisiana[2]
- John Pickering, a federal district judge, in 1803, for intoxication on the bench and unlawful handling of property claims[3]
- Samuel Chase, a Supreme Court justice, in 1804, for arbitrarily and oppressively conducting trials when sitting as a trial court judge[4]
- James Peck, a federal district court judge, in 1830, for abusing the contempt power[5]
- West Humphreys, a federal district court judge, in 1862, for refusing to hold court and waging war against the US government[6]
- Andrew Johnson, president of the United States, in 1868, for dismissing his secretary of war in violation of the Tenure in Office Act and for taking other actions undermining

Reconstruction enactments, including the Tenure in Office Act, and showing contempt for Congress[7]
- Mark Delahay, a federal district court judge, in 1873, for intoxication on the bench[8]
- William Belknap, secretary of war, in 1876, for bribery[9]
- Charles Swayne, a federal district court judge, in 1904, for abuse of contempt power and other misuses of office[10]
- Robert Archbald, an associate judge on the US Commerce Court, in 1912, for bribery[11]
- George English, a federal district court judge, in 1926, for abuse of power[12]
- Harold Louderback, a federal district court judge, in 1933, for favoritism in appointing bankruptcy receivers[13]
- Halsted Ritter, a federal district court judge, in 1936, for receiving kickbacks, tax evasion, and bringing the federal judiciary into disrepute[14]
- Harry Claiborne, a federal district court judge, in 1986, for income tax evasion[15]
- Alcee Hastings, a federal district court judge, in 1988, for perjury and conspiring to solicit a bribe[16]
- Walter Nixon, a federal district court judge, in 1989, for making false statements to a federal grand jury[17]
- Bill Clinton, president of the United States, in 1998, for lying under oath to a federal grand jury and obstruction of justice[18]
- Samuel Kent, a federal district court judge, in 2009, for sexual assault, obstructing justice, and making false and misleading statements under oath[19]
- Thomas Porteous, a federal district court judge, in 2010, for bribery and perjury[20]

How many of the nineteen people whom the House impeached did the Senate convict and remove from office?

Only eight of the people whom the House impeached were convicted and removed from office. All of them were federal judges: Pickering, Humphreys, Archbald, Ritter, Claiborne, Hastings, Nixon, and Porteous.[21]

How many times has the Senate imposed the sanction of disqualification?

Only three times. West Humphreys, Robert Archbald, and Thomas Porteous were not only convicted and removed from office but also disqualified from holding a future office of honor or trust of the United States.[22]

What exactly is disqualification?

Disqualification is what it sounds like: a formal declaration barring the impeached and convicted official from ever serving again in the federal government and from receiving pensions that had vested because of their federal service.[23]

How many officials has the Senate acquitted or found not guilty and therefore not convicted and removed from office?

Seven. The federal officials that the Senate acquitted or found not guilty and therefore kept their offices are Associate Justice Samuel Chase, Judge James Peck, President Andrew Johnson, Secretary of War William Belknap, Judge Charles Swayne, Judge Harold Louderback, and President Bill Clinton.[24]

How many officials were impeached but avoided conviction and removal because they resigned from office before their impeachment trials commenced?

Three people did this. The first—and most complicated case—involved William Belknap, who had been President Ulysses Grant's longest-serving secretary of war.[25] On March 2, 1876, the House impeached Belknap for bribery.[26] But prior to the House's formal vote on impeachment, he announced his resignation from office.[27] After lengthy debate, the House concluded that a civil officer like Belknap may not escape impeachment by resigning from office.[28] Hence, the House impeached him, and the Senate initiated proceedings against him later that same year.[29] At the start of its trial, the Senate reached the same conclusion as the House on the question of whether it could hold the trial in spite of Belknap's resignation. Voting 37–29 to retain jurisdiction, the Senate proceeded with its trial.[30] But, when the trial concluded, only a simple majority of the Senate voted Belknap guilty on all the impeachment articles, falling short of the two-thirds majority required for conviction.[31] Because the vote fell short of the two-thirds required for conviction, Belknap was acquitted.[32]

The Senate's report on Belknap stated that, of the twenty-five senators who voted "not guilty," twenty-two claimed to have done so because they believed that the Senate had no jurisdiction over an official who had resigned from office prior to his impeachment trial.[33] The other three senators voting "not guilty" explained they did so because they believed Belknap was innocent of the charges against him.[34] Some scholars read this report as indicating that the Senate acquitted Belknap (treating votes of not guilty the same as those for acquittal), but others construe it as indicating that Belknap simply avoided conviction because of a substantial number of senators voting on the procedural ground that the Senate no longer had jurisdiction—or the power—to conduct an impeachment trial on the charges against him.[35]

Two other officials were able to avoid Senate impeachment trials by resigning after their impeachments by the House but before the Senate began their trials. In 1926, George English resigned from a federal district judgeship after the House had impeached him for various abuses of power.[36] Shortly thereafter, the Senate dismissed the trial without reaching the merits of the charges against him.[37] In 2009, Samuel Kent, then a federal district judge in Texas, was convicted and sent to prison for lying to investigators about sexually abusing two female employees.[38] Kent made an offer to resign as long as he was allowed to stay in office long enough to have his pension fully vested.[39] Outraged, members of the House Judiciary Committee voted unanimously to send four impeachment articles to the full House in June 2009.[40] After the House approved the articles, Kent submitted a new letter of resignation that President Barack Obama accepted.[41] On July 20, the House approved a resolution asking the Senate to end his impeachment trial.[42] The Senate ended the trial two days later.[43]

Were there any other officials who were impeached but somehow avoided having the Senate hold an impeachment trial or convict them for impeachable misconduct?

One other federal official was able to get his impeachment trial dismissed in the Senate for reasons other than the merits of the charges against him. This was William Blount, the first federal official ever to be impeached by the House.[44] Blount was a colorful figure who participated in the constitutional convention as one of North Carolina's delegates,[45] served as governor of the Southwest Territory,[46] and was selected as one of Tennessee's first two senators in 1796.[47] At around the same time, Blount was seeking ways to deal with extremely heavy indebtedness (due to the loss in value of considerable land he had acquired on credit).[48] Blount was impeached for one of his schemes—conspiring to assist the British in their war with Spain in spite of the United States' official neutrality.[49] When the Senate became aware of a letter he had written to help the British acquire the then Spanish-owned Louisiana, Blount asked for a delay to consider his answer. The Senate granted the request, but Blount used the time to flee to Tennessee.[50]

In Blount's absence, the House of Representatives impeached him on July 7, 1797, for conspiring with the British against Spain, in contravention of American policy.[51] The next day, the Senate, based on a report it had completed on July 6, voted 25–1 to expel Blount for "disorderly behavior."[52] The Senate subsequently commenced an impeachment trial, though Blount's counsel argued that the Senate lacked the jurisdiction to do so because only "civil officers of the United States" were impeachable, that such officers had to be appointed by the president, and that of course he was an elected senator, not a presidential appointee.[53] On January 11, 1798, the Senate, with then Vice President Thomas Jefferson presiding, voted 14–11 to dismiss the charges for lack of jurisdiction.[54]

The significance of the vote dismissing jurisdiction in Blount's trial has been debated over the years. Because the 14–11 vote was on the question of whether the Senate lacked jurisdiction on the basis that Blount had argued, the Senate itself construed the vote as establishing an important early precedent recognizing that senators are not "civil officers of the United States" and therefore are not subject to the impeachment process.[55] But the fact that not every senator explained his vote has left uncertainty over the significance of the dismissal. As a result, the vote could be construed as having been based at least in part on the fact that Blount had been expelled and was no longer in the Senate at the time that his impeachment trial commenced and therefore the matter of his removal had become moot. Some scholars question whether the Blount precedent is either binding or correctly decided.[56] Some urge the Senate to stand by the decision, others argue that a different Senate is entitled to reach a different judgment, and still other scholars dispute that the conclusion that members of Congress are not to be counted among the "civil offers of the United States."[57]

Was Andrew Johnson the first president to be threatened with impeachment?

No, several presidents before Andrew Johnson had been threatened with impeachment. One of the first was Andrew Jackson. Many of Jackson's political opponents feared that he had become a tyrant as president and supported their claim by pointing to several of his actions, including firing many of the previous administration's appointees and replacing them with his political friends and allies, forcing the resignation of all but one of his cabinet officials in response to the snubbing of the wife of his secretary of war,[58] directing the forcible removal of more than 7,000 Native Americans from their lands in apparent disregard of a Supreme Court order otherwise,[59] and wielding his nominating and veto powers ruthlessly. One of Jackson's most controversial actions involved his aggressive efforts to undermine the National Bank, which had been created by Congress and had its constitutionality upheld by the Supreme Court. Jackson vetoed the rechartering of the National Bank and then dismissed his treasury secretary, William Duane, when he refused to remove its deposits and place them in state banks instead.[60] The Senate rejected Jackson's nominee to replace Duane with his attorney general, Roger Taney;[61] however, Taney, at Jackson's bidding, redirected the National Bank's deposits into state banks.[62]

In 1834, President Jackson's Democratic Party controlled the House, but the opposition party, the Whigs, controlled a bare majority of the Senate seats.[63] This meant that impeachment by the

House was a practical impossibility as long as Democrats remained unified in opposition, while conviction and removal by the Senate similarly appeared unrealistic as long as Democrats held together, which they did. In response, the Whigs in 1834 censured Jackson for withholding documents relating to his actions defunding the National Bank.[64] Outraged, Jackson declared the censure unconstitutional.[65] He argued that the impeachment process was the exclusive process for punishing presidential misconduct and dared Congress to use it, knowing that there were not enough votes for impeachment, much less for conviction and removal.[66] In the next two cycles of elections, he campaigned successfully to return the Senate to Democratic control. Consequently, the Democrats, led by Thomas Hart Benton, once a political foe but by then an ally of Jackson's, expunged the censure in 1837, just a few months before the inauguration of Jackson's vice president, Martin Van Buren, as president.[67]

Another president to face the serious threat of impeachment before Andrew Johnson was John Tyler. Tyler had left the Democratic Party to become the running mate of the Whig candidate William Henry Harrison, who won the presidential election of 1840, defeating Martin Van Buren in his bid for a second term.[68] Harrison died thirty days later, thus elevating the vice president to the presidency for the first time in history.[69] From that moment until the end of his presidency four years later, Tyler was despised widely by both parties— the Democrats because he had left them to run with Harrison, and the Whigs because they did not trust him. Throughout his presidency, Congress pushed back hard each time that Tyler attempted to aggressively exercise his presidential prerogatives, including his nominating and veto authorities.

The first impeachment attempt against Tyler arose immediately after he vetoed the popular Little Tariff Bill. It had increased tariffs as Tyler wanted, but at the cost of implementing a scheme of "distribution of proceeds on the public lands" that he had long opposed as bad policy and unconstitutional.[70] Tyler issued his veto on June 29, 1842.[71] John Botts, then a Whig member of the House from Virginia, introduced a resolution on July 10, 1842, to appoint a special committee to consider whether Tyler had committed any impeachable offenses.[72] Botts felt confident that the Whig leaders in Congress, including Jackson's great nemesis, Henry Clay, would support the resolution, but the leaders felt it was premature.[73]

Instead, they provoked Tyler to cast other vetoes, including one against an enactment rechartering the National Bank.[74] When Tyler defended his veto in a message to the House, the House referred it to the special committee that had been formed to consider whether he had committed an impeachable offense.[75]

A week later, the committee issued a report harshly rebuking Tyler for his vetoes, which it condemned as a "gross abuse of constitutional power and bold assumptions of power never vested in him by law" and for having "assumed . . . the whole Legislative power to himself[.]"[76] Though the report found that Tyler's actions constituted impeachable offenses, it did not recommend impeachment because "in the present state of public affairs, [it would] prove abortive."[77] The committee's report included a minority report that defended the legality of Tyler's actions.[78] The House approved the report, with virtually no discussion, by a vote of 100–80.[79] The report effectively censured Tyler. Though Tyler responded with a formal protest, the House refused to publish it.[80] In a second attempt at impeaching Tyler, the House considered an impeachment resolution, pushed by Botts (who, by this time, had lost his seat in the House), that listed nine grounds for Tyler's impeachment.[81] On January 11, 1843, the House rejected the resolution, by a vote of 127–83.[82] It was the first time the House ever voted on an impeachment resolution.[83]

How many presidents have been impeached?

Only two American presidents have been impeached by the House. The first was Andrew Johnson (1868),[84] and Bill Clinton (1998) is the other.[85] The Senate acquitted both.[86]

Why was Andrew Johnson impeached?

It is an understatement to say that Andrew Johnson was unpopular when he ascended to the presidency because of the assassination of President Lincoln. Prior to becoming Lincoln's vice president for his second term, Johnson had been a relatively undistinguished Democratic senator from Tennessee, known mainly for his refusal to abandon his seat when the state of Tennessee seceded and for his insistence on maintaining his fidelity to the Union.[87] He left the Senate in 1862 when Lincoln appointed him the military governor of Tennessee.[88] In 1864, Lincoln wanted a Southern Democrat as his running mate. He chose Johnson.[89] Upon Lincoln's assassination in 1865, Johnson became president.[90]

Over the next few years, Johnson battled Congress for control of Reconstruction policy.[91] Johnson had a narrow view that Reconstruction policy should be minimal, doing nothing more than quickly restoring the seceded states and abolishing slavery. Congress disagreed. It wanted much more. One measure, which Congress enacted over Johnson's veto to limit his authority, was the Tenure of Office Act, which prohibited the president from removing officials confirmed by the Senate without the Senate's approval.[92] Johnson's decision in February 1868 to dismiss Edwin Stanton, his secretary of war, in violation of the Tenure in Office Act, set the stage for his impeachment by the House.[93] Less than a month after Johnson had fired Stanton, the House, on February 24, 1868, voted 126–47 to impeach Johnson.[94] The House approved eleven impeachment articles against Johnson, nine of which cited his dismissal of Stanton and efforts to replace him (with Ulysses Grant) as violations of the Tenure in Office Act.[95]

Why didn't the Senate convict Andrew Johnson and remove him from office?

President Johnson's chances for avoiding conviction and removal did not look good. Republicans controlled both the House and the Senate.[96] The House managers, who were tasked with presenting the case for Johnson's conviction and removal in the Senate, included Thaddeus Stevens and John Bingham, two of the most prominent Republicans in Congress.[97] Indeed, of the Senate's fifty-four members, forty-two were Republicans.[98] Had the Republicans been united, Johnson would have become the first president to have been convicted and removed from office. But, because ten Republicans joined the nine Democrats in voting 35–19 to acquit Johnson,[99] the Senate fell one vote shy of the requisite two-thirds to convict Johnson and remove him from office.

A popular explanation for why Johnson was acquitted has focused on the actions of seven prominent Republicans, including William Fessenden of Maine, Lyman Trumbull of Illinois, and Edmund Ross of Kansas, who expressed concerns about the evidence against

Johnson and the push to oust him from office. Because Ross had been threatened that, if he voted for acquittal, he would be subject to a bribery investigation and the other six all faced hostile voters and state legislatures back home, their votes have often been construed as "profiles in courage," to quote from the title of John F. Kennedy's book, which includes a chapter on Ross.[100] Indeed, none of the Republican senators who voted to acquit Johnson ever served again in elective office.[101]

The popular view further posits, as Chief Justice William Rehnquist did in his book on the impeachment trials of Samuel Chase and Andrew Johnson, that the Senate's acquittal vindicated the principle that Johnson's remarkable cadre of lawyers—including Henry Stanberry (who had served previously as Johnson's attorney general) and Benjamin Curtis (who had dissented in *Dred Scott v. Sandford* and resigned from the Court in protest over the decision), asserted in his defense—that a president may not be impeached, much less convicted and removed, on the basis of mere partisanship or a policy difference with the Congress. Johnson's learned counsel argued that it is within a president's authority to refuse to abide by a law that he considers to be unconstitutional.

There are, however, other possible explanations for Johnson's acquittal. The eminent historian Michael Les Benedict suggests that senators voting for Johnson's acquittal did not want him removed because that would have elevated to the presidency the president pro tempore of the Senate, Benjamin Wade. Wade would then have been in a position to win the Republican nomination in 1868. But moderate Republicans hated Wade, who had been a harsh critic of President Lincoln. Lincoln's allies preferred a weakened, ineffectual Johnson in office than an emboldened Wade. Moreover, there is conflicting evidence on whether there is a different, less noble explanation for the Senate's vote. After the trial, Benjamin Butler, one of the House managers, held a series of hearings that produced some evidence showing that some Republican senators might have been bribed (by promises of patronage or money) to vote for acquittal.[102] But no charges were ever made on the basis of the hearings, and other evidence indicates that some Republican senators had been pressured (by Butler, among others) to switch their acquittal votes to conviction.[103]

Would Richard Nixon have been impeached had he not resigned?

Richard Nixon experienced one of the most dramatic shifts of any president in history: he won re-election by a historic landslide in 1972,[104] and then, less than two years later, he resigned from office in disgrace.[105] The turnaround is due to the nearly unanimous perception that Nixon had abused his powers and committed impeachable offenses, including authorizing and attempting to cover up a burglary of the Democratic Party headquarters in the Watergate hotel.[106]

The investigations revealed that Nixon had been engaged in a breathtaking range of wrongdoing. The House Judiciary Committee and a Senate select committee had each undertaken meticulous fact-finding, which ultimately uncovered the evidence that Nixon had taped every conversation in the White House.[107]

Three days after the Supreme Court ordered Nixon to turn over dozens of taped conversations, the House Judiciary Committee approved three articles of impeachment, including one charging that Nixon obstructed justice by paying hush money to the burglars and another that Nixon had abused his powers by ordering the Central Intelligence Agency and the Federal Bureau of Investigation to harass his political enemies.[108] Twelve days later, Nixon resigned.[109]

Had Nixon not resigned, almost everything we know indicates that he would have been impeached, convicted, and removed from office. Though its chair was a Democrat, the House Judiciary Committee employed a single staff, underscoring through its joint report the extent to which it was nonpartisan and professional.[110] Shortly after complying with the Supreme Court's order that he turn over the taped conversations in the White House, Nixon was visited by several congressional leaders, including Republican senator Barry Goldwater of Arizona, a widely respected party elder, who told Nixon that they expected if he were impeached by the Senate he could not hope for more than ten to twelve senators to stick with him.[111] Resign, they suggested, and he did.[112] Ever since, people on both sides of the aisle have had confidence that the outcome accords with a proper understanding of impeachment.

Why was Bill Clinton impeached?

Bill Clinton's impeachment was based on misconduct relating to his efforts to hide the sexual relationship he had with a White House intern, Monica Lewinsky. The relationship came to light during the discovery phase of a lawsuit brought by Paula Jones, a former Arkansas state employee, who claimed that Clinton had sexually harassed her when he was governor of Arkansas.[113] Though the lawsuit had been filed against Clinton shortly after he became president in 1993, his lawyers argued that as president that he was entitled to special immunity from being sued for civil damages for as long as he held that office.[114] The District Court judge in the case, Susan Webber Wright, agreed to delay the lawsuit until President Clinton's term of office ended.[115] Jones's lawyers appealed to the US Court of Appeals for the Eighth Circuit, which ruled in Jones's favor that the lawsuit should proceed while Clinton was president.[116] Clinton's lawyers then appealed to the Supreme Court, which ruled, shortly before Clinton's second inauguration, that a sitting president was not entitled to any immunity in a civil case based on his pre-presidential conduct.[117]

Before Judge Webber Wright granted President Clinton's motion for summary judgment in April 1998, Jones's lawyers had become aware of Clinton's inappropriate relationship with Lewinsky.[118] Jones's lawyers asked Clinton under oath about the relationship.[119] They construed his denial to be a lie under oath and reported the matter to Kenneth Starr, who had been appointed as independent counsel to look into business transactions involving the Clintons that dated back to well before Bill Clinton was president.[120] Starr expanded his investigation to look into whether Clinton lied in the Jones case.[121] Starr and his team eventually drafted a formal report to Congress claiming that, in the course of trying to hide the relationship he had with Lewinsky from authorities, Clinton committed as many as eleven offenses for which he could be impeached, including perjury, obstruction of justice, and abuse of power.[122]

The Starr Report became the basis for the House Judiciary Committee to consider, in the fall of 1998, whether Clinton had committed any impeachable offenses.[123] Clinton's vulnerability to impeachment was evident from the outset, given that Republicans held a majority of seats in the House and believed that Clinton was a philanderer and a moral degenerate whom they had long derided as "Slick Willie."[124] The Judiciary Committee focused its inquiry on the question of whether the president's conduct, as set forth in the Starr Report, provided a basis for impeachment.[125] With no additional fact-finding beyond that described in Starr's Report, the committee approved four articles of impeachment against Clinton.[126] On a nearly straight party-line vote, the House voted on December 19, 1998, to impeach Bill Clinton based on two articles of impeachment, one charging obstruction of justice and the other perjury.[127] In doing so, it made Clinton the second president in American history to be impeached by the House of Representatives.[128]

Why did the Senate not convict President Clinton?

Throughout Clinton's impeachment proceedings in the House, it had been evident that, even if he were impeached, his conviction and removal in the Senate would be highly unlikely since the numbers favored him—Democrats held forty-five seats and were united in opposing his conviction and removal from office. Once the House impeached Clinton, Senate Majority Leader Trent Lott began developing a streamlined trial procedure to ensure that the Senate would be done with the matter as quickly as possible. After five weeks of arguments from the lawyers on each side (and interviews of a few witnesses), the Senate voted on February 12, 1999, to acquit Clinton on both articles of impeachment.[129] Needing two-thirds for a conviction, the House managers failed to achieve a bare majority on either article.[130] Ten Republicans joined the forty-five Democrats to vote "not guilty" on the charge of perjury, and five Republicans joined all the Democratic senators to vote "not guilty" on the charge of obstruction of justice.[131]

Most but not all senators explained their votes. Of the forty-five Democrats who voted not guilty on both articles of impeachment, thirty-eight explained their reasoning.[132] Of the latter, twenty-seven senators explained that they did not consider the misconduct alleged in each article to constitute an impeachable offense (essentially arguing that Clinton committed "low," not "high," crimes).[133] Sixteen of the thirty-eight Democrats explained that the partisan zeal of the House managers in the Senate impeachment trial affected their votes,[134] and fifteen Democrats and one Republican senator (Arlen Specter of Pennsylvania) said they did not believe that the House managers had proven the misconduct alleged in each article of impeachment.[135] Two other Republican senators said they had voted not guilty even though they believed that all the charges against President Clinton had been proven,[136] and Republican senator Fred

Thompson of Tennessee (a former prosecutor) explained that he had voted not guilty on the first article because he believed its vagueness and failure to specify Clinton's statements as false made it impossible for Clinton to defend himself against them.[137]

Two months after Clinton's impeachment trial, Judge Webber Wright held Clinton in contempt of court for making false statements under oath.[138] It was the first time that a sitting president had been sanctioned for disobeying a court order.[139] She referred her finding to the State Bar of Arkansas, which suspended the president's law license for five years.[140]

Two decades later, we can speculate further about extent to which social, political, and cultural developments explain what happened in Clinton's impeachment proceedings. First, the political parties had to reconsider the importance of moral character and sexual indiscretions to their agendas and conceptions of the presidency. Almost everyone in Congress was disgusted by Clinton's misconduct, but it was a challenge for each party (and ultimately each senator) to figure out the pertinence of their disgust. Democrats and liberals, who positioned themselves as the champions of women's rights, struggled to explain away the president's misconduct as not pertinent to the impeachment process and as merely a consequence of a consensual relationship. Republicans struggled to maintain their championing of the importance of moral character to presidential leadership at a time when it appeared the nation regarded Clinton's misbehavior as sordid, sadly predictable, yet irrelevant to his performance as president. As a cultural matter, Clinton's misconduct was widely viewed as reprehensible, but for many people his misconduct said more about his private flaws than his public leadership. Yet, the failure to remove Clinton (while conceding he testified falsely under oath) has been hard to reconcile with a legal and constitutional culture that respects the rule of law, including civil laws creating liability for sexual harassment. Many people believe that Clinton broke the law, degraded the presidency, and undoubtedly committed an impeachable offense, but the Senate Democrats let him get away with it. The Senate might have set a potentially disturbing precedent that allowed a powerful man to avoid responsibility not only for his misconduct but also for demonizing a woman who had worked for him and who lacked anything close to the same resources and stature that he had to defend her virtue. Indeed, more than a few scholars and many Americans continue to believe that a president's perjury and obstruction of justice are appropriate grounds for impeachment, conviction, and removal and that Clinton's acquittal tarnished Democratic senators, who were unable to bring themselves to toss him out of office.

Why wasn't George W. Bush impeached?

George W. Bush was president when the terrorist attacks that brought down the World Trade Center occurred on September 11, 2001.[141] In response to the attacks, Congress approved a resolution authorizing the president to take military action against the perpetrators of the attack.[142] President Bush and several high-ranking officials within the administration argued that such action was necessary to bring down the Iraqi government led by Saddam Hussein in order to protect the United States and the rest of the world from "weapons of mass destruction" that Hussein had developed but hidden from United Nations inspectors.[143] Citing photographic and other evidence (not all made public), President Bush argued that because Hussein posed an immediate threat to the security of the United States he had to order a preemptive invasion.[144] After American forces had invaded Iraq had toppled Hussein, they discovered no weapons of mass destruction.[145] When evidence came to light from British sources that they and the Americans had reason to believe there were no weapons of mass destruction, many Americans claimed that Bush should be impeached for having lied to the American people in the run-up to the American invasion of Iraq.[146]

There are several reasons that could explain why no serious movement to impeach President Bush ever materialized in the House. First, even though Democrats had retaken control of both the House and the Senate in 2006, Republicans controlled enough seats in the Senate to make conviction and removal highly unlikely. Mobilizing support for impeachment in the House was considered futile given the practical impossibility of securing a conviction in the Senate. Second, it is possible some senators might have lost any taste for impeachment in the aftermath of President Clinton's impeachment proceedings. Third, successfully impeaching and removing President Bush from office would have elevated to the presidency Bush's vice president, Dick Cheney, who was more unpopular than Bush.[147] Moreover, even if President Bush had made false statements, he could argue that he had not made them in bad faith—that is, that he was acting in good faith when he erred in authorizing the Iraqi invasion in the aftermath of the terrorist attacks against the United States on 9/11. Last but not least, many members of Congress supported the invasion of Iraq and were not disposed to say, at least at that point, that either they or the president had been mistaken in doing so.

Why wasn't Barack Obama impeached?

President Obama was, from the moment he entered office, harshly criticized by Republican leaders on many different grounds. Among the more persistent complaints were claims that Obama made illegal recess appointments,[148] lied when he said that everyone could keep their current health plans under the Affordable Care Act,[149] exceeded the boundaries of his powers and usurped legislative power when he authorized executive actions deferring deportation for the children of people who had illegally entered the United States,[150] approved secret surveillance of American people in the name of national security,[151] and authorized drones to kill people, including some American citizens, who had joined the forces fighting against the United States in Iraq and Afghanistan.[152]

In some cases, such as recess appointments and immigration, the courts ruled against President Obama.[153] In other cases, the courts upheld President Obama's actions, as they did with the most controversial provision of the Affordable Care Act, the individual mandate to purchase private health care insurance.[154] In many cases, such as his ordering of the drone strikes, President Obama had claimed a legal basis for his actions.[155] In any event, Republicans used their criticisms of the president to rally their base and to retake control of the House in 2010 and the Senate in 2014. Once back in power, Republicans stepped up their opposition to the president, but they did not initiate impeachment inquiries against him. A majority of Americans never expressed support for impeaching President Obama, who remained popular throughout his terms in office, and in spite of the stiff Republican opposition and criticism he faced for years as president.[156]

Chapter 3

WHICH FEDERAL OFFICIALS ARE IMPEACHABLE

Who is subject to impeachment?

The Constitution provides that "The President and all civil officers of the United States, shall be removed from Impeachment for and Conviction of, Treason, Bribery, or other high Crimes and Misdemeanors."[1] While expressly specifying that the president and the vice president may be subject to impeachment, this clause challenges subsequent generations to figure out who are "all civil officers of the United States." This has turned out to be a tricky question. We can look to several things to guide us. For example, we can look at how the term "civil officers of the United States" is used throughout the Constitution. Presumably, the terms should mean the same thing throughout the document, and the contexts in which they appear might provide clues about its meaning. Another possible source of meaning to consider is how Congress has construed the phrase historically in the course of exercising its powers in the field of impeachment or how presidents and Congress have construed the terms in other contexts. Yet another place to look for clues to the meaning of this phrase is how the framers and ratifiers understood that language in their discussions in the constitutional and ratification conventions. The answer to the basic question of who is subject to impeachment depends on which of various different techniques for determining the meaning of particular language in the Constitution seems to be the most persuasive.

Are members of Congress subject to impeachment?

The Senate has answered this question in the negative. Indeed, the Senate faced that question in its first impeachment trial. The subject of that proceeding was William Blount, who had been impeached by the House but expelled from the Senate before the beginning of his impeachment trial.[2] The significance of the Senate's 14–11 vote to dismiss the matter because of a lack of jurisdiction is not entirely clear, though the Senate treats its vote as deciding that senators were not "civil officers of the United States" and therefore not impeachable for their misconduct.[3] Before we consider more extensively the question of whether the Senate was correct in reaching that judgment on the impeachability of members of Congress, there is another argument or two that support the Senate's vote to dismiss Blount's impeachment trial.

Consider the structure and design of the Constitution and whether it makes sense that the framers would have allowed two different ways for a member of Congress to be ejected by Congress. One way is explicit in the Constitution—the process for expulsion of a senator by his colleagues for disorderly conduct.[4] Blount was the first member of the House or the Senate to be expelled.[5] The House has subsequently expelled five of its members, and the Senate has expelled fifteen of its members: Blount and fourteen others were expelled because they abandoned their offices to join their states in seceding from the Union during the Civil War.[6] No senator has been expelled since the Civil War.[7] It is possible that both expulsion and impeachment were intended to be used to deal with a senator's corruption—expulsion for "disorderly conduct," which sounds like something different from breaking the law or doing something criminal or dishonest. Indeed, both chambers of Congress have determined they each may censure or reprimand their respective members for conduct that is worthy of condemnation but does not constitute "disorderly conduct."[8]

Yet, in the absence of debates or other evidence from the constitutional and ratification conventions demonstrating the intention that both processes may be used to redress the corruption or misconduct of a member of Congress, we are left to wonder why the members of the first Congress, which was composed of a number of people who had participated in drafting and ratifying the Constitution, would have wanted two different methods for senators to be ousted from office. Is it possible that it would be absurd to think that there should be two methods for ousting senators, not just one, and that the House would have a role in determining whether senators should be removed for their misconduct? Did the First Congress make a mistake in Blount's case? Is it possible that the methods address different kinds of misconduct? Was the close vote on Blount an indication that perhaps subsequent generations should not give undue weight to the Senate's determination that members of Congress are not impeachable? None of this is to say that a differently constituted Senate, many years later, would be unable to reconsider this question and reach a different result. It could, though in fact no subsequent Senate has found a sufficiently persuasive reason to conclude that the first Senate erred in concluding that members of Congress were not impeachable, a question of constitutional law that everyone in the Senate at the time understood was important and would establish a significant precedent for Congress and the future of the Constitution.

For purposes of impeachment, to whom does the phrase "all civil officers of the United States" refer?

The significance of this phrase is that it denotes the class of people who, in addition to both the president and vice president, are impeachable. This phrase is obviously not self-defining, though some authoritative interpreters of the Constitution agree on its meaning. Indeed, the Senate, the executive branch, the Supreme Court, and many scholars agree that the Senate correctly dismissed Blount's impeachment trial and that the language "civil officers of the United States" refers to certain high-ranking officials within the executive and judicial branches.[9] There are several arguments in support of that position.

First, several provisions of the Constitution use rather plain language that excludes members of Congress from being counted among "all civil officers of the United States." For example, Article II, Section 2, provides that the president "shall Commission all the Officers of the United States."[10] It is safe to say that the president does not have the power to appoint or commission members of Congress and therefore the latter do not fall within the category of "officers of the United States." Similarly, Article I, Section 6, provides that "no person holding any office under the United States shall also be a member of either house during his continuance in office."[11] This language obviously prohibits someone who has accepted an appointment as an "officer of the United States" from also serving as a member of Congress (and presumably vice versa). The conflicts of interest that this clause seeks to eliminate can be avoided only if the clause is also read to prohibit members of Congress from serving at the same time as "officers of the United States." Moreover, the appointments clause in Article II, Section 2, indicates that members of Congress are not "officers of the United States."[12] It speaks of two kinds of federal officers, neither of which likely includes members of Congress. On the one hand, the fact that the president "shall nominate, and by and with the Advice and Consent of the Senate, shall appoint [all] other officers of the United States . . ." raises the plain inference that "officers of the United States" are presidentially appointed officials who occupy offices created by Congress. On the other hand, the "inferior officers" to which the appointments clause refers in contradistinction to "officers of the United States" are less important officials whose appointment Congress may, pursuant to this clause, vest in other, non-legislative authorities. Members of Congress are not appointed by presidents; nor do they occupy offices created by Congress. Hence, Congressmen do not fit into what appears to be the plain meaning of "officers of the United States."

The Supreme Court has adopted this same construction of the Constitution. It has ruled several times that the phrase "civil officers of the United States" refers to executive and judicial officials who wield substantial authority.[13] Pursuant to this reading, high-ranking officials within the executive branch, such as cabinet officers, and federal judges, including Supreme Court justices, are subject to the federal impeachment process. But, members of Congress are not.

Beyond this, the prestigious Office of Legal Counsel in the United States, which serves as the constitutional lawyers for the Department of Justice, the president, and the heads of executive departments and agencies, concluded, on the basis of its own study of the question, that members of Congress are not civil officers for purposes of the impeachment process but that certain high-ranking executive and judicial branch officials may be subject to impeachment.[14] As a practical matter, the opinions of the Office of Legal Counsel are binding throughout the executive branch. Although their opinions are not technically binding on subsequent Offices of Legal Counsel, the office itself and subsequent attorneys general and presidents tend to defer to earlier opinions because the office has a tradition of nonpartisanship in delivering its opinions. The office is considered to have developed special expertise on questions of constitutional law that face the executive branch.

If there is not universal consensus on the meaning of "all civil officers of the United States," who disagrees with that interpretation of the Constitution and why?

Some scholars have disagreed with the conclusion that the constitutional language "all civil officers of the United States" excludes members of Congress and refers solely to certain high-ranking executive and judicial branch officials. One of the most prominent of these scholars was Raoul Berger, who wrote an influential treatise on the impeachment process in 1974.[15] Berger argued that the framers were familiar with the British practice in which "the vast bulk of impeachments" were brought against members of the House of Lords, the upper chamber of Parliament.[16] Berger further cited arguments from the ratification conventions in which several delegates appeared to presume, at least to Berger, that senators were impeachable given the concern they expressed over the Senate's being given the power to expel its own members.[17]

Seth Barrett Tillman, a prolific constitutional scholar who is a lecturer at Maynooth University in Ireland, has also taken issue with the construction of the phrase "all civil officers of the United States." He argues that these words were actually written to exclude the president and the vice president and other elected officials in the federal government, including members of Congress.[18] Hence, for Tillman, the Senate reached the right result in the case of William Blount, but his construction of the phrase leads to the conclusion that the president is not covered by this same language, which he reads as directed at people who had been appointed to federal offices, such as the members of the president's cabinet.

Tillman supports his construction of the terms "civil officers of the United States" through several arguments based on the Constitution's text and history and early historical practices. First, he finds it meaningful that the clause setting forth the class of impeachable officials expressly mentions the president and the vice president and then is followed by the terms "all civil officers of the United States." Tillman infers from this phrasing that the president and the vice president are distinct from "all civil officers of the United States." He argues that, if the president and vice president were part of the same class as "all civil officers of the United States," there would have been no need to list them explicitly among the federal officials who may be subject to impeachment.

Second, according to Tillman, several early presidents—George Washington, Thomas Jefferson, James Madison, and James Monroe—accepted gifts from foreign states without asking for congressional approval, which would have been required if they were included among the "officers of the United States," to whom the foreign emoluments clause applies. Tillman accords special weight to this fact because, in constitutional interpretation, we tend to defer to how early figures of authority, such as our first few presidents, understood their powers.

Third, Tillman contends his reading of the text—as indicating that neither the president nor the vice president counts among the "officers of the United States"—is consistent with the original meaning of "officers of the United States," which, he argues, was based on the phrase "office under the Crown."[19] The latter phrase, used in the English practice prior to the drafting of the federal Constitution, referred not to the king or to elected offices but rather to appointed offices whose authority derived from the appointing authority.[20] Moreover, in 1792, the Senate asked then Treasury Secretary Alexander Hamilton to produce a financial statement listing all people within the federal government holding "Office . . . under the United States."[21] As Tillman has demonstrated, Hamilton did not include in that list "the President, the Vice-President, or members of Congress."[22] This fact, too, reinforces Tillman's reading that the phrase "officers of the United States" excludes federally elected officials but instead applies to appointed positions in the executive or judicial branches. Last but not least, Tillman and a coauthor, Professor Josh Blackman, have argued that Tillman's construction of the language "all civil officers of the United States" is consistent with how three early state constitutions used the similar phrase "under the state."[23] Altogether, Tillman finds that these arguments support the conclusion that "officers of the United States" does not include the president, the vice president, or members of Congress.

So, who is right about the meaning of "all civil officers of the United States"?

To begin with, let's be clear about where there is agreement about the meaning of this phrase. There is significant scholarly agreement that "all civil officers of the United States" includes federally appointed officials in the executive and judicial branches but excludes members of Congress. That leaves the Senate's dismissal of the Blount impeachment trial intact, while clarifying that the range of officials who may be subject to the impeachment process includes the president, the vice president, and at least some appointees in the executive and judicial branches. But there is disagreement with respect to at least two things: which federal appointees are subject to the impeachment process (recall the Supreme Court says that it is those who wield substantial or significant authority) and whether federal judges may be disciplined in ways other than through the impeachment process (and, if so, for what).

First, there are two strong counterarguments to Berger's claim that the framers were familiar with the English practice of allowing impeachment of members of Congress and consequently meant for the Constitution to adopt that understanding. The first problem is that one objective of the framers in fashioning the impeachment process, perhaps the main objective, was to distinguish the American from the English system of impeachment. The framers of our Constitution did not want to follow the English practice in all particulars; they wanted to establish a uniquely American process that applied to a narrower range of people than the English system did. Moreover, Berger's argument could lead to absurd results, which the people drafting and ratifying the Constitution never would have wanted, and it would be a mistake to implement. His argument actually leads to the conclusion that anyone may be subject to impeachment, since the reason why members of Parliament were impeachable is that everyone was impeachable in the English system.

Yet we know this is not what the framers wanted. Again, the framers deliberately narrowed the class of people subject to impeachment. Berger's argument disregards that effort. And while some people made the claim during the ratification conventions that members of Congress were impeachable, these people were the anti-Federalists who were attempting to undermine support for the Constitution. In fact, every time someone asserted during the conventions that members of Congress were impeachable they were met with stiff resistance.[24]

The question of whether Tillman is right in his construction of the range of officials to whom the foreign emoluments clause applies has significant ramifications for the scope of impeachable offenses. If Tillman is right, then that clause does not apply to the president and the vice president and they therefore cannot violate that clause. Accepting income or any benefit from a foreign state might still pose a problem for a president, but not, at least according to Tillman, because it violated the foreign emoluments clause. Knowing who is impeachable still does not resolve the question for what things may they be impeached. Here, I will consider the counterarguments made against Tillman's construction of the class of people to whom the foreign emoluments clause applies.

The place to begin any examination of the foreign emoluments clause is with its text, which provides that "no Person holding any Office of Profit or Trust under the United States shall, without consent of Congress, accept any present, Emolument, Office, or Title, of any kind whatever, from any King, Prince, or foreign State."[25] The first thing to note is that this clause is not worded exactly like the principal impeachment clause, which applies to "all civil officers of the United States." The difference in wording might be inconsequential, as Tillman suggests, or perhaps it might have been drafted to apply to a broader class of people than "civil officers of the United States."

Several arguments have been made to support interpreting the foreign emoluments clause more broadly than Tillman does. First, the argument could be made that Tillman is mistaken in assuming that the Americans who drafted the Constitution merely borrowed the language and concept underlying the foreign emoluments clause from the British. Whereas the British used the phrase "office under the Crown" to denote people appointed by the sovereign, the key language "under the United States" used in the foreign emoluments clause was meant to encompass anyone who exercised any power on behalf of the federal government and whose authority derived from the "general government's democratically legitimated sovereign power."

Second, the Constitutional Convention debates suggest a broader, rather than a narrower, reading of the class of people to whom the foreign emoluments clause applies. In fact, Edmund Randolph, who would later serve as the United States' first attorney general, declared during the convention that the foreign emoluments clause was meant to "exclude corruption and foreign influence" and to "prohibit any one in office from receiving or holding emoluments from foreign states."[26] During the Virginia ratifying convention, Randolph underscored the importance of the problem of "the president receiving emoluments from foreign powers."[27] He explained that "it is impossible to guard better against corruption" than by having a president who "is restrained from receiving any present or emoluments whatever."[28]

Zephyr Teachout, a Fordham University law professor who has engaged in an extended debate with Tillman over the scope of the foreign emoluments clause, contends that fighting corruption was one of the Constitution's principal objectives.[29] She argues that the Constitution has a "structural commitment to combat corruption." She argues that the framers talked about corruption more than anything else during the Constitutional Convention, and that, as a result, there are "nearly two dozen features of the original Constitution that were designed to combat corruption," including two other clauses restricting emoluments, including the restriction that the president may not receive any "emolument" from the United States besides the official compensation authorized to be paid to the president by the government of the United States.[30] It thus makes no sense, in her judgment, to maintain, as do Tillman and Josh Blackman, that the foreign emoluments clause does not apply to the president. In contrast, the Office of Legal Counsel agrees that this clause applies to the president, and, whatever might have been the case in the early days of the Republic, the modern practice has been to treat the president as subject to the foreign emoluments clause.

But even assuming that Teachout has the better of this argument, what about Tillman's argument that George Washington, Thomas Jefferson, James Madison, and James Monroe accepted foreign gifts without asking Congress for permission? Perhaps whatever they thought is not dispositive, though it is hard to ignore a constitutional understanding they all seemed to share. For example, the First Congress authorized the National Bank, which the Supreme Court later upheld, but President Jackson vetoed its rechartering because he thought it was unconstitutional.[31] The point is not that President Jackson was right or wrong; the point is that other, later authorities may reach different conclusions about matters of constitutional law, just as the Office of Legal Counsel has done with respect to its construction of the foreign emoluments clause.

It is, however, impossible to ignore entirely the fact that these presidents actually accepted gifts of any serious value. Put differently, it is doubtful anyone could have made a serious case that the receipt of these gifts in any meaningful way corrupted any of these early presidents.

Perhaps there is a different explanation for Hamilton's choosing not to include the president and the vice president on his list of federal officials who were "civil officers of the United States." Perhaps it could be argued that Hamilton might have understood the question he was being asked as directing him to list the "civil offices" that "federal legislators would be barred from accepting, and which offices those standing for election to Congress for the first time in 1792 would be obliged to surrender if elected."[32] In any event, whatever answer Hamilton gave, we know that it was not in response to the basic question whether the foreign emoluments clause applies to the president.

Yet another argument countering Tillman's claim that the foreign emoluments clause does not apply to the president is that it would lead to absurd results. For example, it follows from his argument that there would be no constitutional prohibition against the president serving as a member of Congress while he was also serving as president. As Frank Bowman, a law professor at the University of Missouri, suggests, it is equally absurd to construe the Constitution, as Tillman's theory allows, as prohibiting the "U.S. ambassador to France from accepting a jeweled snuff box from the French government, but would allow the King of France to award the President of the United States a title of nobility accompanied by a grant of land and revenues." Other equally, if not more absurd, results could follow, including foreign states' granting titles or substantial revenue to a vice president in exchange for his siding with them in disputes with the United States. While Tillman might respond that the receipt of such gifts might provide a basis for impeachment, his own argument provides the defense that such receipt did not violate any part of the Constitution.

Tillman might counter that the examples given of possible corruption of the president fail to recognize that the president's conduct in each instance is problematic not because of the foreign emoluments clause but rather because it might be considered bribery and therefore may provide a basis for impeachment. Tillman might argue that, if foreign powers are successfully inducing the president to act in ways that are counter to the interests of the United States—to sell out American interests, it in effect sounds an awful lot like bribery. Indeed, Gouverneur Morris said as much when he talked of the need to protect against royal briberies, which had been a problem for the English:

> Our Executive was not like a Magistrate having a life interest, much less like one having an hereditary interest in his office. He may be bribed by a greater interest to betray his trust; and no one would say that we ought to expose ourselves to the danger of seeing the first Magistrate in foreign pay, without being able to guard against it by displacing him. One would think that the King of England will be secured against bribery. He has as it were a fee simple in the whole Kingdom. Yet Charles II was bribed by Louis XIV.[33]

Twice in the same passage, Morris characterizes the "crime" being committed as bribery.

One must be cautious not to over-interpret Morris's statement. For one thing, there were instances in which delegates described a president's receipt of gifts as a problem addressed by the foreign emoluments clause. When the latter clause is mentioned in the constitutional and ratification conventions, it is in reference—in virtually every instance—to the president. If the foreign emoluments clause is part of an overall scheme within the Constitution to combat corruption, the principal concern underlying that scheme was to keep the president in check. The framers were consumed with limiting a president's vulnerability to corruption, not the potential for corruptibility of those serving with him. Recall Randolph's express declaration that a fundamental purpose of the foreign emoluments clause was to combat presidential corruption. It would have been perverse for the framers to express their concerns about presidential corruption throughout the convention and then discover that the president was not somehow covered by the very provisions they had fashioned to prevent his corruption.

And what about the few state constitutions that used language similar to "officers of the United States," which Tillman and Blackman read as having been used to distinguish appointed from elected officers? It could well be that the phrase was used to distinguish executive and judicial officials from legislative ones—but how do we know whether this or the Tillman-Blackman reading is the correct one? And, if Tillman and Blackman are right in their interpretation, how much difference should it make to the overall construction of the foreign emoluments clause and meaning of the language "all civil officers of the United States?"

The objective in constitutional interpretation is always to see which reading of the Constitution makes the most sense of all the different sources of meaning. Tillman and Blackman would argue that their reading makes the most sense of the Constitution's text, using original meaning, and early practices as sources of meaning, while Teachout and others would argue that their reading makes better sense, because it coordinates several different modes of constitutional analysis—Supreme Court precedent, modern practices, structure, and the consequences of the different constructions of the pertinent constitutional language.

Are Article III judges subject to impeachment?

The discussion of who are included among "all the civil officers of the United States" suggests that the answer is yes. Virtually everything we know about the history and early practices of impeachment point to the fact that federal judges may be subject to the impeachment process. No one seriously questions that the phrase "during good behavior" distinguishes judicial tenure from that executive and legislative branch officials, including the president and members of Congress. Presidents, vice presidents, and members of Congress have fixed terms, whereas federal judges do not. They have unlimited terms.[34] The phrase "during good behavior" is a term of art, familiar to the framers, that defined the length of judicial tenure. The framers were concerned with protecting the federal judiciary from political reprisals, and so vested judges with life tenure as long as they did not commit "Treason, Bribery, and other High crimes and misdemeanors."[35] Though federal judges therefore have different kinds of tenure as compared to that of presidents and vice presidents, federal judges may have their tenure interrupted if they commit impeachable offenses.

The framers of the Constitution were familiar with the three different kinds of judicial tenure that were used in England and the states. These were removal by the executive at will; by the executive upon "address" by the legislature; and by legislatures through impeachment. Easy dismissal of judges undermined their independence, making them less effective and vulnerable to losing office if the sovereign did not like their decisions. The framers knew that allowing the executive to easily remove judges had been a major grievance among the English in the seventeenth century, and indeed the Declaration of Independence cited the vulnerability of judges to being removed at the king's pleasure as one of its justifications.[36] Moreover, the framers considered but rejected legislative address to the executive.[37] That left the third option, subjecting judges to impeachment, as the one adopted by the framers.

The disagreements that arise among commentators have to do with whether impeachment is the exclusive means for addressing judicial misconduct or whether other means may be used, particularly with respect to misconduct that falls short of "Treason, Bribery, and other High crimes and misdemeanors." There is a good deal of authority supporting the exclusivity of impeachment as the means for disciplining judges. For example, Hamilton argued in the Federalist Papers that "the article respecting impeachments" in the Constitution was the "only provision on the point which is consistent with the necessary independence of the judicial character, and is the only one which we find in our Constitution in respect to our own judges."[38] On more than one occasion, the Supreme Court has suggested that impeachment is the exclusive means for addressing judicial misconduct.[39]

Yet, constitutional authorities have long recognized the need for the judiciary to police itself, particularly with respect to misconduct that falls short of an impeachable offense. Judges agree that they have some inherent authority to address problems with the performance of their colleagues (e.g., failures to do the job, becoming seriously ill, or allowing inexcusably long backlogs) or misconduct (e.g., drunkenness). The Congress, with the support of the federal judiciary, enacted the Judicial Conduct and Disability Act of 1980, which empowers anyone to bring a complaint against a judge for "conduct prejudicial to the effective and expeditious administration of the business of the courts" or has become, by virtue of mental or physical disability, "unable to discharge all the duties of the judicial office."[40] This act allows the judiciary to investigate these complaints itself and even implement some sanctions, such as a suspension, which is supposed to be temporary.[41] If a determination is made that a judge engaged in impeachable misconduct, the act allows the judges who have made this finding to refer the matter to the House of Representatives, so that it may consider impeachment.[42]

Judges have generally followed the procedures of this statute, though the more extreme sanctions it authorizes—suspension or referrals to Congress—have concerned some judges. Their concern is that impeachment is the exclusive means the Constitution authorizes for judicial removal and therefore the act's authorization of suspensions is unconstitutional.[43] Interestingly, the first successful impeachment was the removal of Judge John Pickering for insanity and intoxication.[44] President Jefferson had initiated the matter,[45] and a number of commentators have pointed out that, even though Jefferson and his fellow Republicans wanted to use Pickering as the first in a series of efforts to remove ardent Federalists who were on the bench, Pickering's son pleaded with Congress not to impeach him because the aberrant behavior he exhibited was the result of his growing feeble.[46]

Ever since that impeachment, Congress has been reluctant to use impeachment to address a judge's infirmity, and so the Judicial Conduct and Disability Act of 1980 was designed in part to provide a mechanism for addressing mental or physical disability by means other than impeachment. The principal argument supporting the federal law in making this arrangement is the acknowledgment that mental or physical disability may not be grounds for impeachment. Such infirmity might pose a problem, but, echoing the concerns of Judge Pickering's son, using impeachment as a solution taints the judge's reputation forever even though the supposed misconduct was not deliberate and was likely beyond the judge's control. This justification does not appease every judge, and there lingers, to this day, concerns among some judges that the disciplinary mechanisms authorized by the law make it possible for judges to be subject to sanctions without the safeguards available in the impeachment process, including having a majority in the House and more than two-thirds of the Senate agreeing on the severity of the offense and ensuring that those imposing the punishment are politically accountable.

To what extent are officials subject to impeachment for misconduct before their election or appointment to impeachable offices?

We know that private citizens are not subject to the impeachment process, but what if someone who is now an impeachable official did something bad before assuming office and it came to light *after* the person assumed office? Imagine, for example, a presidential candidate who lied about committing a murder during the campaign but then later is discovered to have been responsible for that crime. May that person be impeached for the pre-presidential misconduct?

This question turns out not to be completely hypothetical. Although the framers never directly considered this question, it has come up with respect to both judges and presidents over the last few decades, and this issue came up during the 2009 impeachment proceedings brought against Thomas Porteous, who at the time was a federal district judge in Louisiana.[47] Years after his appointment as a federal judge, Porteous faced the prospect of impeachment. Prosecutors had cut a deal with a man who claimed the judge had engaged in a wide range of misbehavior both before and after his appointment as federal district judge, including receiving kickbacks as a state court judge.[48] When the matter came before the Congress, Porteous tried to deflect some of the charges by arguing that even if he had done something wrong as a state court judge it was irrelevant to his current office.[49]

The House rejected that argument. It took the position that there was a connection between the misconduct and his current office, for he had lied about the misconduct to the president, who nominated him to the office; to the Federal Bureau of Investigation, which did his background check; and to the Senate, which confirmed him.[50] As a judicial nominee, he was bound, under penalty of perjury, to be forthcoming with the FBI doing his background check, and he had pledged under oath to the Senate that he was not withholding any evidence that would impact negatively on his character or judgment.[51] Of course, he was doing just that. It was obvious that had Porteous made this disclosure while his nomination was pending before the Senate, it would have never confirmed him. So, he defrauded the Senate to get the job. There was, in other words, a connection between the misconduct and the judge's securing the federal judgeship he held. The House unanimously impeached the judge, and the Senate convicted him on the basis of several impeachment articles, including lying to the Senate.[52]

The Porteous example illuminates how we should deal with the question of whether a president can be impeached for having lied or engaged in some other kind of misconduct during his campaign. Assuming that the lie or the misconduct concealed from the public some kind of serious misconduct, the answer is yes. (If he hid something trivial, it is hard to imagine why he would have lied or why the lie would have made any difference to the outcome of the election.) The critical thing is to establish a clear connection between the misconduct and the president's securing the office he occupies. If, for example, the people elected a president with full knowledge of the misconduct (e.g., they had known he had killed someone in a duel, which happened to be the case with President Jackson), then impeachment would seem inappropriate because the public appeared to have effectively ratified (or accepted) the misconduct. Given that impeachment is not supposed to be a substitute for elections, it seems improper to punish a president for the misconduct, which the voters had a chance to use against him but chose not to (for whatever reason). If, however, the voters did not know about the misconduct until after the election or it turns out that only after the election did the voters discover that what the president told them was untrue, a good argument could be made that the president effectively defrauded the voters to secure office. In this latter case, the president's misconduct seems analogous to that of Judge Porteous, who had defrauded the Senate to secure his appointment as a judge.

The difficult question in the Porteous case or the hypothetical in which the president lies during a campaign is how close a connection must there be between the misconduct and the federal office currently being occupied. There has to be a close connection or nexus between the misconduct and the office, but how close must it be? The closest possible connection the law can require is called the "but for" test, which asks whether something would not have happened but for the misconduct in question. While this test ensures the closest possible fit between cause and effect, it might be difficult, if not impossible, as a practical matter, to establish that a president might not have been elected, or someone might not have been appointed as a judge, but for the misconduct in question. If we adopt a slightly less demanding fit between cause and effect, it can be easier to show, but at the risk of allowing for too much play between the joints. In any event, if the Congress treats this issue as it does other questions about evidence or burdens of proof, then it would leave it to the discretion of each individual member of Congress to decide for himself or herself how close the connection must be between the misconduct and securing the office in question.

To what extent are officials subject to impeachment for misconduct after they have left office?

The initial reaction to this question might be of course not. After all, we are talking about someone who has returned to private life, and we have already established earlier that private citizens are not subject to impeachment in this country. But what if the misconduct was to suppress information about other misconduct committed while the person was in office? At this point, we might be inclined to fall back on the reasoning used to support recourse to impeachment in cases where a close connection can be shown between the misconduct committed prior to entering office and the office currently occupied. It might be equally plausible to think that former officials might be vulnerable to impeachment for misconduct that came to light after they left office. Here it is important to recall that one of the sanctions in the impeachment process is disqualification from serving in any federal office in the future. The imposition of that sanction seems appropriate in the case of someone who had engaged in misconduct while in office but whose misconduct did not come to light until after they left office.

As we wrestle with this question, we should keep in mind the basic nature of the impeachment process. The Constitution does not impose a duty on Congress to initiate an impeachment proceeding whenever there is evidence of wrongdoing constituting an impeachable offense. There is no language or history suggesting that Congress has any such obligation. Instead, members of Congress have the discretion to initiate impeachment proceedings, and the history of impeachment practices is a history of how that discretion has been used over time. The fact that impeachment is possible does not mean that the Congress must use it. There could be many reasons why Congress does not make recourse to impeachment, including the belief of many members that a forced resignation might be preferable.

Richard Nixon is the most famous example of a forced resignation, but he is not the only one. In 2017, a well-known and widely respected federal court of appeals judge, Alex Kozinski, resigned immediately after the press published a series of charges made by former law clerks and others of decades of inappropriate behavior, including sexual harassment, asking about sexual proclivities, uninvited displays and discussions of pornography, and non-consensual touching and grabbing.[53] The resignation short-circuited an investigation into the charges authorized by the chief judge of the US Court of Appeals for the Ninth Circuit, on which Kozinski had served for more than thirty years. The resignation foreclosed impeachment proceedings. Nonetheless, it does not relieve us of the question of to what extent misconduct like that of Judge Kozinski may serve as the basis for impeachment.

Chapter 4

DEFINING IMPEACHABLE OFFENSES

What do the study of the origins of the Constitution and our experiences with impeachment teach us about the meaning of the terms "other high crimes or misdemeanors"?

From the British and colonial understandings of impeachment, the constitutional and ratification convention debates, and late-eighteenth-century and early-nineteenth-century commentaries on the federal impeachment process, we can identify several distinctive features of the kinds of misconduct for which people may be impeached, convicted, and removed from office. Coordinating that historiography with Congress's historical practices in the impeachment process enables us to sketch a good, albeit not perfectly consensus-commanding, understanding of the scope of impeachable offenses.

First, not all crimes are impeachable offenses. Some crimes are just not serious enough, especially when we consider that the purpose is to identify the grounds allowed by the Constitution to cut short a high-ranking official's tenure. Again, jaywalking is a good example of a crime that does not rise to the level of an impeachable offense. Another might be a moving violation in a car or destroying a mailbox. These are all crimes, but none is sufficiently serious to constitute an impeachable offense.

Second, we know that not all impeachable offenses are crimes. The framers were familiar with the English tradition in which the phrase "other High crimes and misdemeanors" was understood as referring to political crimes, which were acts that caused serious injury to the State (or the Republic, in the case of the United States) but that were not necessarily codified as crimes by the State. Political crimes do not require the perpetrator to be sent to jail. Many abuses of power cause damage but are not criminal offenses. A good example is the second impeachment article that the House Judiciary Committee approved against Richard Nixon, which charged Nixon with having abused his powers to order the Central Intelligence Agency and the Federal Bureau of Investigation to go after his political enemies.[1] The misconduct alleged here was not criminal, but it was serious.

Third, we know from the debates in the constitutional and ratification conventions that the proponents of the Constitution used similar examples to illustrate the kinds of offenses for which presidents and others may be impeached, convicted, and removed from office. They frequently referred to impeachable offenses as "great" offenses injuring the country, and they stressed that impeachment would apply if an official such as the president "deviates from his duty" or if "he dare to abuse the powers vested in him by the people."[2]

Alexander Hamilton made similar observations in explaining and defending the scope of impeachable offenses in the Federalist Papers, often treated as either an important source to consult for understanding how the framers understood the Constitution they had just drafted or brilliant exercises in propaganda that may, or may not, convey the genuine constitutional views of Hamilton, Madison, or the framers generally. Hamilton noted, for example, that the "subject [of the Senate's] jurisdiction [in impeachment trials] are those offenses which proceed from the misconduct of public men, or, in other words, from the abuse or violation of some public trust. They are of a nature which may with peculiar propriety be denominated POLITICAL, as they relate chiefly to injuries done immediately to the society itself."[3]

Hamilton further commented that the Senate, as the impeachment court, could not be "tied down" by strict rules, "either in the delineation of the offense by the prosecutors [who would probably come from the House of Representatives] or in the construction of it by the judges," that is, the senators.[4] If the Federalist Papers are genuinely reflective of the original meaning of the scope of impeachable offenses, then they can be read to suggest that the range of impeachable misconduct could not be neatly specified in advance of actual proceedings; it would be worked out over time through congressional practices. If, however, the Federalist Papers' constitutional arguments should be taken with a grain of salt, because they were designed to appease concerns about the newly drafted Constitution during the ratification process, then we should take care not to fetishize them or to place too much weight on them in trying to determine the ultimate meaning of the Constitution.

Justices James Wilson and Joseph Story, widely regarded as two of the most thoughtful early commentators on the Constitution, shared Hamilton's views, as expressed in the Federalist Papers, that impeachable offenses were political crimes, the specifics of which had to be worked out over time like the common law. The common law is how judges have developed, on a case-by-case basis, the particular rules or standards that might be used to resolve to particular legal contests, such as those relating to contracts, torts, or property. In the shared understanding of Hamilton, Wilson, and Story, the scope of impeachable offenses had to be worked out in a similar way, incrementally, on a case-by-case basis.

For example, in a series of lectures on the Constitution given immediately after his appointment to the Supreme Court, Justice James Wilson, who had been a widely respected delegate from Pennsylvania at the constitutional convention, referred to impeachments as encompassing, among other things, "political crimes and misdemeanors."[5] Justice Wilson understood the term "high" that described the "crimes and misdemeanors" for which someone could be convicted and tossed out of office as "political" in the same sense as Hamilton had discussed in the Federalist Papers.

Similarly, Justice Story, in a widely respected series of commentaries on the Constitution, suggested that the "political injuries" that could serve as the basis for impeachment and removal were to be "[s]uch kinds of misdeeds . . . as peculiarly injure the commonwealth by the abuse of high office or trust."[6] Story explained further that "no previous statute is necessary to authorize an impeachment for any official misconduct," nor, in his judgment, could such a statute ever be drafted because "political offenses are so various and complex a character, so utterly incapable of being defined, or classified, that the task of positive legislation would be impracticable, if it were not almost absurd to attempt it."[7] Justice Story believed, like Hamilton and Wilson, that besides the fact that impeachable offenses had to entail abuses of power, injuries to the Republic, and breaches of trust, Congress would end up working out on a case-by-case basis the specific misdeeds that actually were the abuses of power, injuries to the Republic, and breaches of trust for which impeachable officials could be impeached and removed from office.

In impeachment proceedings, how have the members of Congress understood the meaning of "other high crimes and misdemeanors"?

The short answer is: a lot. Each and every time the House has considered initiating an impeachment inquiry, one or more members have given some thought to the question of what constitutes "other high crimes and misdemeanors." Perhaps even more important, we know that when the House has actually impeached someone, a majority of its members must have thought (and routinely said) that the misconduct charged fit within the constitutional scope of impeachable offenses. The House has never decided to go forward with an impeachment without the majority's belief that the misconduct in question qualified as an impeachable offense.

One of the more interesting, widely repeated observations made about impeachment nicely captures this essential fact about impeachment. In 1970, Gerald Ford, then the Republican minority leader in the House of Representatives, pithily said that an impeachable offense "is whatever a majority of the House [considers it] to be at a given moment in history; conviction results from whatever offense or offenses two-thirds of the other body considers to be sufficiently serious to require removal of the accused from office."[8] Over the years, many commentators have pilloried Ford for this comment, often deriding his intelligence and dismissing the comment for merely stating the obvious.[9]

Yet, as I have thought about this comment over the many years I have studied impeachment, I think Ford was exactly right. He was not saying that a majority of the House just gets to make up whatever it wants to serve as the basis for an impeachment, and there's more to it than that. Ford was suggesting something different. He was saying that, over time, one good place to look for determining what may qualify as an impeachable offense is what the House has found to be sufficiently serious to serve as a basis for impeaching someone. So, if the House has impeached someone, we can infer from that the belief a majority must have thought an impeachable offense was involved. This is exactly what Justice Story said. He was suggesting that impeachment law would likely develop much as the common law of contracts or torts (personal injuries) has developed. The common law comprised judicial decisions on a particular subject over time, and these judicial decisions build on and feed off each other. A similar dynamic applies in the field of impeachment; Story was suggesting that in the field of impeachment, Congress, not courts, makes the critical decisions and so, in his view, congressional practices would comprise something akin to the common law of impeachment. Ford captured this same dynamic with his comment.

So, what do we discover when we look at how Congress has exercised its impeachment authorities over time? When we look at these practices in the field, we find that the Congress has generally agreed on several basic concepts: that not all crimes are impeachable offenses; not all impeachable offenses are crimes; and that impeachable offenses encompass serious abuses of power, breaches of trust, and serious injuries to the Republic. We know further that there are at least two serious requirements, or elements, for misconduct to qualify as an impeachable offense: there must be bad intent or bad faith, and there must be some bad act. The impeachment articles against every officer who has been impeached by the House and convicted and removed by the Senate have set forth these two basic elements. These elements are consistent with the framers' objective to narrow the scope of impeachable offenses from the English system in which anything could serve as the basis for impeachment.

Although there is ample evidence to suggest that the framers did not intend for the impeachment process to track the criminal law in all essential respects, the criminal law did provide a backdrop, as did the impeachment experiences in England and the states, for the drafting of the Constitution. The influence of these disparate sources on the impeachment clauses is evident in both the language adopted and post-ratification historical practices.[10] Both the original meaning and historical practices, including Hamilton's commentary on impeachment in the Federalist Papers and Justice Story's *Commentaries on the Constitution of the United States,* have indicated that the "bad acts constituting impeachable offenses are what the Founders understood to be political crimes."[11] Political crimes include serious offenses against the State and include not only serious felonies, which are codified as crimes and indictable, but also abuses of power and breaches of the public trust, which are not indictable.

Is the Congress bound by its prior practices or could it deviate from, or even abandon, those practices in the future?

Congress is not bound by its prior practices any more than a court of law is bound by its precedents. Judicial precedents are persuasive authority in courts, but courts, particularly the Supreme Court, sometimes overturn prior decisions that it has come to believe are mistaken and require overturning for other good reasons, such as proving to have been unworkable in practice.

A future Congress could decide, for example, that it no longer agrees with the Senate's judgment in the Blount trial or perhaps that impeachable misconduct should consist of both bad faith and bad actions. Indeed, this is another good example of Gerald Ford's insights into the process: the House could decide at one time that certain misconduct does not rise to the level of an impeachable offense and then reconsider that determination and reach a different conclusion at a later time. The Senate, of course, could do the same with respect to its own prior judgments made in impeachment trials.

This does not mean that all bets are off, and that anything may then serve as the basis for impeachment. Indeed, there are only two instances that have been considered in any way to have been possible abuses of the impeachment power. If anything, Congress appears to have underused, rather than overextended, its power of impeachment.

One of these cases was the impeachment, conviction, and removal of John Pickering in 1803–1804. The initial movement to impeach Pickering came from President Jefferson and Secretary of State James Madison, who wanted to use the impeachment process to get rid of judges they thought had become too partisan.[12] Pickering made a good target because of his odd behavior on the bench. Though he was impeached, convicted, and removed from office, it is unlikely that Congress would use the impeachment power in the same in a similar case now, because it has allowed courts to develop other mechanisms for addressing physical or mental infirmity, which seems to have been Pickering's most serious deficiency.

The other case where some people think the Senate went too far is the impeachment, conviction, and removal of federal district judge Halsted Ritter, in 1936. Though Ritter had been suspected—and impeached—for receiving kickbacks and other misconduct, the Senate convicted and removed him solely on the basis that he had brought the federal judiciary into disrepute.[13] Those grounds might trouble some people, who might worry that they were too broadly framed, effectively allowing members of Congress to oust Ritter for any reason any of them might have had. But the counterargument is that in Ritter's case, there was specific misconduct identified in the record that provided the basis for the catch-all impeachment article on which he was ultimately convicted. It could be further argued that it is essential for federal judges to be beyond reproach ethically and that once they have engaged in behavior that robs them of that essential quality they have degraded their office—that is, they have brought the federal judiciary into disrepute.

Interestingly, the Ritter precedent has not opened the door for Congress to extend the grounds on which it has subsequently impeached, convicted, and removed other judges. Since Ritter, the House has impeached five judges, all for serious alleged misconduct in office, including bribery, perjury, and sexual assault.[14] The Senate convicted and removed four of these five.[15] The only one of these judges it did not convict or remove was Samuel Kent, who resigned in order to avoid the disgrace of an impeachment trial for sexual assault, perjury, and obstruction of justice.[16] It is safe to assume that the grounds for which Kent had been impeached are universally considered legitimate grounds for impeachment. Congress retains the discretion not to move forward on an impeachment for several reasons, including its decision that an official's resignation that has eliminated the necessity for an impeachment trial.

Must an impeachable offense have a connection to an official's office or duties?

It is tempting simply to answer yes to this question, but the determination of whether certain misconduct may serve as the basis for an impeachment is more complex. To be sure, every example that the framers and ratifiers used to illustrate the kind of misconduct that would serve as an impeachable offense had some connection to an official's office or duties. For example, several delegates cited the bribery of the president by foreign interests as an example of the necessity for treating that kind of offense as impeachable because it corrupted the president's judgment and injured American interests.

But do these examples mean that officials may not face impeachment for misconduct that does not have any connection to their office or duties? In President Clinton's impeachment proceedings, his lawyers argued that his lying under oath and other acts to hide his sexual relationship with Monica Lewinsky from the public, his wife, and other authorities did not constitute impeachable misconduct because, they claimed, his sexual relationship with Lewinsky had nothing to do with his job as president.[17] But, that argument ignores or elides the fact that Clinton was one of Lewinsky's supervisors and thus the relationship revealed something about his attitude about and approach to the presidency.

The extent to which arguably private misconduct may serve as a legitimate basis for impeachment depends on the misconduct. For example, "bribery" serves as the basis for impeachment regardless of whether an official was being bribed or was attempting to bribe someone else. Moreover, at least two federal judges were impeached, convicted, and removed from office based in part on misconduct that had no direct relationship to their office or their formal duties. One impeachment article against Harry Claiborne charged that he had committed income tax fraud, while the charge against Walter Nixon was that he had made false statements to a grand jury to help the son of a business partner.[18] The House not only impeached those officials, but the Senate also convicted and removed both judges on those grounds.[19]

During President Clinton's impeachment proceedings, one point on which every expert witness agreed is that murder would provide an appropriate basis for impeaching the president even if it had nothing to do with his job. The same can be said of many other kinds of serious misconduct, including sexual assault or sexual harassment, which served as one of the bases for impeaching Samuel Kent. There are, in other words, certain bad acts that are legitimate grounds for impeachment even though they have nothing formally to do with an official's position or duties. The critical question is not *whether* misconduct unrelated to an official's job or duties may serve as a basis for his impeachment; rather, the important question is *which kinds* of misconduct unrelated to offices or duties may serve as a legitimate basis for impeachment.

Impeachability depends on several factors, including the seriousness of the offense and the damage it has done to an official's ability to maintain the trust or respect he or she needs in order to remain in office. With presidents and federal judges (or, for that matter, any officials), it is not difficult to see how murder or sexual harassment is sufficiently serious as an offense that it plainly undermines the moral authority they need to remain in office.

May someone be impeached for gross incompetence?

The discussion of the range of impeachable offenses raises a question about their boundaries or limits, including the extent to which malicious intent or bad faith is required. Is there any kind of bad behavior that is so awful that the accused's intent would not matter? Murder is often mentioned as an answer, but it is reasonable to assume that the defenses to a charge of murder are likely to be that the accused did not commit the bad act of murder and/or the accused acted in self-defense or did not commit the act with a malicious intent. What about a president or cabinet officer who was just awful as an administrator or oversaw a department or administration that was filled with corruption but did nothing? Does good faith matter in that instance, or is it possible to argue that the sheer magnitude of the incompetence provides a sufficient basis for an impeachment action?

These questions have turned out not just to be bothersome hypotheticals raised by scholars. They came up when the House considered the possible impeachment of John Koskinen, then the head of the Internal Revenue Service, in 2016.[20] At that time, Jason Chaffetz, a Republican member of the House of Representatives from Utah, urged his colleagues on the House Judiciary Committee to consider impeaching Koskinen for gross incompetence.[21] Chaffetz and several other Republican members of Congress were concerned that a few years earlier certain officials at the Internal Revenue Service had targeted conservative groups to deny them tax exemptions as nonprofit organizations.[22] When President Obama first appointed John Koskinen as the commissioner of the IRS in late 2013, Chaffetz was among the House members who pressed Koskinen to find out how the targeting had occurred, including the names of the officials who had been responsible for it.

When the House discovered that one of the officials involved, Lois Lerner, had lost hundreds of emails that might have been pertinent to the investigation, Chaffetz was displeased. He pressed Koskinen further to determine what had happened and why.[23] Koskinen promised he would do so.[24] But, when House members found out later that Koskinen had given misleading testimony before the House on what he had known and done to investigate the matter (and to keep it from ever reoccurring), Chaffetz asked the House Judiciary Committee to consider initiating an impeachment inquiry against Koskinen.[25] Koskinen insisted he had acted in good faith, prompting Chaffetz to argue that at the very least Koskinen merited impeachment based on the gross incompetence of his leadership of the IRS.[26]

In making a determination of whether to initiate an impeachment action against Koskinen, the House Judiciary Committee had to consider whether gross incompetence or negligence could serve as the legitimate basis for an impeachment. Chaffetz argued that Koskinen had a legal obligation to prevent files from being deleted (as they apparently were) after they had been placed under a protective order. Chaffetz disputed that bad intent had to be shown, and noted comments made during the Constitutional Convention and from Justice Joseph Story in his *Commentaries on the Constitution of the United States* indicating support for gross negligence as an impeachable offense. Some Democratic members of the House Judiciary Committee countered that, in rejecting "maladministration" as a basis for impeachment and instead adopting the standard of "Treason, Bribery, and other high crimes and misdemeanors," the framers had expressly refused to allow the scope of impeachable offenses to include anything akin to gross incompetence.[27]

As an expert witness before the House Judiciary Committee, I agreed with the latter argument and testified further that allowing an impeachment on the basis of gross incompetence to proceed, as Chaffetz was urging, broadened the basis for impeachment too far.[28] In my view, allowing gross negligence to serve as a basis for impeachment would not only make it easier to bring impeachments but also deviate from the long-standing practice within the House to require bad faith in addition to a bad act as a basis for impeachment.[29]

I suggested the possibility that Koskinen's superiors at the Treasury Department and the president could determine the level of his competence. I emphasized that bad faith, rather than incompetence, was an essential element of an impeachable offense.[30]

In late 2016, the Freedom Caucus, of which Chaffetz was a member, tried to force a vote in the House on Koskinen's impeachment, but it never came to a vote. The significance of that outcome remains a question. It is uncertain whether the committee's or the House's refusal to proceed with an impeachment attempt against Koskinen may serve as a precedent on the question of whether gross incompetence or negligence can serve as a basis for an impeachment. Even if it does, it is unclear how weighty a precedent it could be, given that the issue arose during a presidential election year in which the outcome could provide a solution to whatever problem was posed by having Koskinen remain in office. President Trump did not extend Koskinen's service as the commissioner of the IRS.

So, how are we supposed to determine what qualifies as "serious offenses" against the Republic or breaches of the public trust?

Case-by-case is the answer. This approach might not satisfy everyone, or perhaps even most people, but it is the most sensible method we have. Our experience with impeachment confirms the wisdom of Justice Story's insight that it would be impossible to codify—that is, to spell out in a statute or in one definitive list—all the specific misdeeds that would count as an impeachable offense. Through its experience, Congress makes determinations about whether to authorize an impeachment based on the context in which the misconduct arose.

The lack of certainty about what exactly comprises the full set of impeachable offenses, but thinking about there being a spectrum of the kinds of misconduct that officials might commit, might help our understanding even if it makes some people uneasy. At one end are those things we can all agree are inappropriate grounds for impeachment, such as jaywalking or a moving violation. At the other end are those things we can all agree are clearly legitimate grounds for impeachment, such as bribery, obstruction of justice, murder, and perjury. Whenever some misconduct comes before Congress whose seriousness it has not yet had the chance to consider in the context of an impeachment, the critical question it will ask is where does this misconduct fit on the spectrum of misconduct? Is it closer to the jaywalking end or to the bribery, murder, and obstruction of justice end? The closer it is to this latter end of the spectrum, the more likely it is the offense may serve as a legitimate basis for impeachment.

What is an example of an abuse of power that is impeachable?

The articles of impeachment that the House Judiciary Committee approved against President Nixon make two charges that are paradigmatic examples of impeachable offenses. One article charged that Nixon had ordered the heads of the Internal Revenue Service and the Federal Bureau of Investigation to harass his political enemies. Nixon's conduct was not illegal, but it was a clear abuse of power. As president, he had authority to give directions to the heads of these agencies, but that authority did not extend to investigating or auditing people solely because they were not popular with the president. The ability to direct these officials was unique to the presidency, and the abuse of that authority could only have been addressed through impeachment.

The House Judiciary Committee also charged President Nixon with obstruction of justice, which entails attacking or undermining the administration of justice. Nixon's efforts to use the power of the presidency to interfere with the investigations into the break-in of the Watergate complex and his own role in that affair were serious offenses against the country.

A harder question is whether the House Judiciary Committee's third article of impeachment against Nixon constituted an impeachable offense. It charged Nixon with violating a legislative subpoena. Whether or not Nixon had a viable defense against that article—namely, that complying with the order would have aggrandized the Congress at the expense of the presidency—requires looking more closely at executive privilege.

Who is Joe Isenberg, and why do his writings come up in some discussions of the scope of impeachable offenses?

Joseph Isenberg is a retired professor who taught tax law for many years at the University of Chicago Law School (indeed, I was one of his students). When he was a student at Yale Law School, he published an intriguing note about impeachment in the *Yale Law Journal*,[31] and in 1999, he published an intriguing review of the law of impeachment and presidential immunity. According to Isenberg, the Senate *must* remove an official for the enumerated offenses of "Treason, bribery, and other high crimes and misdemeanors," but it also had the power to remove him or her for misconduct other than the grounds specified in the Constitution. Based on Isenberg's review of the English law of impeachment, the framers' debates on impeachment, and the early practice of impeachment, "Congress has the power to impeach AND REMOVE civil officers for a wide range of serious offenses other than high crimes and misdemeanors."[32] His study of the historiography suggests that "Article II, Section 4, is not plausible as a comprehensive definition of impeachable offenses," and he notes that "In the entire body of impeachment cases and commentary in England impeachable offenses are not once held out as congruent with 'high crimes and misdemeanors.' "[33]

I, however, have not been persuaded by his arguments or his evidence. There are many reasons I think his scholarship is flawed, but three should suffice here. The first is based on the Constitution's text. The Constitution provides that "the President, the Vice-President, and all civil officers of the United States may be removed upon impeachment and conviction for Trial, Bribery, and Other High Crimes and Misdemeanors."[34] The language suggests, quite straightforwardly, that impeachment and conviction are restricted to, or conditioned on, a certain range of misbehavior. If the framers had wanted, as Isenberg argues, to provide for a broader basis for impeachment, they could have done so. Indeed, they had many opportunities to do so during the constitutional convention but rejected them. They settled on language that narrowed the scope of impeachable offenses.

Though Isenberg says at one point that the "framers did not consider high misdemeanors to be a grab-bag of offenses, but crimes directed against the state," he suggests that the language of "high crimes and misdemeanors" is nothing more than "an incantatory phrase, not an element of substance." [35] In other words, Isenberg believes the phrase is not meant to actually constrain or limit the grounds for removal. He suggests further that judges have been subject to removal for misdeeds other than "high crimes and misdemeanors." But, once we have acknowledged that the text is not meant to confine or constrain the entities to which it has been addressed, it loses its meaning for all practical purposes.

It is one thing to argue that the Constitution's text authorizes specific things not mentioned within it, such as implied congressional powers or unremunerated rights, but it is quite another to suggest that the text has a specific meaning that does not define the outer boundary or limits of federal power. Isenberg would no doubt point to the broader language defining judicial tenure "during good behavior" as encompassing or allowing for judges to be removed—through impeachment—on grounds other than or in addition to "high crimes and misdemeanors." Assuming this is true, it does not explain why presidents, vice presidents, and other nonjudicial officers may be impeached, convicted, and removed from office on grounds other than "high crimes and misdemeanors." The problem is that Isenberg's construction makes it easier for judges to be ousted than any other officials, a possibility that seems impossible to square with their unique tenure, which was designed to insulate them from political reprisals rather than to make it easier to remove.

Second, Chief Justice John Marshall declared ours to be a system of "enumerated powers" in his landmark opinion in *McCulloch v. Maryland* (1819) upholding the constitutionality of the National Bank.[36] If Marshall was right, it would follow that no branch has unlimited or uncircumscribed power. Yet this is what Isenberg is arguing, that the Constitution sets forth no practical limits on the grounds for impeachment other than the fact that the "crimes" must be "against the state."

Third, none of the delegates at the constitutional and ratification conventions said that they expected the Constitution to allow for conviction and removal on grounds besides or beyond "other high crimes and misdemeanors." When they spoke of impeachment, those who supported the Constitution spoke of particular kinds of misconduct, which makes sense since their objective was to narrow the scope of impeachable offenses from what it had been in England.

Chapter 5

EXPLAINING THE PROCEDURES IN IMPEACHMENT

How does an impeachment begin?

Generally, impeachments can begin in at least two ways. The first is that someone or some group outside the House of Representatives asks the House or some members in it, or makes a referral to the House, to consider impeachment. Almost anyone can do this, including presidents, prosecutors, citizens, and judicial councils. For example, President Jefferson and his secretary of state, James Madison, urged their fellow Republicans in the House to consider impeaching Federalist judges, including Justice Samuel Chase and Judge John Pickering.[1] Referrals have been made to the House by two special prosecutors—Leon Jaworksi, who, as special prosecutor appointed by the attorney general, referred to the House several boxes of materials demonstrating possible impeachable offenses committed by President Nixon;[2] and Kenneth Starr, who, as independent counsel, referred evidence to the House showing that President Clinton might have committed as many as eleven impeachable offenses.[3]

Half a dozen times since 1986, the Judicial Conference of the United States has made referrals to the House to consider impeaching judges who had gotten into serious trouble, including Harry Claiborne (1986), Walter Nixon (1989), Alcee Hastings (1989), Robert Collins (who had been convicted in a criminal trial of accepting money to influence his sentencing of a drug smuggler and who resigned the day before the House was supposed to initiate an impeachment inquiry in 1993), and Samuel Kent (2009).[4] In

1993, the House delayed impeachment proceedings against another federal district judge, Robert Aguilar, after a federal appellate court overturned his conviction for obstruction of justice.[5]

The second way in which impeachments can begin is when some member(s) of the House, on their own initiative, recommend that the House considers initiating an impeachment inquiry, as, for example, Representative Jason Chaffetz did when he urged his colleagues on the House Judiciary Committee to consider impeaching IRS commissioner John Koskinen.

Regardless of who is pressing the House to consider an impeachment, the Constitution provides that the House has "the sole power of impeachment."[6] Congress takes this language literally, as it should. It means that, although the House can get recommendations on whether to impeach someone or not, it is the House and the House alone that must actually conduct and take responsibility for impeachment. Though there is nothing in the Constitution barring people or authorities outside of the House from recommending that the House considers impeachment, none of these recommendations is binding on the House; that is, none of these outside authorities has the power to require or force the House to initiate impeachment hearings. Having the "sole power of impeachment" means the House remains free to disregard any recommendations that it considers an impeachment if it so chooses.

What is the House's role?

The House has "the sole power of impeachment" and thus performs a different function than does the Senate, which has "sole power to try impeachments," but House members and commentators have differed on the exact nature of the House's role in the impeachment process. Does it function like a grand jury, which may indict or charge someone with criminal misconduct? Does it function more like a prosecutor, who has some duty to investigate criminal charges and make recommendations, based on the evidence it has found, on whether or not to proceed with a criminal prosecution? What factors should the House take into account in exercising its "sole power of impeachment"?

Though many members of the House liken its role in the impeachment process to that of a grand jury, the House differs from a grand jury in several important respects, all of which suggest that the House should function differently. Laypeople serve on grand juries, whereas many House members are lawyers and are otherwise presumably more sophisticated than the general public when it comes to the question of assessing political or other similar misconduct. Indeed, given that the House helps to write the federal criminal laws, its members are much more likely than the typical grand jury member to know a good deal about the criminal law and criminal process. In further contrast with grand jurors, House members are likely to be familiar with the targeted official and have political, if not personal, interests in the outcomes. These relationships do not disqualify them; presumably, it makes them more informed.

Moreover, grand juries tend to do whatever the prosecutors who assembled them tell them to do. In contrast, no one outside of the House, not even the president, may tell the House members what they should do in an impeachment proceeding. To be sure, prosecutors cannot command grand juries to do anything, but many people worry that grand juries (who are said to be disposed to indict even a "ham sandwich" if prosecutors asked them to do so) are extremely vulnerable to prosecutorial persuasion.

Once the House of Representatives formally impeaches someone, it appoints several members to act as House managers, whose job is to serve as prosecutors in the ensuing Senate impeachment trials. In the House, some of these members are likely to have had leadership or influential roles in its impeachment proceedings. House members may choose to function even in the House as prosecutors, though this is a choice they make; the Constitution does not command or require this.

Indeed, the House allows its members to decide for themselves what role the House has in impeachment. The House's own website says that the "House brings impeachment charges against federal officials as part of its oversight and investigatory responsibilities."[7] It describes House managers as "prosecutors in the Senate" once the House has chosen to deploy its "sole power to impeachments."[8] In any given impeachment inquiry, House members, particularly those undertaking leadership roles, will often explain to the public how they conceive their functions.

Does the House have a constitutional obligation to do any fact-finding?

It is not clear that the House has a duty to do this. To understand why, we need to be clear on what constitutional constraints apply to or restrict the House's discretion in fashioning or adopting procedures when it exercises the "sole power of impeachment." The latter clause does not, on its own terms, seem to oblige the House to do anything in particular other than to exercise discretion over the awesome power of impeachment. This clause does not, in other words, impose any particular procedural obligations on the House. If there are any such obligations, they will arise because House members choose to impose those obligations on themselves and/or because other constitutional provisions impose them.

There are two constitutional clauses that might restrict the discretion of the House in adopting or fashioning any particular procedures for impeachments. The first is the Fifth Amendment's due process clause. The other clause, which obviously applies in the impeachment context, is Section 5 of Article I, which provides in pertinent part that "Each House may determine the Rules of its Proceedings."[9]

In the context of impeachment, the question is whether the House's power "to determine the Rules for its proceedings" obliges it to do anything specific, including undertaking any particular actions or adopting any special procedures, such as conducting its own fact-finding and investigation. The answer, in all likelihood, is no. This clause seems to vest the House with ample if not complete discretion over the rules it adopts for internal governance, including but not limited to the procedures or rules to be used in impeachment proceedings, such as determining whether a special committee will be assembled to consider the impeachment of a particular official, or whether the matter will be assigned to the House Judiciary Committee. Generally, the House construes this clause as giving it plenary, or complete, power over the formulation of the procedures and rules that it uses in doing its business.

It is highly doubtful the House could formulate rules or procedures that expressly discriminated against people because of their race or religion, but this is because the Fifth Amendment imposes those constraints through its due process clause. In constitutional law, this is called an "external" constraint on a power to differentiate it from whether the power itself has any "internal" limits—referring to whether a power on its own terms has some inherent boundaries. For example, when Congress enacts a law pursuant to its power to regulate interstate commerce, there are external constraints (e.g., the Fifth Amendment's restrictions on racial discrimination) and internal constraints (the law must be confined in some way to a realm of "commerce" that concerns more than one state).

The internal constraints on the scope of the House's power to fashion rules for its own proceedings appear minimal. The grant to the House to exercise "the sole power of impeachment" includes discretion over not only how but also whether to wield that power. As long as a rule or procedure used as part of the impeachment process makes any sense, then the House will likely seem to have stayed within the inherent boundaries of both its impeachment power and its power to determine rules for its impeachment proceedings. In practice, the House makes decisions on a case-by-case basis whether fact-finding is required in a particular impeachment inquiry, a practice that we all would have to concede makes sense even if we disagree with it.

In fact, the question of whether the House has a duty, or just the discretion, to do fact-finding was debated at length during the House's consideration of the impeachment of President Clinton. The majority likened the House's role to a grand jury and did not do any fact-finding or investigation of its own. Instead, it passed along to the Senate the referral from the office of Independent Counsel Starr. The House managers, among others, figured that the House's function was basically to formulate the charges against the president, which it then became the responsibility of the Senate to investigate further in its impeachment trial of the president.

The Clinton impeachment was only one of three instances when the House impeached someone without doing any fact-finding or investigation of its own. Three days after President Andrew Johnson dismissed his secretary of war, Edwin Stanton, the House impeached Johnson, without having done any investigation or fact-finding beyond reading (and submitting for the record) the letter of dismissal that President Johnson had forwarded to it.[10] The House also did no fact-finding in the case of Judge Harry Claiborne. Because Claiborne asked the House to impeach him so that he could present evidence to the Senate showing his innocence, the House obliged.[11] Things did not turn out as Claiborne expected, however, in the Senate, which voted to convict and remove him from office.[12]

Some commentators and some members of Congress believe that the failure of the House to do any of its own fact-finding or to do any investigation of its own can undercut how the Senate or others perceive the legitimacy of its decision to impeach. Some commentators, as well as Democratic members of the House in the 1990s, complained that the House merely rushed to judgment in Clinton's case.[13] They argued that rush to judgment cast doubt on the legitimacy of the House's vote of impeachment. (The fact that the referral arrived shortly before the midterm elections and that Congress was just two or three months away from the start of a new legislative session made it seem, at least to the Clinton defenders, as if the whole affair was pushed through before the leadership in the House might change.)

Those defending the House's choice to forgo independent fact-finding argued that the extraordinary detail in the Starr referral made any fact-finding by the House unnecessary and that, in any event, once the House made formal charges against the president it was the Senate's duty to conduct a trial. In other words, the House had enough reason to take the position that an impeachment trial was warranted.

What is the Senate's role in the impeachment process?

This question turns on the answers to several other questions: What does it mean for the Senate to have the "sole power to try impeachments"? What must the Senate do when it sets out "to try impeachments"? Must the Senate do anything at all if the House impeaches someone, or could it ignore the matter entirely? Must the Senate hold an actual trial of the impeached official?

The Senate has answered some of these questions. Whether it must do anything at all in response to an impeachment by the House and what its power "to try an impeachment" means are questions that the Senate has asked itself before and answered. Article I, Section 5, empowers "Each House to determine the rules for its proceedings."[14] So, as the eleven House managers prepared to go to the

Senate to present their impeachment articles against William Blount, Thomas Jefferson, then the vice president of the United States and presiding officer of the Senate, forged a rule that ensured their respectful reception. After receiving the impeachment articles, the Senate developed other rules to govern the impeachment trial.[15]

Years later, three days after the House impeached President Johnson, the Senate, with Chief Justice Salmon Chase presiding, adapted its rules of procedure for a presidential impeachment trial.[16] The Senate followed these same rules for President Clinton's impeachment trial. For example, the Senate rules tell us what the Senate will do once the House has impeached someone. There is a special process for receiving the House managers when they formally present the House's impeachment articles to the Senate. In practice, the Senate has taken the position that it must at least welcome the House managers when they come to present their impeachment articles to the Senate. This respectful reception underscores the solemnity of the occasion and the respect due to a coordinate branch of government.

Once the Senate formally receives the impeachment articles from the House, then it must consider its next steps. It still has the discretion, because of its plenary power to try impeachments, to decide what to do next. It might adjourn without doing anything more, as it did when William Belknap resigned shortly after his impeachment by the House; or it might consider arguments on the necessity for dismissal for lack of jurisdiction, as it did at the outset of William Blount's trial.[17]

But what if, when all is said and done, the Senate does not dismiss the matter? This means it must "try" the matter, but what does that mean? This turns out to be a big question, which the rules will help to answer.

What does it mean for the Senate to have the power "to try an impeachment?" Must it hold an actual trial for the impeached official?

These questions have received close attention from senators, particularly in the form of the Senate rules, Supreme Court review, and leading constitutional scholarship. Let's consider what each of these three sources has said about the nature of the Senate's power in the realm of impeachment. Our concern here is with the extent to which the word "try" imposes any kind of internal constraint on the Senate's discretion in this realm.

The Senate's impeachment rules and its special procedures for presidential impeachment trials provide clear guidelines for the Senate to follow. For example, Rule XI of the Senate's impeachment rules provides that the Senate may, if it chooses, appoint a special committee of senators to take testimony and gather evidence and then issue a report with recommendations that goes to the full Senate for its consideration.[18] Under these rules, the Senate could recall witnesses already interviewed by the House and take testimony or do further fact-finding on its own, if it saw fit.[19] In contrast, the special rules for presidential impeachment trials require that the full Senate sit as the trial body. Indeed, this is how the Senate proceeded in every impeachment trial until the 1930s, when it amended its rules, including the adoption of Rule XI.[20] The Senate's experiences in earlier trials were not good; many senators did not bother attending the trials. The Senate adopted Rule XI to deal with the problem, and it has been followed in every impeachment trial since the 1930s except for that of President Clinton in 1999.

Not everyone agrees that the Senate's use of trial committees is a good practice. The three judges who were convicted and removed from office in the late 1980s—Harry Claiborne, Alcee Hastings, and Walter Nixon—each objected to the Senate's reliance on a twelve-member trial committee to gather evidence and take testimony rather than require the entire Senate to do that work and conduct a trial of the impeached official.[21] They argued that the word "try" meant what it said, namely, that the full Senate had to actually hold a trial for the impeached officials.[22]

The Senate rejected the judges' procedural challenges (as did the Supreme Court later). Instead, the senators agreed that Article I, Section 5, of the Constitution vested the Senate with the authority to design whatever procedures and rules they deemed fit for impeachment trials. Walter Nixon, one judge convicted by the Senate, filed a lawsuit challenging the constitutionality of the Senate's use of trial committees pursuant to rather than holding a full trial, where all the senators heard all the evidence and deliberated together on the questions of whether Nixon had engaged in misconduct, whether his misconduct provided a legitimate basis for impeachment and removal, and whether he should be convicted and removed from office.[23] Nixon's counsel, David Stewart, pointed to the tendency of senators not on the trial committee to defer to the findings and recommendations of those on the trial committee.[24] Stewart argued the patterns of deference reflected an abdication of responsibility of all senators to participate and consider the evidence presented in the trial.[25] He further claimed that a full trial conducted with every senator present and the opportunity for counsel on both sides to present their arguments and evidence in full protected judicial independence.[26]

Interestingly, Kenneth Starr, then the solicitor general of the United States, defended the constitutionality of Rule XI trial committees before the Supreme Court,[27] which rejected Nixon's challenge.[28] The Court unanimously concluded that it would be inappropriate for the Court to consider the challenge's merits.[29] The Court's opinion was delivered by Chief Justice Rehnquist, who had published a book the year before on the impeachment trials of Justice Chase and President Johnson.[30] For the Court, Rehnquist explained why the word "try" in the Constitution vested the Senate with special, non-reviewable authority over the procedure the Senate should follow rather than impose an obligation on the Senate as a whole to conduct a full trial on the charges set forth in the impeachment articles approved by the House against Nixon.[31]

To begin with, the chief justice explained, the Constitution expressly authorized the Senate to adopt Rule XI and the Senate's use of a trial committee.[32] Recall that the Constitution specifies only a few details of what is required for an impeachment trial, including that (1) the senators voting on the impeachment must be on oath or affirmation,[33] (2) two-thirds of the senators present must concur in order for there to be a conviction,[34] (3) the only permissible punishments that may be imposed upon a conviction on impeachment are removal from office and future disqualification,[35] and (4) the chief justice of the United States should preside when the president is tried.[36] These requirements leave a lot to be worked out with respect to the specifics of an impeachment trial, which the Constitution leaves to the full, unreviewable discretion of the Senate, as provided in Article I, Section 5, that "[e]ach House may determine the Rules of its Proceedings."[37]

Second, Thomas Jefferson's *Manual of Parliamentary Practice*,[38] the Federalist Papers,[39] and the states' practices prior to the drafting and ratification of the Constitution[40] all show that, in designing the American impeachment process, the framers used the British procedure as a model;[41] they were aware of but did not reject the practice of the House of Lords in the seventeenth century to use committees to gather evidence for impeachment trials.[42]

The concern driving Nixon's judicial challenge was that, without the full Senate actually participating in the trial, there could be no guarantee or assurance that it took the matter as seriously as it should. In fact, the whole Senate had the discretion to accept, reject, or question any of the committee's findings of fact; two-thirds of the Senate voted to convict Nixon on two articles of impeachment; and the full Senate exercised its judgment in Nixon's impeachment (as it can in any impeachment trial) not to call witnesses other than the judge himself to testify before the entire body.

Moreover, if the Senate's use of trial committees were unconstitutional, then there would be doubt about the constitutionality of delegations of authority within each branch. Such delegations are common, and indeed are necessary to ensure the efficient and effective operation of each branch and the administration of its responsibilities. This is especially true in the House and the Senate, though each branch does it. For example, the Senate routinely delegates fact-finding authority to committees to assist it in rendering judgment on various matters over which it has exclusive control, such as treaty ratifications and judicial nominations; the Supreme Court has relied on special masters in cases of original jurisdiction;[43] the federal district courts have delegated fact-finding responsibilities to special masters and others "[f]rom the commencement of our Government;"[44] and the House and the Senate have long used committees to gather evidence when acting as "the Judge of the Elections, Returns and Qualifications of its own Members"[45]—a role in which the House or Senate is clearly acting as "a judicial tribunal."[46] If the Court ever were to hold Rule XI unconstitutional because it violated an express limitation that only the full Senate could conduct any aspect of an impeachment trial, then the constitutionality of these (and many) other delegations is in trouble because the delegations might conflict similarly with explicit grants of arguably non-delegable authority to the full membership of a branch to perform an important function.

Is it possible to appeal an impeachment conviction to the Supreme Court?

The answer is no. Many people may wonder what if any role the Supreme Court may perform in this area. Given that the Constitution clearly vests the responsibility for impeaching in the House and conducting an impeachment trial in the Senate, the only potential role for the Supreme Court might be as a court of last resort to consider the appeal of a judicial challenge to alleged illegalities in an impeachment proceeding.

The Supreme Court's unanimous opinion in *Nixon v. United States* (1993) settled that question. It unanimously rejected any role for judicial review over an impeachment trial. The decision aligned with the thinking and research of several prominent scholars, who had argued against judicial review in these circumstances.

To understand both why the Court reached the conclusion that it did in *Nixon* and why prominent scholars, such as Charles Black of Yale Law School, agreed with the result, we need to review a line of decisions that the Court has delivered that is known collectively as the political question doctrine. This doctrine says that there are some matters of constitutional law that the courts do not decide; these are called political questions, on which the Constitution vests final, non-reviewable discretion in certain actors other than the courts. By "final, non-reviewable," we mean that these actors literally have the final say on these questions and that courts may not review or second-guess the judgments or decisions these actors make on these matters. A classic example is whether courts may adjudicate the meaning of war, a matter that historically has been left to the final, non-reviewable discretion of presidents and members of Congress. Until Walter Nixon's challenge, it was commonplace for scholars to mention the judgments in impeachment trials as another classic example of a political question.

Walter Nixon's challenge to his removal from office by the Senate required the Supreme Court to consider for the first time whether these scholars were right. Six justices held Nixon's claim to be a "political question," a special matter that courts do not decide.[47] They determined that the word *try* did not represent an "implied limitation on the method by which the Senate might proceed in trying impeachments."[48] Instead, they determined, based on their application of some of the factors for determining a political question set forth in *Baker v. Carr* (1962),[49] that the word *try* "lack[ed] sufficient precision to constitute a judicially manageable standard of review of the Senate's actions,"[50] especially when contrasted with the three "precise" limitations set out in the impeachment trial clause[51]—that Senate members shall "be on Oath or Affirmation"; that the chief justice shall preside at a presidential impeachment trial; and that conviction requires a vote of at least two-thirds of the members present. Other language in the same clause— giving the Senate the "sole" power to try impeachments—constituted what the Court regarded as a straightforward "textual commitment" of authority to a coordinate branch. Finally, the Court emphasized that judicial review was inappropriate for several reasons: it would upset the framers' decision to allocate to different forums the powers to try impeachments and to try crimes; it would disturb the system of checks and balances, under which impeachment is the only legislative check on the judiciary; and it would create a "lack of finality and [a] difficulty [in] fashioning relief."[52]

The Supreme Court distinguished its 1969 decision in *Powell v. McCormack*[53] on the basis that it involved a constitutional provision authorizing that "each House shall be the Judge of the Elections, Returns and Qualifications of its own Members,"[54] which was limited by Article I, Section 2. This provision "specified three requirements for membership in the House: The candidate must be at least 25 years of age, a citizen of the United States for no less than seven years, and an inhabitant of the State he is chosen to represent."[55] Hence, "[t]he decision as to whether a member satisfied these qualifications *was* placed in the House, but the decision as to what [they] consisted of was not."[56] In contrast, the clause vesting the Senate with the authority to conduct contained no separate provision that provided a standard or "could be defeated by allowing the Senate final authority to determine the meaning of the word 'try.' "[57]

Concurring in the judgment, Justice Byron White, joined by Justice Harry Blackmun, thought the case presented a justiciable question, though in his view of the merits the Senate had "very wide discretion in specifying impeachment trial procedures,"[58] so that as a practical matter a successful judicial challenge was unlikely. Still, Justice White believed that proper checks and balances were best preserved when Senate impeachment trials helped control the largely unaccountable judiciary, "even as judicial review would ensure that the Senate adhered to a minimal set of procedural safeguards in conducting impeachment trials."[59] The requirement that the Senate "try" impeachments created judicially manageable standards, which would be violated "[w]ere the Senate, for example, to adopt the practice of automatically entering a judgment of conviction whenever articles of impeachment were delivered from the House."[60]

Concurring separately in the judgment, Justice David Souter agreed that the case presented a nonjusticiable political question, but he thought that this determination should be made on a case-by-case basis. If the Senate were to convict upon a coin toss, or (borrowing an example from Justice White) upon a summary determination that the official was a "bad guy," Justice Souter thought that "judicial interference might well be appropriate."[61]

Among the leading scholars whose thoughts on this question were vindicated, none was more renowned than Charles Black of Yale Law School, whose book on the subject of impeachment remains a classic. Applying the different factors that the Court has traditionally employed for determining whether a particular issue is a political question, Black made a forceful case against judicial review of impeachment proceedings many years before. For example, he argued that the need to treat the Senate's judgment as final is compelling: if it were not, he asks, imagine the military's uncertainty about whom to obey if the Senate convicted and removed a president but the president was challenging that judgment at a time when the nation was at war. There could be an endless series of lawsuits seeking to obstruct or delay the implementation of the Senate's order. As a practical matter, it is absurd, Black argued, that there would be no finality on the question of who is legitimately the president.

What role does the chief justice of the United States have in the impeachment process?

According to the Constitution, the chief justice of the United States presides over presidential impeachment trials.[62] The framers provided for this arrangement in order to ensure that the presiding officer would not be the vice president, who clearly would have a conflict of interest in overseeing the trial of the one person standing between him and the presidency. Moreover, having the chief justice preside over the president's impeachment trial would underscore the seriousness of the occasion. The chief justice's special protection of life tenure would help to insulate him from any political reprisal for any decisions he made when presiding over the president's impeachment trial. He would also, presumably, not be a political ally of any of the senators and presumably would command their respect throughout the trial.

Chief Justice Salmon Chase and Chief Justice William Rehnquist approached their responsibilities as presiding officer differently. From the start, Chase believed that the Senate sat as a court to try President Johnson, and he thus pushed the Senate to follow legal procedures. As a result, Chase provided the senators with the opportunity to test the rules, which allowed the rulings of the presiding officer to be appealed to the body as a whole, which could overrule him by a majority vote. In contrast, Chief Justice Rehnquist, no doubt informed by the research he had done for his recently published book on the Chase and Johnson impeachment trials, understood that the trial was a unique political process within the Senate, and he gave the House managers and senators considerable leeway in arguing the case for and against the president's conviction and removal. Whereas there had been conflicts between a number of senators and Chief Justice Chase during the Johnson impeachment trial, there were none between the Senate and Chief Justice Rehnquist. Whereas some of the tension involving Chase arose because of his own political ambitions (indeed, he would run for the presidency again shortly thereafter), Chief Justice Rehnquist ended the hearings with levity and was happy to return to the "very structured environment of the Supreme Court" from "the more free-form environment of the Senate."[63]

What if the chief justice himself is the subject of an impeachment process?

The president is the only official for whose impeachment the Constitution establishes special safeguards. The Constitution therefore does not specify any special safeguards for any other officials, including the chief justice of the United States. No chief justice has ever been impeached, but it is safe to assume the impeachment of the chief justice of the United States would command considerable public attention, to say the least. As a result, it is possible that the House and the Senate would, in their respective proceedings, be careful to use fact-finding and other procedures that would be designed to inspire public confidence and to earn the respect of subsequent congresses and generations.

Who presides over a vice president's impeachment trial, given that the Constitution makes the vice president the presiding officer of the Senate?

This is a popular trivia question. It is often asked in order to illustrate a perceived oversight of the framers who had made the vice president the presiding officer of the Senate. Because the Constitution makes no exception for the vice president to step down as the Senate's presiding officer, it seems to follow that he would preside over his own impeachment trial. But such a reading of the Constitution is a good example of the problem that Professor Akhil Amar of Yale Law School called "blinkered textualism," referring to reading constitutional clauses on their own terms without considering how they might be coordinated with other constitutional text.[64]

When he was vice president, Thomas Jefferson, in drafting the first manual of Senate rules, provided that the Senate could designate someone else to preside over a vice president's trial. The authority for doing this derives from Article I, Section 5, which empowers each chamber of Congress with the power "to determine the rules of its proceedings."[65] This express delegation of authority to the Senate plainly allows it to make a rule or adopt a practice allowing someone other than the vice president to preside over his impeachment trial.

What difference, if any, does the Fifth Amendment make to impeachment proceedings?

Most impeachment commentators do not consider the possibility that the Fifth Amendment's due process clause applies to impeachment proceedings, much less what it requires. I believe that the clause does apply to impeachment procedures, but it is not clear that it requires anything more than what the House and the Senate have traditionally done in this area.

The most obvious indication that the due process clause applies to the impeachment process comes from the language of the clause itself: it expressly applies to Congress when it deprives a person of "life, liberty, or property without due process of law," and it makes no exceptions to its application to congressional actions, giving rise to the inference that it must apply in *all* contexts, including impeachment.

If the clause applies, then the Supreme Court has directed that we ask two questions. The first is whether the interest being deprived without due process of law is a protected "life, liberty, or property" interest for purposes of the Fifth Amendment. The likeliest kind of protected interest that an impeachable official's position, whether it be the presidency, judgeship, or cabinet office, could be is a protected "property" interest. (It seems ludicrous to argue it would be covered by "life," which has to do with living or dying, or "liberty," which, in this context, has to do with the freedom of movement.) Whether something is a protected "property" interest for purposes of the Fifth Amendment due process clause depends on whether federal law gives rise to a reasonable expectation of entitlement to keep the position as long as the conditions of the legal protections are met. Hence, cabinet officials might not have a protectable interest here since they can be fired at will by the president. In contrast, presidents and judges cannot be fired at all. They appear to be entitled to keep their jobs until the expiration of their terms or unless they have been impeached, convicted, and removed from office because they committed impeachable offense(s).

If we conclude that the impeachable official's position is a protected Fifth Amendment property interest, then we ask a second question—what process is due. This question entails determining the kind of process that must be given by the federal government before it takes the interest (the position) away from the official. In the jurisprudence of procedural due process, the minimal due process required prior to the deprivation of a protected Fifth Amendment interest is the existence of a neutral decision maker and a hearing.

It appears that, even if we apply the due process clause to the impeachment context, due process of law is satisfied as long as there is an impartial decision maker *and* some kind of hearing. These are remarkably easy safeguards to provide in this context: first, because the Constitution expressly designates the House in impeachment proceedings and the Senate in impeachment trials as the decision makers, the framers made the decision for us that these authorities are more "neutral" than any other possible decision makers. The framers rejected the Supreme Court as the decision maker here, in part because it would have had a vested interest in impeachment proceedings brought against any of its members. Indeed, of the three branches the Congress is the only one without any impeachable members, thus ensuring it had less of a vested interest than if either of the other branches, many of whose members were impeachable, were vested with the impeachment authority.

Second, both the House and the Senate hold hearings during their respective impeachment proceedings, during which the accused has an opportunity to make his or her case. The hearings that either the House or the Senate provide might not be perfect, but perfection is not the constitutional requirement here. The minimal requirement is that a hearing is required, and the House and the Senate do hold impeachment hearings. Thus, assuming that the Fifth Amendment due process clause applies in the impeachment context, it appears to have been satisfied in those cases in which it applied.

However, there remains a good argument that the Fifth Amendment due process clause does not apply to the impeachment process. The Fifth Amendment requires that due process of law be followed prior to the deprivation of a protected interest, but impeachment is *not* a legal proceeding. It is a unique constitutional process, which provides a unique sanction for impeachable misconduct. This is the point that Supreme Court justice James Wilson, who had served as a delegate in both the constitutional and ratification conventions, made when after ratification he emphasized impeachments were "proceedings of a political nature . . . confined to political characters, to political crimes and misdemeanors, and to political punishments."[66] He explained further that the framers believed that "[i]mpeachments, and offences and offenders impeachable, [did not] come within the sphere of ordinary jurisprudence. They are founded on different principles; are governed by different maxims; and are directed to different objects; for this reason, the trial and punishment of an offence on an impeachment, is no bar to a trial and punishment of the same offence at common law."[67] Impeachment proceedings do not bar subsequent legal proceedings. The point of Wilson's comment is that it underscores the fact that impeachment proceedings are unique, and as such, are not to be treated as tantamount to or the same as legal proceedings. Perhaps significantly, Justice Wilson died after the Fifth Amendment took effect, but nowhere in his discussions of the impeachment process did he ever indicate that, much less discuss how, the due process clause applied to the impeachment process.

Is there a burden of proof required in impeachment proceedings?

Members of Congress agree on at least two things about the burden of proof required in impeachment proceedings. First, they agree that there is a burden of proof required in impeachment proceedings. More important, they agree that it is practically impossible to enforce a single, uniform burden of proof on every member of the House and the Senate. In the absence of any such standard, members of Congress agree that it is up to each House member and each senator to decide for themselves on the appropriate burden of proof to be applied in their respective proceedings.

Members of Congress have three choices with respect to the burden of proof they believe is required in impeachment proceedings. The first is preponderance of the evidence. This is the burden used in civil proceedings. The second possible burden of proof is beyond a reasonable doubt. This is the burden used in criminal proceedings. For some members of Congress, the fact that impeachment is a hybrid proceeding, with some things in common with civil and others with criminal proceedings, leads them to adopt a burden of proof that is a combination of both the civil and criminal burdens of proof. The cross between these burdens would require clear and convincing evidence of misconduct or, as Charles Black once suggested, "overwhelming preponderance of the evidence."[68]

Would the application of the Fifth Amendment due process clause to impeachment proceedings make a difference to the outcome of this analysis? I think not. Burdens of proof—or rules of evidence—are not requirements of the law of procedural due process. Even if they were, they would not make any difference, given the intractability of guaranteeing that each member follow them.

Are any rules of evidence required in impeachment proceedings?

A major reason courts adopt rules of evidence is that they help lay-people on juries, who are not trained in the law, to figure out the trustworthiness of particular kinds of evidence introduced at trial and to weigh them accordingly. Rules of evidence also are important for defining the limitations on the use of evidence illegally obtained by state or federal authorities.

None of these reasons apply in the context of impeachment. The members of Congress who are the decision makers are presumed to be sufficiently legally sophisticated so that they can appreciate the qualitative differences in the kinds of evidence that might be introduced, such as hearsay. After arguing that "the House and the Senate ought to hear and consider all evidence, which seems relevant, without regard to technical rules," Charles Black bluntly observed that "Senators are in any case continually exposed to 'hearsay' evidence; they cannot be sequestered and kept away from newspapers, like a jury. If they cannot be trusted to weigh evidence, appropriately discounting for all the factors of unreliability that have led to our keeping some evidence away from juries, then they are not in any way up to the job, and 'rules of evidence' will not help."[69] Moreover, given that impeachment proceedings are uniquely political, rather than legal, proceedings, members of Congress may be informed, but not bound, by how the latter operate.

Consequently, there are no required rules of evidence in impeachment proceedings in either the House or the Senate. Besides the Constitution's leaving each chamber the authority to determine rules for their respective proceedings, the long-standing practices in the House and the Senate have been for each chamber to allow almost any kind of evidence to be admitted into its impeachment proceedings and for each member to determine its relevance.

Does double jeopardy apply to an impeachment?

The Fifth Amendment provides in pertinent part, "nor shall any person be subject for the same offence to be twice put in jeopardy of life or limb."[70] This means that no one may be criminally tried twice for the same crime. This clause makes no mention of any exceptions, but it does not have to. By its terms, double jeopardy only applies to criminal proceedings; they are the only kind of proceeding in our legal system in which either "life or liberty" is put in jeopardy. Because impeachment is not a criminal proceeding, the Constitution does not forbid someone from being subjected to it more than once, even for the same offense.

May an impeachment come before civil or criminal proceedings?

Yes, it may. After setting forth the range of permissible sanctions in impeachment proceedings, Article I provides, "but the Party convicted shall nevertheless be liable and subject to Indictment, Trial, Judgment, and Punishment, according to Law."[71] A plain inference from this language is that impeachment may precede criminal prosecution for the same offense. It is less clear, however, whether the criminal prosecution must always follow the impeachment action. What if the House of Representatives fails to impeach or if the Senate fails to convict—is it permissible to proceed with a criminal action? Or must any such action be brought only after the person has left office and returned to private life? What about civil actions? May they precede impeachments or must they be brought against impeachable officials only after they have left office?

All these questions concern the proper sequencing of impeachment proceedings on the one hand, and civil or criminal proceedings on the other. Their answers depend on the extent to which impeachable officials have immunity from certain legal actions while they are in office. The extent of such immunity depends in turn on the kinds of officials and legal actions involved. The arguments and likely sequencing of proceedings are different for judges and cabinet- or subcabinet-level officials than for presidents.

First is the question of whether judges may be subject to civil or criminal proceedings before they have been impeached and removed from office. The matter of civil liability has been dealt with by the courts for years through their recognition of an absolute immunity for judges for civil lawsuits based on their exercise of any official functions.[72] This immunity extends to any judicial acts related to the cases that have come before them. It does not extend to anything unofficial or that arises over matters that are not connected to their official duties, such as sexual harassment or alimony payments.

A more difficult issue involves criminal prosecutions of federal judges. This issue came to a head in the late 1980s when two federal judges, Harry Claiborne and Walter Nixon, were criminally prosecuted, found guilty, had exhausted their appeals, and were both sitting in jail but still being paid as federal judges before impeachment inquiries were initiated against them.[73] Because the Constitution guarantees federal judges undiminished compensation,[74] they could have their caseloads, but not their pay, suspended. It was partly the outrage over the judges' audacity in not resigning but instead retaining their titles and still being paid that triggered their respective impeachment proceedings.

The textual argument against pre-impeachment criminal prosecutions of federal judges is similar to the one that is used to prohibit criminal prosecution of the president. They attempt to read the language of Article I as presuming impeachment would precede criminal prosecution, because Article I says the "party convicted shall nevertheless be liable." Some attempt to infer from the language that "the party convicted" refers to someone who has been convicted in an impeachment trial but who is "nevertheless" still liable in civil or criminal proceedings for their misconduct. Indeed, this language applies to every official who may be subject to impeachment, including judges and presidents. Judges and others are also concerned that allowing criminal prosecutions of sitting judges because they can be used to harass or target judges whom the prosecutors do not like. The need to protect against overzealous prosecutors trying to undermine judicial independence arguably could militate in favor of allowing federal judges to continue receiving their salaries until such time as they are formally removed from office.

But ultimately reading the Constitution as requiring impeachments to precede criminal prosecutions of judge is strained. First, the pertinent constitutional text could also be read as merely anticipating (but not requiring) that impeachments would precede criminal prosecutions, and that, regardless of the order in which they proceed, an impeachable official may be subjected to both in appropriate cases. Second, the Bribery Act of 1790, which declared judges would be "disqualified" if they were convicted for bribery,[75] conceivably reflected the understanding of the First Congress—commonly regarded as representative of the framers' generation—that criminal prosecutions of judges could occur prior to impeachment proceedings because the law is premised on such a sequence.[76] Third, reading the pertinent constitutional language as mandating that impeachments must precede criminal prosecutions would produce some peculiar outcomes, including barring any criminal prosecution of an impeached judge whom the House failed to impeach or the Senate acquitted on facts that could support a criminal conviction.[77]

An even more serious problem with this reading is that it is based on a misunderstanding of how impeachment works. The framers believed that impeachment and the criminal law served different purposes. The function of the first half of Article I, Section 3, Clause 7, is to signal the distinction between the American system and the English practice, under which it was permissible to impose criminal sanctions in an impeachment. The second half of Clause 7 of Article I, Section 3, does not immunize impeachable or impeached officials from criminal prosecution.

Have any courts addressed the question of whether impeachment may precede or must follow a criminal indictment?

A few federal appellate courts have rejected arguments that impeachment of federal judges must precede their indictment, prosecution, conviction, and/or imprisonment. The claimants in these cases argued that doing any of these to federal judges should be barred before an impeachment because the targeted judges are effectively disabled in violation of the constitutional principle that impeachment is the only constitutionally permissible means of depriving federal judges of their constitutional powers.[78] They further argued that allowing such prosecutions threatened judicial independence because it allowed prosecutors to use their prosecutorial powers to harass judges they disliked.[79]

United States v. Isaacs (1974)[80] was the first case in which a defendant claimed that indictment prior to impeachment was tantamount to removal without an impeachment conviction. Denying Judge Otto Kerner's application to stay his prosecution for criminal activities committed before he had entered judicial office, the Seventh Circuit in *Isaacs* explained that "[p]rotection of tenure is not a license to commit crime or a forgiveness of crimes committed before taking office."[81] The court also rejected the argument that judicial independence could be protected only by recognizing impeachment as the only means by which to punish judicial misconduct, because judicial independence "is better served when criminal charges against [judges] are tried in a court rather than in Congress. With a court trial, a judge is assured of the protections given to all those charged with criminal conduct."[82]

In 1985, in *United States v. Claiborne*,[83] the federal court of appeals for the Ninth Circuit rejected Harry Claiborne's argument that his conviction and imprisonment before his impeachment were unconstitutional because they violated the supposed constitutional principle that judges could not be removed by any means other than impeachment.[84] Claiborne buttressed his claim with three arguments. First, he argued that the "Party convicted" language in Article I, Section 3, Clause 7, presupposes that any disruption of a federal judge's life tenure should occur first through impeachment and only later through criminal prosecution; otherwise, the past participle "convicted" has no meaning.[85] The problem with this reading is that it conflicts with the framers' view of impeachment and criminal proceedings as separate actions unfolding in no particular sequence.

Second, Claiborne argued that prosecuting judges subjects them to a level of intimidation that violates their independence.[86] In his view, even if one were exonerated, the rigors and expense of a criminal investigation are so great as to give the executive leverage over federal judges. To be sure, there is little doubt that the vulnerability of sitting judges to criminal prosecution could potentially compromise judicial independence by effectively subjugating judges to the political branches. Indeed, the ability of federal prosecutors to use criminal investigations or prosecutions to pressure or intimidate federal judges who have been hostile to the federal government or prosecutors is hardly unknown.[87]

The problem with this second argument is that judicial independence is not the only constitutional value that is relevant to judicial performance. The framers also sought to secure judicial integrity. In fact, every federal court ever asked to consider the constitutionality of pre-impeachment prosecutions of federal judges has deemed the impropriety of placing judges "above the law" to be the dominant constitutional value involved.[88] In other words, these courts concluded that judicial vulnerability to criminal prosecution prior to impeachment does less to compromise judicial independence than immunity does to avoiding legal accountability.[89]

Claiborne's final argument against pre-impeachment criminal prosecution was that imprisoning him while he was still a federal judge effectively removed him from office.[90] He maintained that his pre-impeachment imprisonment skirted the constitutionally mandated procedural safeguards for removal and created a "constitutional . . . collision between two branches of our government" by compelling an Article III judge "to surrender to the custody of the attorney general, an officer of the executive branch; . . . [and to] be confined outside his district, disenabled from performing judicial functions."[91] This argument rests on a presumption that life tenure means that "a judge has judicial authority unless and until that power is stripped by congressional impeachment."[92] On this view, only Congress has the power of judicial removal; therefore, the attorney general's bypass of the impeachment process violated the procedural safeguards the Constitution accords to judges.[93] Claiborne concluded that because criminal prosecution necessarily presupposes the potential for imprisonment (a de facto removal from office), prosecution must be prohibited.

The Ninth Circuit appellate court found an unusual basis for rejecting the argument that impeachment of federal judges must precede their prosecution and imprisonment. Maintaining that "federal judges [may] be removed from office only by impeachment," the court reasoned that because the Seventh Circuit had ruled in *Isaacs* that criminal prosecution and conviction of a senator does not ipso facto "vacate the seat of the convicted Senator, nor compel the Senate to expel him or to regard him as expelled by force alone of the judgment," neither were judges automatically removed "by force alone of the judgment."[94]

Some commentators are not persuaded by this analogy. They do not believe it helps to clarify whether imprisonment (as opposed to conviction) prior to impeachment is constitutionally permissible.[95] They argue further that the analogy disregards the key protections uniquely conferred upon the judiciary collectively and individually. The protections accorded by Article III are meant to ensure judicial independence require that judges must be treated differently for purposes of both criminal prosecution and imprisonment. In sum, these critics argue that in the area of criminal prosecution and imprisonment, senators are not analogous to judges, because senators lack an equivalent to judicial independence.

Arguing for different treatment of judges and senators for purposes of criminal prosecution is, however, not supported by either constitutional structure or history. First, just as judges are protected in their official status by Article III's guarantee of judicial independence, senators enjoy immunity for their official acts through the speech and debate clause.[96] But neither judicial independence nor the speech and debate clause protects judges or senators from prosecution for violating the criminal law.[97] In effect, the *Claiborne* decision's critics contend that judges should have a special immunity from criminal prosecution until they are impeached, but the concept of judicial independence only protects judges *as judges.* Judges may have the power to oversee criminal trials, impose or approve punishments for people convicted of committing crimes, and interpret the criminal law, but their official status does not immunize them from complying with it.

Second, imprisonment is not the equivalent of the Senate's convicting and removing someone. Imprisoned, or criminally convicted, judges retain their titles, salaries, pensions, benefits, as well as their ability to return to the bench with full authority to decide cases and controversies.[98] No doubt imprisonment is an impediment to exercising the duties of a federal judge, but it does not have the same permanent or functional consequences as removal and disqualification pursuant to impeachment conviction. In fact, the term *removal* had a specific, formal meaning in 1789, limited to the termination of one's tenure in office.[99] In light of various references made in public documents in or around 1787 strongly indicating that the framers did not equate criminal liability with removal, Stephen Burbank, a prominent legal scholar who was one of the architects of the Judicial Discipline and Disability Act of 1980, concluded that "[i]n the case of 'removal from office,' the framers had in mind the formal termination of a commission or of tenure in office. Yes, they were very concerned about judicial independence and yes, the Constitution should be interpreted so as to accommodate situations unforeseen and unforeseeable in 1787. But criminal proceedings were not a threat to judicial independence unknown to the framers, and . . . they were not a threat the framers deemed serious enough to foreclose."[100]

What about high-ranking executive branch officials other than the president? Are they immune to criminal prosecution while they are in office?

Generally, executive branch officials other than the president have what is called "qualified immunity" from civil lawsuits. The rule recognized in courts (and by Congress through the federal Tort Claims Act) has long been that executive branch officials other than the president are immune from any personal liability for tortious acts or commissions they committed in the course of their carrying out their official duties. But executive branch officials are not immune from civil lawsuits seeking damages based on their unofficial conduct, including anything done in their personal capacities.

The tougher question about whether these officials can claim any immunity from criminal prosecution was largely settled in the Supreme Court's decision in *Morrison v. Olson* upholding the constitutionality of the Independent Counsel Act.[101] There, the Court considered whether the Independent Counsel Act[102] was unconstitutional because it enabled Congress to assert inappropriate pressure on the president—pressure that the Constitution permits only through the impeachment power. According to the solicitor general, the act was a congressional attempt "to bypass the impeachment process that the Framers designed to [ensure] that high officers of government could be investigated and removed from power."[103] In the same vein, Justice Antonin Scalia in dissent suggested "[h]ow much easier for Congress, instead of accepting the political damage attendant to the commencement of the impeachment proceedings against the president on trivial grounds . . . simply to trigger a debilitating criminal investigation of the Chief Executive under this law."[104]

There are several good arguments supporting the Court's rejection of the characterization of the act as an illegitimate bypass of impeachment. First, the dispute did not involve the president. Hence, the real concern had to do with the extent to which executive officials other than the president could be subject to criminal investigation, indictment, and prosecution prior to being impeached, convicted, and removed from office. At the very least, it was widely recognized that any such criminal prosecutions did not cripple or paralyze the executive branch. They could wreak damage on an executive official other than the president, but this damage did not extend to the presidency, much less across the whole executive branch. And whatever damage was done could be defended on the ground that the prosecution was based on illegal criminal activity, that is, actions that the law did not authorize.

Second, the Independent Counsel Act did not authorize Congress to "trigger" a criminal investigation by a special prosecutor.[105] The act gives the attorney general unreviewable discretion to deny any request by Congress to initiate an investigation.[106] Indeed, Congress has the same power under the act to request an investigation by the attorney general as it would have in the absence of the statute to informally pressure the attorney general to commence an investigation. In addition, although the act requires that the special prosecutor turn over evidence that Congress could then use as grounds for an impeachment, the act is not an expansion of congressional power to impeach because it is merely a reporting device rather than a substitute for an impeachment proceeding.

Third, the basic principle long recognized and long followed in the United States that no one is above the law would be decimated as long as the official evaded criminal prosecution. If, for example, impeachment failed, then the official would be able to avoid criminal prosecution for as long as he or she stayed in office. The incentives for using an office to avoid accountability help to produce perverse results.

Moreover, the provisions in the act authorizing investigation and prosecution of impeachable executive officials are neither novel nor unique. Federal prosecution of impeachable officials within the executive branch did not begin with the Independent Counsel Act. Federal prosecutors in the Justice Department have prosecuted impeachable officers, such as federal judges, for years. If those prosecutions are not unconstitutional bypasses of the impeachment process, it is difficult to conceive how the prosecutions of other impeachable officials could be. In addition, prior to enactment of the Independent Counsel Act, the president and the attorney general frequently named special prosecutors pursuant to regulations or statutes that put constraints on their removal by the president.[107] In short, the act did not interfere with or supplant the impeachment process any more than these various law enforcement schemes, whose constitutionality has never been seriously challenged.

Shortly after the Senate acquitted President Clinton, Congress and the president had to decide whether to reauthorize the Independent Counsel Act. They allowed the act to expire. Subsequently, whenever the administration has thought it necessary for a special prosecutor to be appointed to investigate a criminal matter, it has used its long-standing statutory authority to appoint someone, who is subject to removal by the deputy attorney general.

Is it permissible for a sitting president to be subject to civil lawsuits for damages, or to be criminally indicted and prosecuted? Or must a president be impeached and removed from office beforehand?

This has been the most vexing question pertaining to the proper sequencing of impeachment and legal proceedings. The Supreme Court has weighed in on the civil side, so that is where we can start. In *Nixon v. Fitzgerald*, the Supreme Court ruled 5–4 that the president is absolutely immune from civil lawsuits based on his official conduct.[108] The Court reasoned that the unique position occupied by the president required this result.[109] The executive branch is the only branch overseen by a single individual, and allowing civil damage actions to be brought against him based on his conduct as president could make him worry more about avoiding civil liability than doing his job. This immunity helps the president to keep his focus on doing his best for the nation rather than on the financial problems these lawsuits could cause him. The Court suggested that there should be no concern that this immunity would keep the president from being held accountable for the underlying conduct, since there remained a handful of ways of checking any misconduct— impeachment, reduced chances for re-election (for a first-term incumbent or someone, such as Grover Cleveland, who had served one previous term and was running for a second), concerns about historical judgment, the oversight of Congress and the media, and the need to maintain popularity or public support in order to achieve his priorities in office.[110]

In 1997, the Court ruled that a sitting president was not immune from civil lawsuits based on pre-presidential misconduct.[111] The Court rejected the arguments of President Clinton's lawyers that the president should be immune from such lawsuits for all the same reasons that the Court in *Nixon v. Fitzgerald* had found for absolute immunity from civil lawsuits based on official conduct. In that case, the Court's predominant concern had to do with protecting the president's ability to do his job. But, in *Clinton v. Jones*, the need to ensure that the president was not above the law was paramount. The Court reasoned that the presidency should not be used as a shield to deprive these claimants of their day in court.[112] Other Court decisions that upheld subjecting the president to legal process support this outcome as well, and all of them protect against allowing a president to be above the law.[113]

Although these two decisions settled questions about civil lawsuits filed against a sitting president, the question whether a sitting president is immune from criminal process has never come before the Supreme Court—or any court, for that matter. Special Prosecutor Leon Jaworski, during the Watergate investigation, and Independent Counsel Kenneth Starr, in his inquiry into the Lewinsky affair, each reached the conclusion that it was likely that the Constitution barred criminal actions against a sitting president.[114] Most legal scholars who have examined this question have agreed with that conclusion.

The principal argument supporting presidential immunity from criminal prosecutions is that they would effectively paralyze or cripple him and the entire executive branch. Presidents cannot ignore pending criminal investigations, given that their life and their liberty are at stake, not to mention the time and energy required for mounting an effective defense. If presidents require absolute immunity from civil actions based on their official conduct, presidents require at least the same kind of protection from criminal proceedings, where the stakes are higher. Impeachment should therefore come first, and then, once the president has returned to private life, he may be subject to criminal process.

The main argument against granting the president absolute immunity from criminal process is that it would grant the president an entitlement that no one else in our constitutional order, not even the chief justice, enjoys. While the president's position is unique, every other official is subject to criminal process because none of them is above the law. If we take the rule of law seriously, then the president must be subject to it like every other citizen and every other official is. No other principle should countermand its application.

So far, our analysis has been concerned with separation of powers—the relationship among the branches of the federal government. But, if the prosecutor seeking to prosecute the president is a state, not a federal, official, then the problem is not one of separation of powers but rather of federalism, which pertains to the proper relationship or balance between the federal and state governments. A zealous state prosecutor cannot be dismissed by the president or prone to pressure from Congress. At the same time, a state prosecutor can use his or her power to make it harder for the president to do his job. States generally do not have the authority to cripple the federal government any more than the federal government has the power to cripple the states. The risk of a state prosecutor damaging the presidency might lead some courts to stop him if only because there is no other way for a president to be relieved from the damage the prosecutor is wreaking upon the presidency.

For the time being, there is uncertainty as well as substantial disagreement over whether a sitting president may be criminally indicted and prosecuted. Prosecutors who have considered the question in the past have tended to err on the side of allowing the impeachment process to go first. But, if Congress fails to impeach the president, then we are left to trust in the other mechanisms recognized in *Nixon v. Fitzgerald* as the other forums for holding a president accountable for his misconduct.

Does a prior conviction or judgment from a court carry any weight in an impeachment proceeding?

A prior conviction carries no formal weight, but a criminal conviction of a judge or other impeachable official would be hard for lawmakers to ignore or discount. As we consider the extent to which, as a formal matter, criminal convictions are entitled to any weight in impeachment proceedings, we should not forget their practical effects.

In the law, the special doctrines of *res judicata* and collateral estoppel apply when there has been some prior judicial proceeding or court decision on the same subject. *Res judicata* bars the parties from relitigating the same matter they have previously litigated; collateral estoppel bars someone from relitigating or rearguing an issue that has already been decided.

One question that came up in the late 1980s was whether the criminal proceedings that had already been brought (and succeeded) against Harry Claiborne and Walter Nixon were entitled to have the effect in their impeachment proceedings of either *res judicata* or collateral estoppel. After some deliberation, the Senate rejected the application of either of these doctrines in an impeachment trial.[115] Giving such effects to the earlier proceedings would have allowed them to bind the House or the Senate, which was thought to be unfair and to allow these other proceedings to displace the roles that the House and Senate had in the impeachment process. Individual members of Congress could take note of prior claims and proceedings, but were not bound by them.

By refusing to allow prior convictions or court proceedings to have any binding effect on the House or Senate, senators underscored the separateness and independence of impeachment from these other processes.

Do any special privileges apply in impeachment proceedings?

No, but this does not prevent presidents or others from trying to invoke them. Executive privilege pertains to the entitlement of the president to maintain the confidentiality of information produced on his behalf. In *United States v. Nixon*, the Supreme Court unanimously rejected Richard Nixon's claim that he was entitled to an absolute executive privilege—entitling him to keep information of any kind confidential if he wanted it to be.[116] Instead, the Court recognized that presidents had qualified executive privileges, meaning that their claims of entitlement to keep information confidential would be balanced against the need for it to released or published. In *United States v. Nixon*, the Court did the balancing and ruled that Nixon's asserted need to keep information about the Watergate break-in confidential was outweighed by the need for the criminal defendants in that case to mount a defense.[117]

The third impeachment article approved by the House Judiciary Committee shortly thereafter charged that Nixon's refusal to comply with a legislative subpoena to turn over the taped conversations in his possession (the same tapes the Court ordered him to turn over to the Watergate special prosecutor and the defendants in *United States v. Nixon*).[118] The Committee echoed the Court's rejection of the president's entitlement of an absolute executive privilege, something the committee felt would enable him to undermine or impede investigations into his misconduct. Nixon's rejoinder was the same as every president has made after *United States v. Nixon*—that the decision pertained to executive privilege in judicial proceedings. Nixon (and other presidents since) argued that an absolute privilege was essential in interactions with Congress or else the president would effectively become subservient to the will of Congress, indeed that he would be required to make it easier for Congress to investigate him by having to give up the information produced on his behalf whenever Congress felt it had a greater entitlement to it.

The Judiciary Committee's approval of an impeachment article against Nixon for refusing to comply with a legislative subpoena does not yet settle the question of whether such refusal may serve as a legitimate basis for impeachment. The full House has yet to endorse that view, which in turn has meant that the Senate has never had the chance to consider whether to convict and remove a president on the basis of such a refusal. In the absence of impeachment proceedings that arguably settle this question once and for all, we are left to consider the arguments made for and against grounding an impeachment, conviction, and removal on this basis. A president will likely argue that he is entitled to refuse to comply with a legislative subpoena as a means not only to protect his entitlement to assert executive privilege but also to ensure that the presidency can maintain an equilibrium, or stay on an equal footing, with Congress, particularly on questions of presidential power. Congress may respond that allowing a president to refuse compliance with a legislative subpoena enables him to avoid accountability for his misconduct, particularly in an impeachment proceeding. Congress's concern is that a president's refusal could undermine congressional investigations into his misconduct. Presidents may defend their refusals on the grounds that they prevent the presidency from being made subservient to the Congress.

What is the right answer, or where does or should the Constitution draw a line on whether Congress may compel a president to testify or produce evidence in an impeachment proceeding? I am inclined to think the question virtually answers itself. Impeachment is the principal check on a president's misconduct or abuse of power. It is therefore the one forum recognized in the Constitution where a president should not be entitled to refuse to appear or to constitutional privileges that undermine or eviscerate this check against his misconduct. Thus, a qualified privilege makes the most sense under these circumstances. A president can make his assertions for the need to maintain confidentiality, but his claims are entitled to inspection, or review, within the impeachment process. Indeed, any such inspection or review provides a means to assess the credibility of a president's assertions of privilege. No other result seems to make as much sense, particularly since the framers rebelled against a king and had no agenda of re-creating here the same potential for despotism and tyranny that they rebelled against. A qualified privilege attempts to strike the right balance between presidential and congressional entitlements. A qualified privilege allows a president to have his cake but not the entitlement to eat it all too.

Are there any other privileges that might apply in impeachment proceedings?

The other privilege that some witnesses or parties in impeachment proceedings might be interested in invoking is the Fifth Amendment's privilege against self-incrimination. (The Fifth Amendment provides in pertinent part that "no person . . . shall be compelled in any criminal case to be a witness against himself.") This privilege entitles someone from refusing to answer questions in criminal proceedings because answering them might incriminate the person in some criminal activity. Though some prosecutors might insist that this privilege applies only to criminal ones, witnesses have long been counseled not to answer questions in non-criminal proceedings, such as civil discovery, that could be used against them later in criminal proceedings. Indeed, it has long been the practice in non-criminal proceedings to allow witnesses to invoke their Fifth Amendment privileges in non-criminal proceedings but to allow the other parties to draw negative inferences from the silence ensuing from their invoking their Fifth Amendment privilege against self-incrimination.

A similar principle applies in congressional hearings, including impeachment proceedings, but it should be clarified that the principle works differently for compelled testimony and documents. In general, the Congress has taken the position that the Fifth Amendment privilege may be invoked with respect to testimony that is compelled and that is "incriminating."[119] Usually, most questions that arise with respect to this privilege have to do with what constitutes incriminating testimony. The scope of the privilege has tended to differ when a committee is attempting to compel or subpoena documents. The case law provides that the Fifth Amendment privilege against self-incrimination does not apply to voluntarily created documents that are incriminating, but courts do allow witnesses to invoke the Fifth Amendment to protect themselves from being incriminated because of the compelled "act of production." In practice, the relative scope of the asserted privilege tends to be worked out between the parties based on the particular facts of the circumstances in which it is invoked, and members of Congress may still seek to draw negative inferences from the invocation of the privilege.

Does the pardon power extend to impeachment proceedings?

Luckily, this is an easy question to answer. The Constitution expressly says no. It provides that the "President shall have power to grant Reprieves and Pardons against the United States, except in cases of impeachment."[120] The pardon power extends to federal criminal offenses but not to impeachable offenses or state crimes. The president therefore does not have the authority to use the pardon power to insulate himself or anyone else from the impeachment process.

Chapter 6

EXPLAINING WHAT PUNISHMENTS THE SENATE MAY IMPOSE

What punishments may be imposed in an impeachment proceeding?

The Constitution provides that "Judgment in cases of impeachment shall not extend further than to removal from Office, and disqualification to hold and enjoy any Office of honor, trust or profit under the United States."[1] The first is, of course, removal from office. We have already identified the most important question about removal, that is, whether it automatically follows from conviction. The Senate has answered this question definitively. The second sanction is disqualification. Both its nature and imposition raise questions that have not been answered as clearly as those relating to removal.

What happens when the Senate acquits someone?

An acquittal by the Senate brings its impeachment trial to an end and allows the impeached official to retain the office he or she currently occupies. Whether the Senate has voted to acquit or convict, the Senate still must take the further step of formally adjourning in order for the Senate to cease functioning as the trial court and to move on to other business. Acquittal does not, however, foreclose subsequent civil or criminal proceedings or liability for the same or different matter. In addition, acquittal does not foreclose another impeachment proceeding based on some other offense. Indeed, the Constitution restricts double jeopardy only for criminal proceedings, not for civil or impeachment proceedings focusing on the same misconduct.

What happens when someone is convicted?

From 1789 until early 1936, the Senate took two votes at the end of impeachment trials.[2] It first asked each senator whether or not the impeached official should be convicted of the misconduct charged in the impeachment articles.[3] Next, it asked if the person should be removed. As a practical matter, the bifurcation of the votes at the end of the trial allowed senators to vote to convict someone but then to reach a separate determination on which grounds to vote for their removal. In every case where at least two-thirds of the Senate voted to convict an official, the Senate voted to remove that official.[4]

After the 1936 impeachment trial of Judge Ritter, the Senate took the position that removal was automatic upon conviction and did not require a separate vote.[5] Ever since, the Senate has conflated the two votes into a single one, and it has asked at the end of each impeachment trial only whether the impeached official should be convicted. If more than two-thirds of the Senate voted to convict the impeached official, he has been automatically removed from office. Automatic removal means that at that moment, the official is stripped of his office and is no longer entitled to the compensation for that position, to exercising the power of that office, and to the protections and immunities that come with that office.

While the practice of bifurcated votes seems to cut against the Senate's conclusion that removal follows automatically upon conviction, there is other constitutional text to support the Senate's current practice. Article II provides that "the President, the Vice-President, and all civil officers of the United States shall be removed from Office on Impeachment for, and Conviction of, Treason, Bribery, or other high Crimes and Misdemeanors."[6] This language suggests rather clearly that removal is not discretionary, a point on which there is nearly universal agreement. If an official is convicted at the end of his impeachment trial, the official is automatically removed from office (assuming, of course, that the person has not yet resigned).

What is disqualification?

The common answer is that disqualification entails prohibiting the convicted official from ever serving in any other federal office again.[7] Yet the wording of the Constitution suggests that there is more to disqualification than this. In fact, disqualification further prohibits the disqualified official from receiving any federal pensions to which they would have been otherwise entitled deriving from their service in their previous federal office.

Does the Constitution require that the sanctions of removal and disqualification be imposed at the same time, or may (or must) they be imposed separately?

Both the text of the Constitution and the Senate's practices suggest that the sanctions of removal and disqualification are separately imposed. "Removal" is mentioned twice in the Constitution as a sanction following upon conviction, but disqualification is mentioned only once. Each time that removal is mentioned, it follows, as the text of Article I, Section 3, shows, immediately after the term conviction, with the proximity of the terms of removal and conviction suggesting that they are closely connected in practice. In contrast, the only constitutional provision mentioning disqualification provides that "Judgments in Cases of Impeachment shall not extend further than removal from office, and disqualification to hold and enjoy any Office of honor, trust, or profit under the United States."

One obvious purpose of this provision is to clarify the two particular sanctions that may be imposed at the end of an impeachment trial. This textual provision, standing alone, does not link disqualification so closely to conviction as to suggest that it automatically follows upon a conviction. Moreover, disqualification is mentioned in the second half of the clause, separated from removal by a comma. The separation of disqualification from removal into two different parts of the same clause could be construed as separating these two sanctions in practice as well. Indeed, this reflects the current Senate understanding and practice, in which removal always follows impeachment but disqualification is not compulsory.

How many times has the Senate disqualified an official it convicted?

The Senate has formally disqualified only three officials in American history—West Humphreys, Robert Archbald, and Thomas Porteous.[8] All three were federal judges.

In 1853, President Franklin Pierce appointed Humphreys a federal district judge in Tennessee.[9] When Tennessee seceded from the Union in 1861, Humphreys abandoned his federal judgeship to accept an appointment as a judge on the Confederate district court in Tennessee.[10] On May 19, 1862, the House impeached Humphreys, and on June 26, 1862, the Senate held an impeachment trial, after which it voted unanimously to convict and remove him, followed by another vote to disqualify him.[11] Though none of the impeachment charges alleged he had engaged in treason, they did charge him with providing aid to a rebellion against the United States; undoubtedly, this was one of the most serious charges that could be brought against someone.[12] Humphreys's action to follow the secessionist movement and join the rebellion against the Union made him an ideal person to be the first federal official removed and then disqualified from ever holding another federal office.

Robert Archbald was the second judge to be disqualified by the Senate. At the time, he was serving as a judge on the US Commerce Court after having served for a brief time as a federal district judge.[13] In 1912, the House became aware that Archbald had entered into agreements with litigants appearing before him to benefit himself financially.[14] The House approved thirteen impeachment articles against him, with only a single member of the House voting against them.[15] After an impeachment trial, the Senate convicted Archbald on five of the thirteen impeachment articles, followed by a vote of 39–35 to disqualify him from further service in a federal office.[16]

Judge Porteous was appointed by President Clinton to a federal district judgeship in Louisiana in 1994. He faced impeachment in January 2010 for a wide range of misconduct, including receiving kickbacks from cases that had come before him, committing fraud when declaring and seeking bankruptcy relief, and lying to the Senate and the FBI when he was considered for his appointment to the federal district court in 1994.[17] In December 2010, the Senate voted to convict and remove him from office.[18] The Senate then formally disqualified him from further federal service by a vote of 94–2.[19]

Why is disqualification rarely imposed?

No one knows the answer for sure, because the historical record is sparse. One possibility is that members of the House simply had not thought of disqualification when they were drafting their impeachment articles. Another is that perhaps the House did not consider the misconduct to be serious enough to justify both removal and disqualification. In any event, another complication that has arisen is whether the House must expressly mention the necessity for disqualification in its impeachment articles. Indeed, this issue arose during the House's impeachment proceedings against President Clinton, during which the majority members drafting the impeachment articles concluded they needed to include disqualification as among the sanctions that they wanted the Senate to consider if it ultimately convicted President Clinton of misconduct. Since the Senate takes the position it does not have the authority to amend the impeachment articles approved in the House, it does not seek to impose disqualification as an afterthought; it does so only if the House has specified not just removal but also disqualification as the desired sanction.

Does disqualification require at least two-thirds approval in the Senate, as removal does, or may it be done by a majority vote?

A tough question that has arisen with respect to disqualification is whether it requires at least two-thirds approval of the Senate or merely a bare majority vote. Because the Senate currently treats removal as the automatic consequence of a two-thirds vote to convict, the Senate logically regards a two-thirds vote as a prerequisite to the imposition of the punishment of removal. Yet, on each of the three occasions on which the Senate imposed the punishment of disqualification, it did so after a simple majority vote, though in two of the cases the vote was not close.[20] The Senate defends this practice on its reading of the relevant text, and on its belief that the officials subjected to a separate disqualification vote are adequately protected from abuse through both the requirement of a supermajority vote prior to a conviction and through the political accountability of senators. With a conviction as a necessary precondition, a vote on disqualification never arises unless at least two-thirds of the senators already have agreed on removal.

It is possible, however, to read the relevant constitutional text and structure differently. First, the fact that removal follows automatically from an impeachment conviction by a two-thirds vote does not suggest anything determinative about the requisite vote for disqualification. The Senate's authority for its practice of conducting different votes on removal and on disqualification is premised on the inference from the facts that the Constitution mentions removal twice, once in connection with a conviction, which may occur only through a two-thirds vote, but mentions disqualification only once, in a separate clause, as one of the two punishments permissible in an impeachable proceeding. Yet, an equally plausible inference from the pertinent text is that, given the framers' expectation that the two-thirds vote requirement would make it less likely for impeached officials to be convicted and punished for improper motives, both punishments should be applied by the same voting requirements. Otherwise, allowing a simple majority of the Senate to choose to disqualify a convicted official eliminates the important safeguard that the framers sought to provide against intemperate impeachment by empowering slightly more than one-third of the body to check its wanton use. The Senate's practice of requiring only a majority vote for disqualification precludes a significant number of senators, who would normally have the power to prevent a conviction, from blocking the harsh punishment of disqualification if they saw fit.

Who is Alcee Hastings and why is he relevant?

In 1979, President Jimmy Carter appointed Alcee Hastings as a federal district judge in Florida.[21] Just two years later, a federal grand jury indicted Hastings for conspiracy and obstruction of justice for soliciting a bribe in exchange for reducing the criminal sentence of two mob-connected felons who had been convicted in his court.[22] Even though the jury had convicted his friend and co-conspirator William Borders, it acquitted Hastings.[23] Subsequently, a special committee of judges from the circuit in which he served investigated charges that Hastings had lied and falsified evidence in his criminal trial.[24]

Based on its findings, the Judicial Conference of the United States recommended that the House of Representatives consider his impeachment for bribery and perjury.[25] On August 3, 1988, the House of Representatives voted 413–3 to impeach Hastings on the basis of seventeen impeachment articles.[26] In 1989, a special twelve-member trial committee of the Senate, composed of an equal number of Republicans and Democrats, investigated the charges and issued a report to the full Senate in early October 1999.[27] On October 18, the Senate conducted its trial of Hastings, during which the House managers and Judge Hastings and his lawyers presented their arguments behind closed doors.[28] The next day, more than two-thirds of the Senate voted to convict Hastings on eight of the impeachment articles, and he was removed from office.[29]

However, the impeachment articles did not recommend disqualification, and the Senate voted only to convict and remove the judge.[30] Subsequently, Hastings ran successfully for Congress in 1992, and he has served as a representative in the House ever since.[31]

During President Clinton's impeachment in 1998 and Thomas Porteous's impeachment in 2010, a majority of the House decided it would not make the same mistake it had made in Hastings's case not to consider including a recommendation on disqualification in its impeachment articles. The House included the recommendation of disqualification in the impeachment articles it approved against Clinton, and it has included a recommendation for disqualification in every subsequent impeachment.[32] Thus, the Senate not only convicted and removed Porteous from office but also, by an overwhelming vote, disqualified him as well.[33]

What is censure?

Censure is a declaration of misconduct made by the House or Senate. It takes the form of a simple resolution, which each chamber has the power to approve by a simple majority vote. The only time that a majority of the House or Senate has approved a censure of a president was the Senate's 1834 censure of Andrew Jackson for withholding classified documents his cabinet had put together regarding his veto of the rechartering of the National Bank.[34] The Senate expunged the censure shortly before President Jackson's second term ended in 1837.[35]

Is presidential censure constitutional?

In considering the constitutionality of censure, we should keep in mind that there are two basic approaches to analyzing constitutional issues relating to separation of powers, or the distribution of powers in the Constitution. The first is called formalism, which takes the approach that the Constitution spells out all the ways in which power may be shared or distributed among the three branches of the federal government. For formalists, the Constitution sets out all the permissible ways in which power may be distributed among the three branches. Some formalists may argue that censure is unconstitutional because the Constitution does not mention it at all, much less as an alternative to impeachment. The point is that the specific mentioning of impeachment as a mechanism for addressing official misconduct excludes the possibility of there being any others.

An alternative approach in separation of powers debates is called functionalism, which balances the competing considerations of any proposed mechanism. Functionalists ask whether the innovation or alternative being considered unduly impedes the functioning of another branch. So functionalists would probably argue that, on balance, censure does not unduly aggrandize the legislature at the expense of the presidency. The arguments over censure's constitutionality are based on one or the other of these approaches.

There are, however, several arguments that support the constitutionality of censure that are consistent with both of these approaches to constitutional analysis. First, the text of the Constitution appears to answer the question about the legitimacy of censure, for it provides that "Judgment in cases of impeachment shall not extend further than" the sanctions of impeachment, removal, and disqualification. A plain inference from this language is that something that falls short of them both might be permissible.

Second, if we think of censure as nothing more than a simple resolution, which each chamber may approve by a majority vote, the Constitution does not bar resolutions and sets forth no restrictions on the content that they may be used to express. Third, historical practices, which are more important and valid to functionalists than they are to formalists, are nonetheless a widely acknowledged source of constitutional meaning, and each chamber has condemned presidents in resolutions in the past, arguably establishing historical practices in support of them. For example, the House of Representatives had adopted the committee report criticizing President Tyler.[36] Moreover, there is no question members of the House or the Senate may deliver speeches or make statements critical of a president (or some other official). It seems odd for the Constitution to allow them to do that, because of the speech or debate clause and the First Amendment, but not to allow them to record the fact that they have done so. Indeed, they must, because of the constitutional requirement for Congress to keep a journal of its proceedings.[37] Then, we are left with the question whether a resolution recording the fact of condemnation is different from the mere routine recording of the fact of members' criticizing the president or other official(s). If there is no meaningful difference between a congressional record filled with critical statements about a particular official or event and an official censure resolution, then a censure resolution seems constitutional.

For the sake of thoroughness, we should note that there are at least two counterarguments that may be made against the constitutionality of censure. The first is the formalist claim that censure is illegitimate because impeachment is the only constitutionally authorized means for Congress to punish a president. This argument might have struck many people as disingenuous (indeed, most Americans supported censure as an alternative to impeachment throughout President Clinton's Senate trial[38]). This was the argument made by President Jackson against his censure.[39] But, if censure is merely an effort to bypass the requirements for impeachment, then it seems suspect.

Another argument made against censure is that it violates the constitutional prohibitions of bills of attainder. If a censure is nothing more than a bill of attainder, Congress may not do it. The question, then, is whether it is one or not.

What is a bill of attainder?

A bill of attainder is the act of a legislature declaring someone guilty of a criminal act and imposing punishment in lieu of a trial. For example, neither chamber of Congress, nor Congress as a whole, had the authority to declare that President Clinton was guilty of perjury and then to sentence him to a prison term or to impose a fine.

Is censure a bill of attainder?

The question that is often asked about any resolution purporting to criticize a president for misconduct is whether that is only a resolution or whether it is actually something more. If it literally does nothing more, it is in all likelihood not a bill of attainder. But if, for example, the House approves a resolution merely criticizing a president for some wrongful conduct, it still could be a bill of attainder if it damages the president in any way. Even assuming there is no confinement or fine imposed, the resolution might damage the president's reputation, leading some people to conclude that the injury to the president is enough damage to treat the resolution as a bill of attainder rather than as a harmless resolution, such as the House's celebration of a holiday, event, or individual.

However, reputation is not something that the prohibition of bills of attainder was designed to protect;[40] the prohibition has historically been understood as having the narrower purpose of precluding fines, physical punishment, or imprisonment imposed by a legislature as a substitute for a judicial proceeding. Even if there were damage to a president's reputation, it is likely to have resulted from expression that is undoubtedly protected by the First Amendment and the speech or debate clause. A censure is the functional equivalent of the latter action. Although one could object that censure might be a futile act politically or could be overused to harass a president (or another official), these are prudential—not constitutional—objections. The calculation of whether a censure is constitutional is separate and distinct from whether it makes political sense to use it in any given case.[41]

Is it permissible for the Senate to issue or approve findings of fact?

At one point during President Clinton's impeachment proceedings in the Senate, the senators considered a proposal to allow a vote on findings of fact before the vote on conviction and removal. The proposal derived its inspiration from the Senate's long-standing practice, prior to 1936, to take two votes at the end of an impeachment trial, one on whether the person was guilty or not guilty and the other on whether the Senate should convict and remove the official.[42] This alternative analysis intrigued some senators who were interested in declaring the president guilty of misconduct but not in voting him from office. In the views of its supporters, the finding of fact would have been indistinguishable from censure, for it would have embodied nothing more than an expression of criticism of an official's conduct. Thus, a finding of fact arguably would have been constitutional for the same reasons as censure.

The proposed finding of fact in Clinton's trial was problematic, since it was unclear what purpose it served. Indeed, its timing— prior to the adjournment of the impeachment trial—raised concerns about whether it was an attempt to exact some sanction on Clinton in the absence of a conviction. As long as the Senate's vote on the finding of fact occurred during the impeachment trial, it could easily have been confused with a vote of conviction, and some senators understood it as tantamount to the latter. Undoubtedly, many senators who supported the finding of fact were motivated in part by their desire to prevent the president from claiming vindication or acquittal if the Senate failed to convict him for perjury or obstruction of justice. The finding of fact would have allowed these senators to suggest that the president had been found guilty of certain misconduct (as defined in the finding of fact) by whatever number of senators had voted in favor of the finding of fact. Hence, the finding of fact might have been an effort to produce a conviction but by another name. If the finding of fact were the same as or tantamount to a vote of conviction, then at least two-thirds of the senators would have had to vote in favor of it in order for it to have had the effect of a conviction. If at least two-thirds of the senators had voted in favor of it, it almost certainly would have served as a conviction, and its subject—the president—would have been removed from office. If two-thirds of the senators had not voted in favor of the finding of fact, then the president almost certainly would have been entitled to claim that the vote should have counted as an acquittal.

Indeed, if senators had been required, after having voted on the finding of fact, to take a separate vote on whether to convict (and remove) the president, the president would probably have had good reason to claim a violation of fundamental fairness. That sequence of voting would have appeared to have allowed some senators the chance to try to convict the president on more than one vote—through the vote on the finding of fact and through the subsequent vote on conviction or removal. Subjecting the president more than once to a vote of conviction—in the same proceeding—would simply have subjected him to a dubious and arguably spiteful process, and the result surely would have been perceived as unfair.

Moreover, the fact that the Senate took separate votes on guilt and removal in some earlier proceedings does not necessarily prove that the Senate may convict for a non-impeachable offense. First, in each of the earlier trials in which the Senate took such separate votes, the Senate removed the official from office. It is significant that in each of these proceedings, the Senate took a single vote on whether to remove the official only after the latter had been found by more than a two-thirds vote to have been guilty on the charges set forth in any single article.

For instance, the Senate voted 19–7 to find Pickering guilty on each of four articles and then took a single vote, 20–6, to remove him from office (with Senator William Wells from Delaware deciding to switch sides for the final vote to go with the supermajority because the outcome was a foregone conclusion).[43] Similarly, after a supermajority had found West Humphreys guilty on each of seven articles of impeachment (with the exception of one of the three specifications of misconduct set forth in the sixth article), the Senate voted unanimously to remove Humphreys.[44] In Archbald's trial, the Senate took a voice vote to remove him once a supermajority had found him guilty of the misconduct charged in five of the thirteen articles of impeachment passed by the House.[45] These sequences suggest that as long as two-thirds or more of the Senate had found an official guilty of the misconduct charged in at least one article, removal was inevitable.

Are there any other sanctions falling short of removal and disqualification that Congress may impose on public officials for their misconduct in office?

This is really the same question we considered previously with regard to the constitutionality of censure, since its constitutionality rested entirely on whether it could be fairly described as falling short of impeachment and not constituting an illegal bill of attainder. If you accept censure as nothing more than a simple resolution, which each chamber passes all the time to express its opinion about something (such as expressing condolences to the family of a fallen service member or recognizing Arbor Day), then it follows you would agree there could be sanctions falling short of impeachment, conviction, removal, and disqualification. But, if you think impeachment is the only power the Congress has to express its disapproval of a president's or other high-ranking official's misconduct, then you would likely read the Constitution as precluding any other measures for expressing disapproval.

The difficulty with this latter reading is that it means Congress has no power to do anything about official misconduct falling short of an impeachable offense. Perhaps that was what the Founders intended, leaving these issues to be worked out by the voters or, in the case of judges, perhaps through the inherent powers of courts to deal with administrative issues, such as delays or disability.

In any event, the only other possibility that leaves is the enactment of a law that criminalizes misconduct that Congress believes would be serious enough to provide a basis for impeachment, conviction, and removal. Bribery is one obvious example of Congress's doing so, though of course the Constitution expressly makes bribery one basis for impeachment without saying that it must have been codified as a crime for it to serve this purpose. Alcee Hastings's case illustrates how Congress could remove someone from office on the basis of bribery even though a prosecution on that basis had failed. We know that Congress has the authority to enact federal criminal laws, but the question is, How far may it go in fashioning a law that replaces or somehow supplements the impeachment process? This question leads us to consider the possible relevance and constitutionality of the Bribery Act of 1790.

What about the Bribery Act of 1790? Is that relevant, and was it constitutional?

Shortly after ratification of the Constitution, the First Congress passed the Bribery Act of 1790, which provided that upon conviction in federal court for bribery, a federal judge shall "forever be disqualified to hold any office."[46] The significance of this law is that it might say something about the attitudes of the framers on whether impeachment is the exclusive mode for disqualifying federal judges, because many members of the First Congress had attended the Constitutional Convention or participated in the ratification campaign.[47] Even so, the Bribery Act of 1790 was never enforced, in part because of concerns about its constitutionality,[48] which remains in doubt to this day.[49]

Let's first consider the arguments that support the Bribery Act. It could have been justified as the First Congress's reasonable effort to achieve one or both of two legitimate objectives by combining its powers under the necessary and proper[50] and the impeachment clauses. First, the First Congress might have been trying to clarify the impeachment procedure established in the Constitution by categorically declaring that a conviction in federal court for one of the impeachable offenses specifically listed in the Constitution— bribery—always justifies disqualifying a federal judge from office. In other words, the act might have reflected Congress's expression of its intent to conduct impeachment trials for any federal judges convicted of bribery when it was convinced that it would disqualify any such judges. This reading of the law is also consistent with the view that disqualification requires approval only from a simple majority of the Senate, given that a majority of each chamber is all that would have been required for the bill to be approved in Congress.

Second, the First Congress might have been delegating some of its impeachment authority to criminal juries in a way that actually helped federal judges. Although it is clear that impeachment proceedings are fundamentally different than criminal trials (and vice versa),[51] the act of 1790 might be based on an expectation that the values of judicial independence and integrity normally protected through the supermajority vote required in Senate impeachment trials would actually be adequately protected through the special procedural safeguards that apply in criminal proceedings. In impeachment proceedings, the targeted official is usually not entitled to the kinds of elaborate procedural safeguards governing criminal proceedings.[52]

Moreover, the First Congress might have viewed the delegation entailed in the act as constitutional because it rested on the idea that judges are not immune from the criminal law. Such a notion does not threaten judicial independence because the Bribery Act of 1790 was not directed at any essential judicial activity. Rather, the act focused on judicial misconduct that violated a specific criminal law. The constitutional duties of a federal judge do not require or necessitate any kind of criminal misconduct. In other words, the First Congress might have believed that the act did not threaten judicial independence, because it did not punish or prohibit federal judges for any conduct central to the performance of their constitutional obligations.

Nevertheless, several objections to the constitutionality of the Bribery Act of 1790 are worth examining more closely. The first response is the formalist argument that the Bribery Act violates the Constitution because it usurps the Senate's power to impose disqualification. Only the Senate has that power, and Congress does not have the authority to give that power to anyone else.

Moreover, as the eminent constitutional scholar and lawyer Walter Dellinger once argued, the best way to analyze the constitutionality of the Bribery Act of 1790 is to ask whether it is any more legitimate than a statute that automatically disqualified the president or the vice president once they were convicted in federal court of bribery.[53] Dellinger suggested that the problem with this statute is that it fails to follow the principle that impeachment is the sole means of disciplining and removing the president, vice president, and all federal judges. He suggested that this kind of law would seriously disrupt the administration of justice and domestic tranquility; deprive the president and the vice president of the special securities of an impeachment proceeding, such as a supermajority vote of the Senate prior to a conviction; and redefine the balance of power of the federal government. A similar statute directed at federal judges would, in Dellinger's opinion, likewise be unconstitutional, because it would deprive judges of the unique protections available in an impeachment for ensuring judicial independence, including the chance to give Congress reasons not to remove if it sees fit.

This argument runs into a problem if impeachment is not the sole political means for disciplining and removing federal judges. Given that the Bribery Act of 1790 could be read as subjecting federal judges in limited circumstances to disqualification in a forum in which they could take advantage of greater procedural safeguards than those available in impeachment trials, the act does not necessarily conflict with the distribution of power in the Constitution, at least in cases involving federal district and circuit court judges. If Supreme Court justices were subjected to this statute, an arguably different problem might arise, because they operate, like the president and the vice president, as the heads of their respective branch. Consequently, concerns about the proper distribution or balance of power in the federal government are strongest in those instances in which the removal, disqualification, and disciplining of the most powerful federal judicial officers are at stake. Even so, those concerns are still at stake with respect to lower-court judges, albeit not quite so much as with Supreme Court justices, and concerns about their entitlement to the safeguards and uniqueness of the impeachment process are understandable and justified.

Yet, if impeachment were the sole means allowed for disciplining judges who have engaged in the impeachable misconduct of bribery, the law is obviously attempting to create another venue for redressing such misconduct. If there were such a principle, it would obviously bar Congress from delegating some of its impeachment authority to the courts.

In addition, subjecting the president or vice president to similar legislation poses different concerns: they occupy unique positions under the Constitution as the top two officials in the executive branch. It is especially important to preserve their relationship with, and status in relation to, the other branches by limiting the means by which they may be disciplined, removed, and disqualified by the impeachment process. Making it easier to oust them weakens their stature in the constitutional order. The automatic disqualifications of the president or vice president would have serious political repercussions, for which the key decision-makers are not politically accountable.[54]

Yet another possible constitutional flaw with the Bribery Act of 1790 is that one of the specific safeguards set forth in the

Constitution for the disqualification of federal judges is that at least two-thirds of senators must agree on the propriety of a conviction, which is a predicate for the imposition of disqualification. Even if disqualification is imposed by the Senate through a majority vote, there has to be a conviction first, and it requires a super-majority vote of the Senate.[55] The statute, which needs only a majority vote of both the House and the Senate for passage, would deprive an impeached judge of the constitutional safeguard of allowing formal conviction only through a supermajority vote of the Senate.

Yet another possible constitutional defect with the law is that it allows the House to have a say on the disqualification of judges, which the Constitution had left only to the Senate to impose. True, the Constitution does not say that disqualification is solely a sanction to be imposed by the Senate, as it did with the "sole power of impeachment" to be vested in the House and the "sole power to try" impeachments to be vested in the Senate. Nonetheless, the Constitution clearly vests only the Senate with the authority to impose sanctions after a conviction in an impeachment trial, a delegation of exclusive authority that is frustrated by the statute, which allows a majority of the House to have a say on the imposition of disqualification.

Last but not least, the Bribery Act of 1790 might run afoul of the Fifth Amendment due process clause. The act "forever" disqualifies federal judges convicted of bribery, but convictions can be overturned on appeal.[56] Due process guarantees criminal defendants the right to appeal their convictions without being punished beforehand.[57] It thus appears that the act imposes the constitutional sanction of disqualification, presumably automatically, before courts have settled any judges' appeals.

In any event, it is not insignificant that, as circumstances developed, the First Congress never expressed its understanding of the act, and without its ever having been enforced we can only speculate on how it could be applied. It is unlikely any future Congress would be any more willing to pass a similar statute in light of its uncertain constitutionality and the considerable political fallout its passage would surely engender by circumventing the procedures set forth in the Constitution for judicial disqualification through impeachment.

Are there any other alternatives to impeachment worth knowing about?

Yes, there are. All the states and many countries use different or additional mechanisms for removal, such as petitioning for recall, or for addressing some of the same misconduct that might serve as a basis for impeachment proceedings.

Chapter 7

IMPEACHMENT IN THE STATES AND AROUND THE WORLD

What were the models for the federal impeachment process?

The framers modeled the federal impeachment process in part on the experiences with impeachment in the states and England prior to the drafting and ratification of the Constitution. The states' early experiences with impeachment were mixed: there was considerable frustration and opposition to the English resistance to any checks on the abuses of their royal governors and judges, but the innovations made in the states were useful models for the future. At the same time, the framers purposely differentiated the federal impeachment process from the practice in the English system, in which anyone could be impeached for anything and any sanction could be used. In a parliamentary system like England's, the legislature had the power to remove unpopular leaders, but the framers did not want a parliamentary system. Accordingly, the American Constitution does not allow Congress to undo elections or to oust unpopular leaders. Today, states and other countries learn more from the federal impeachment process and each other than members of Congress learn about impeachment from the states or other countries.

How common is impeachment in the states?

All fifty states provide for impeachment in some fashion. Generally, their impeachment provisions are set forth in their constitutions or laws authorized by their constitutions. Most states use the same language as the federal Constitution does in providing that "judgments in cases of impeachment shall not extend further than removal from office and disqualification to hold and enjoy any office of honor, trust, or profit under the United States, but the Party convicted shall nevertheless be liable and subject to Indictment, Trial, Judgment, and Punishment, according to law." Most states also adopt similar divisions of impeachment authority as does the federal Constitution, splitting it between their respective legislatures' two chambers (except of course for Nebraska, which has a unicameral legislature) and the requirement of at least two-thirds approval of the court of impeachment, usually the state senate, for conviction and removal.

States differ with respect to which public officials are subject to impeachment, the allocation of impeachment authority, the composition of the authorities vested with the impeachment power, the grounds for impeachment, and the officials whom it empowers to preside over impeachment trials. For example, Kansas largely tracks the federal division of authority over impeachment and removal,[1] whereas Alaska provides that an impeachment must originate in the senate and trials are to be held in the state's house of representatives.[2] The official commentary to the Alaska scheme acknowledges, however, that impeachment "is a cumbersome and archaic procedure" that has never been used in Alaska and that the state therefore provides alternative procedures for the removal of judges for incapacity or misconduct.[3]

California empowers its assembly with the power of impeachment, though it does not specify what that chamber may do, and requires trials to be held in the senate and conviction and removal only by at least two-thirds vote of the members of the senate.[4] Arizona and Connecticut have impeachment processes modeled closely on the federal scheme, while Massachusetts has a similar process but worded in a much different manner than in the US Constitution.[5] In Article VI of its constitution, Massachusetts provides that "The house of representatives shall be the grand inquest of this commonwealth; and all impeachments made by them, shall be heard and tried by the senate"; and in the next article it declares that "The senate shall be a court with full authority to hear and determine all impeachments made by the house of representatives, against any officer or officers of the commonwealth, for misconduct and mal-administration in their offices."[6] The article proceeds to require, "But previous to the trial of every impeachment the members of the senate shall respectively be sworn, truly and impartially to try and determine the charge in question, according to evidence. Their judgment, however shall not extend further than to removal from office and disqualification to hold or enjoy any place of honor, trust, or profit, under this commonwealth: but the party so convicted, shall be, nevertheless, liable to indictment, trial, judgment, and punishment, according to the laws of the land."[7]

North Carolina, North Dakota, and Rhode Island have some relatively unusual provisions—and language—relating to impeachment. For example, in describing the court for the trial of impeachments in Article IV, the North Carolina state constitution empowers the state house of representatives with the power to impeach and the state senate with the power to try impeachments and goes further than our federal Constitution to provide that, "When the Governor or Lieutenant Governor is impeached, the Chief Justice shall preside over the Court. A majority of the members shall be necessary to a quorum, and no person shall be convicted without the concurrence of two-thirds of the Senators present."[8] The North Carolina Constitution then adopts the same language as used in the federal Constitution, providing that "Judgment upon conviction shall not extend beyond removal from and disqualification to hold office in this State, but the party shall be liable to indictment and punishment according to law."[9]

New York is a good example of a state's authorizing an unusually constituted court of impeachment. New York provides that "The court for the trial of impeachments shall be composed of the president of the senate, the senators, or the major part of them, and the judges of the court of appeals, or the major part of them."[10] Furthermore, New York expressly makes special arrangements for the impeachments of certain officials, requiring, for example, that "On the trial of an impeachment against the governor or lieutenant-governor, neither the lieutenant-governor nor the temporary president of the senate shall act as a member of the court."[11] Moreover, it provides that "No judicial officer shall exercise his or her office after articles of impeachment against him or her shall have been preferred to the senate, until he or she shall have been acquitted."[12]

What are some examples of the different grounds that states provide as the bases for impeachment?

States differ widely on the grounds they specify may be used as the basis for impeachment and removal. For example, Arkansas provides not only that "The Governor and all State officers, Judges of the Supreme and Circuit Courts, Chancellors and Prosecuting Attorneys, shall be liable to impeachment for high crimes and misdemeanors" but also that those state leaders may be impeached for "gross misconduct in office."[13] Similarly, Colorado provides that "The governor and other state and judicial officers, shall be liable to impeachment for high crimes or misdemeanors or malfeasance in office."[14] (The fact that "gross misconduct" or malfeasance in office is added to "high crimes and misdemeanors" suggests that, at least for those states, "high crimes and misdemeanors" do not encompass those additional kinds of misconduct.)

California merely provides that "State officers elected on a state-wide basis, members of the State Board of Equalization, and judges of state courts are subject to impeachment for misconduct in office."[15] Connecticut does not even mention the grounds for impeachment, except for explicitly providing (in nearly identical language as the federal Constitution has) that "Treason against the state shall consist only in levying war against it, or adhering to its enemies, giving them aid and comfort. No person shall be convicted of treason, unless on the testimony of at least two witnesses to the same overt act, or on confession in open court. No conviction of treason, or attainder, shall work corruption of blood, or forfeiture."[16]

Florida provides that "The governor, lieutenant governor, members of the cabinet, justices of the supreme court, judges of district courts of appeal, judges of circuit courts, and judges of county courts shall be liable to impeachment for misdemeanor in office," which could be read to reach a broader range of misconduct than the federal Constitution's "other high crimes or misdemeanors."[17] Massachusetts provides a broad basis for impeachment that extends to "misconduct and mal-administration in [the covered officials'] offices."[18] New York also provides a broad basis for impeachment by authorizing that "Provision shall be made by law for the removal for misconduct or malversation in office of all officers, except judicial, whose powers and duties are not local or legislative and who shall be elected at general elections, and also for supplying vacancies created by such removal."[19]

North Carolina provides that "Any Justice or Judge of the General Court of Justice may be removed from office for mental or physical incapacity by joint resolution of two-thirds of all the members of each house of the General Assembly."[20] Ohio also provides a broad basis for impeachment: "Laws shall be passed providing for the prompt removal from office, upon complaint and hearing, of all officers, including state officers, judges and members of the general assembly, for any misconduct involving moral turpitude or for other cause provided by law; and this method of removal shall be in addition to impeachment or other method of removal authorized by the constitution."[21] Similarly, Rhode Island provides, "The governor or any other executive officer shall be removed from office if, upon impeachment, such officer shall be found incapacitated or guilty of the commission of a felony or crime of moral turpitude, misfeasance or malfeasance in office. Judges shall be removed if, upon impeachment, they shall be found incapacitated or guilty of the commission of a felony or crime of moral turpitude, misfeasance or malfeasance in office or violation of the canons of judicial ethics."[22]

Do states use other or additional means than impeachment for addressing the misconduct of public officials?

Yes, every state does, making impeachments less likely than its alternatives. States differ in these other or additional mechanisms for addressing official misconduct, including recalls, elimination of judgeships, and special disciplinary processes for certain public officials' misconduct. For example, one popular alternative that is available in all fifty states is empowering state ethics commissions to hear and act upon complaints filed against public officials for violating the states' ethics laws or rules.

North Carolina specifically authorizes a mechanism other than impeachment for removing certain kinds of state judges, which provides a broader basis for the removal of certain judges than the federal Constitution does: "The General Assembly shall prescribe a procedure, in addition to impeachment and address set forth in this Section, for the removal of a Justice or Judge of the General

Court of Justice for mental or physical incapacity interfering with the performance of his duties which is, or is likely to become, permanent, and for the censure and removal of a Justice or Judge of the General Court of Justice for willful misconduct in office, willful and persistent failure to perform his duties, habitual intemperance, conviction of a crime involving moral turpitude, or conduct prejudicial to the administration of justice that brings the judicial office into disrepute."[23]

However, an especially unusual part of North Carolina's impeachment process is set forth in Section 8 of Article VI, which directs that a series of classes of people are "disqualified for office" beginning with "any person who shall deny the being of Almighty God."[24] Usually, state impeachment procedures do not pose a constitutional problem at either the state or federal level, but this provision clearly violates the Constitution's guarantees for freedom of expression and against the establishment of religion.[25] Some of the most dramatic incidents in states' removals of officials over the last few decades have involved these other mechanisms.

Have there been any impeachments in states that are of particular significance?

In American history, states thus far have impeached and removed thirty different public officials for misconduct in office. These have included some interesting, dramatic proceedings. For example, in one of the first significant impeachment efforts made within the states after the Second World War, Arizona governor Evan Mecham served only a few months in office before efforts to oust him began in 1987.[26] Mecham, his opponents charged, had done a number of embarrassing and inappropriate things, including canceling a paid day off for state employees on Martin Luther King Day, using offensive language when referring to African Americans, and mismanaging the state's response to an economic downturn.[27] A recall effort was completed successfully less than a year after he entered office, but he challenged its certification.[28] When the *Arizona Republic*, a leading paper, broke the story of his failure to report a significant loan to his campaign, and a grand jury began investigating whether he had improperly used public funds to help his auto dealerships, the Arizona speaker of the house authorized a special counsel to investigate the charges. Mecham's alleged misdeeds also included ordering the head of the state's Department of Public Safety not to report to the attorney general a death threat that had been made by one of his employees.[29]

The report issued by the special investigation became the basis for Mecham's impeachment.[30] On February 8, 1988, the house impeached Mecham by a vote of 46–14.[31] Later that month, the state senate convened as a court of impeachment and began its trial of the governor. On April 4, the senate convicted Mecham on obstruction of justice 21–9 and on misusing government funds 26–4.[32] The senate next voted 17–13 to disqualify Mecham from serving in any state office in the future, but that vote fell short of the two-thirds majority required for passage.[33] Upon his conviction in the senate, Mecham was removed from office.[34] He was later acquitted in a criminal trial.[35]

Whereas Mecham was a Republican, Rod Blagojevich was a Democrat, elected governor of Illinois in 2003 after serving in the state legislature and the US House of Representatives.[36] In late 2008, he was arrested as a result of a federal investigation into whether he had engaged in criminal acts, specifically to gain financial advantage, from filling the US Senate seat that Barack Obama had vacated upon being elected president of the United States in 2008.[37] Though Blagojevich claimed he was innocent, the state legislature moved quickly to impeach him.[38] On January 8, 2009, the Illinois House of Representatives voted 114–1 to impeach him for abuse of power and attempts to sell gubernatorial appointments, legislative authorizations, and vetoes.[39] In two separate votes on January 29, 2009, the Illinois Senate unanimously voted to remove him from office and to disqualify him from ever serving again in public office in Illinois.[40] He was subsequently convicted of 17 federal criminal charges and sentenced to 14 years in federal prison.

Yet another impeachment that grabbed headlines in its day involved Rolf Larsen, who had been elected to the Pennsylvania Supreme Court in 1977.[41] In 1992, Larsen was accused of improperly communicating with a trial judge about a case.[42] In response, Larsen filed documents showing that Robert Nix, another justice on the Pennsylvania Supreme Court, with whom Larsen had feuded for years, and other justices on the commonwealth's supreme court had engaged in the same kind of misconduct.[43] The Pennsylvania attorney general convened a grand jury to investigate the matter.[44] The grand jury found no evidence of wrongful communication among the judges, but it did find evidence that Larsen had been involved in a conspiracy to fraudulently obtain prescription drugs.[45] A jury subsequently convicted him on two counts of criminal conspiracy.[46] The trial court sentenced him to a year's probation and removed him from office.[47]

Nonetheless, the Pennsylvania General Assembly moved ahead with impeachment proceedings. The Pennsylvania House of Representatives impeached Larsen on seven articles of impeachment, and the Pennsylvania Senate convicted him for improper communication with a trial judge, removed him from office, and disqualified him from ever holding another office of public trust in the Commonwealth of Pennsylvania.[48]

Have there been any notable impeachment attempts in the states that failed?

There have been a few, not including the many times officials have avoided impeachment by resigning from office before the start of any proceedings. Perhaps the most famous instance of a failed impeachment attempt involved Huey Long, who was a popular but controversial public figure in Louisiana and on the national scene during the 1930s. Nicknamed the Kingfish, Long was a populist Democrat who was elected governor of Louisiana in 1928.[49] Once in office, Long dismissed hundreds of political opponents in the administration and replaced them with his personal friends and allies.[50] As he pushed for a number of public works projects and a controversial occupational license tax on the production of refined oil, there was considerable pushback from large oil companies.[51]

Opponents in the Lousiana legislature moved to impeach Long on several charges, including blasphemy, abuses of power, and bribery.[52] Long took his case to the public, which supported him, but the state house referred the impeachment to the senate, which acquitted him but not without charges that both he and his opponents paid off senators for their votes and that Long rewarded several other senators with state appointments and other favors.[53] Subsequently, Long was elected to the US Senate, where he initially strongly supported Franklin Roosevelt's New Deal but then flirted with his own presidential run, which was cut short when he was assassinated in the State Capitol in 1935.[54]

In 2000, the chief justice of the New Hampshire Supreme Court, David Brock, became the first state supreme court chief justice to be impeached. His impeachment dated back to earlier in the year, when the New Hampshire Supreme Court faced an unusual situation: it was asked to review the appeal of a divorce proceeding brought by the ex-wife of one of the justices on the New Hampshire Supreme Court, Stephen Thayer.[55] In a meeting with all the justices present, Chief Justice Brock announced his appointment of two people to substitute for justices who could not hear the case because they knew both parties.[56] Thayer objected to one of the appointments.[57] The court's clerk reported the matter to the state's attorney general, because he knew it was a violation of court procedures for a judge to discuss a case involving a fellow judge with the fellow judge present.[58]

The attorney general's report, issued on March 30, 2000, led to Thayer's resignation and informed the state's House Judiciary Committee that other members of the court had committed other ethical violations.[59] On April 9, 2000, the New Hampshire House of Representatives voted 343–7 to approve an impeachment inquiry against Chief Justice Brock.[60] After its investigation and report, the full chamber voted 253–95 to approve four impeachment articles against Brock, charging "maladministration of practice" in connection with two cases, testifying falsely under oath to the House Judiciary Committee, and "maladministration" by allowing disqualified judges to comment on and influence the proceedings in "cases from which they had been recused and disqualified." After its trial, the state senate acquitted Brock on all four articles of impeachment, as none of them received the two-thirds majority approval for passage.[61] Some senators said they were not convinced of the accuracy of the charges and others that even if Brock had made mistakes, none were serious enough to rise to the level of impeachable offenses.[62]

The Brock trial has potential importance for several reasons. First, the New Hampshire constitution did not set forth the requisite vote for conviction and removal. As a result, the senators decided themselves on the threshold for removal, agreeing it had to be at least two-thirds approval of the senate. Second, judges and some commentators look to the failed impeachment as a vindication of the important principle of judicial independence. Given that the charges might not have been serious enough to justify impeachment and removal, critics of the impeachment believe that the Senate properly left the issues, which largely dealt with the internal operations of the judiciary, for the judiciary to resolve on its own—or for the legislature to establish clear guidelines and restrictions that passed constitutional muster.

Indeed, Brock's acquittal brings to mind three memorable instances in which the effort to impeach prominent judges for their opinions failed (and there was no doubt that Chief Justice Brock was not popular with some senators and some of his fellow judges). The first of these took place in 1766–1788 in North Carolina.[63] This early example was well known among the framers' generation for underscoring the importance of judicial independence from political retaliation. It involved Samuel Ashe, who at the time led the state's superior court judges in weakening ex-Loyalists' claims for restitution in the courts.[64] Some conservative Loyalists drafted impeachment articles against Ashe and the other judges for various kinds of misconduct in cases involving claims brought by ex-Loyalists.[65] The judges defended themselves on the ground that the state legislature had asked them to dismiss the claims and they had simply done what they had been asked to do.[66] The legislature exonerated all the judges except for Ashe, whom conservative legislators still insisted on trying to impeach.[67] Although initially the legislature condemned him for not appearing to answer the charges against him, he eventually appeared, angrily denounced the hearings, and defended himself.[68] The legislature relented, and no impeachment ensued. Later, his defense and the failed effort to impeach him have become among the most notable instances of the vindication of judicial independence and integrity in North Carolina history.

The next notorious incident involved Samuel Chase, whom President Jefferson and Republican leaders wanted impeached and removed from the bench for trying to push through prosecutions under the Alien and Sedition Act even while overseeing trials, as the justices were commonly required at the time to do.[69] The House impeached Chase, but the Senate acquitted him, vindicating the principle that impeachment should not be used to punish judges for their decisions.[70]

Much later, in 1970, then Minority Leader Gerald Ford urged the House of Representatives to initiate an impeachment inquiry against Associate Justice William O. Douglas of the Supreme Court for his colorful lifestyle, extremely liberal opinions, and alleged financial improprieties.[71] The House Judiciary Committee briefly considered but refused to authorize any further inquiry, because it determined that impeachment was not appropriate to use under the circumstances.[72] The committee dismissed the matter based on concerns that partisan motivations had driven the request for an inquiry and on the need to protect judicial independence.[73]

What are some notable instances of states' using mechanisms other than impeachment to address officials' misconduct?

Alabama and Pennsylvania have each had political dramas that culminated in high-profile efforts to discipline high-ranking public officials for misconduct. Both the Alabama and Pennsylvania situations involved the interplay of a number of different laws and authorities.

In Alabama, Roy Moore has been a prominent public figure who has enjoyed substantial popularity among the state's evangelical voters. In 2001, he was elected chief justice of the Alabama Supreme Court after having served as a judge on the Circuit Court for eight years and previously as an assistant district attorney.[74] A graduate of West Point, he was also a veteran of the Vietnam War.[75] A month after his election as chief justice, Moore began arranging for the placement of a 5,280-ton monument to the Ten Commandments that he intended to place in the state's supreme court building.[76] On the evening of July 31, 2001, he authorized the installation of the monument in the rotunda of that building.[77]

In late October, several groups, including the American Civil Liberties Union and the Southern Poverty Law Center, filed a lawsuit in the US District Court for the Middle District of Alabama challenging the constitutionality of the monument's establishment in the Supreme Court building.[78] Myron Thompson, the judge assigned to the case, ruled that the monument violated the federal Constitution's establishment clause and ordered its removal, but he stayed his ruling when Moore indicated his intention to appeal his judgment to the US Court of Appeals for the Eleventh

Circuit.[79] The appellate court affirmed Judge Thompson's order, and Judge Thompson ordered Moore, in compliance with the appellate court's decision, to remove the monument.[80] Two days later, Moore announced his intention to refuse to comply with Thompson's order.[81]

Two days later, on August 22, 2003, the Alabama Judicial Inquiry Commission filed a complaint with the Alabama Court of the Judiciary, a special panel composed of lawyers and judges.[82] The Alabama Court of the Judiciary then held a hearing to determine whether Moore's refusal to comply with Thompson's order violated judicial canons of ethics.[83] Moore argued that Thompson's order was unlawful and that his own construction of the First Amendment was consistent with the religious higher law on which he believed the Constitution, including the First Amendment, had been founded.[84] The next day, the Alabama Court of the Judiciary issued a unanimous ruling stating that Moore had violated the Alabama Canons of Judicial Ethics (which required judges not to engage in partisan activity and to respect the law).[85] Although it had many disciplinary options, including fining the judge, it chose to remove him from office as the Chief Justice.[86]

However, the Alabama Court of the Judiciary did not disqualify Moore from running again for chief justice or any other public office in the state. In 2012, he ran again for chief justice and was re-elected.[87] Three years later, when the US Supreme Court declared that the Fourteenth Amendment due process clause protected the right of same-sex couples to be married,[88] Moore openly criticized the decision and vowed not to comply with its directive.[89] In late January 2016, the Southern Poverty Law Center filed a judicial ethics complaint against Moore.[90] Moore persisted in his criticism. He also directed probate judges and their employees to disregard a ruling from the US Court of Appeals for the Eleventh Circuit that they were obliged to follow the Supreme Court's recent directive and issue marriage licenses to same-sex couples who sought them.[91] He later ordered lower-court judges in the state to comply with Alabama's laws restricting gay marriage that had been enacted before the Supreme Court's decision on gay marriage, and had been nullified by it.[92]

On May 6, 2016, the Alabama Judicial Inquiry Commission forwarded a list of six charges of ethical violations to the Alabama

Court of the Judiciary.[93] Pursuant to state law, Moore was then suspended from his office pending the outcome of the ethics hearing.[94] Though Moore filed a series of legal challenges to the ethics complaints against him, the Alabama Court of the Judiciary held its hearings in August 2016.[95] The court found Moore guilty on all charges and ordered his suspension from office for the remainder of his term.[96] (It did not feel the need to disqualify him from running again for public office, because, once the suspension was over, he would be too old to serve on the Alabama Supreme Court.) Moore appealed the special court's verdict to the Alabama Supreme Court, which appointed seven retired judges to review his appeal of his suspension.[97] On April 20, 2016, the Alabama Supreme Court upheld his suspension.[98]

Moore was not done yet. Six days after the final ruling, Moore resigned from office and declared his candidacy for the US Senate.[99] He won the Republican nomination, but his campaign faltered after an allegation emerged that when he was an assistant district attorney in the 1970s he had so frequently solicited underage women that he had been banned from a shopping mall.[100] On December 7, 2017, in a special election to fill the seat of Jefferson Sessions, he lost the Senate race to Doug Jones, the first Alabama Democrat to win a Senate seat in a quarter of a century.[101]

Earlier that same year, an impeachment resolution had been introduced against the governor of Alabama, Robert Bentley, for misusing state property and other misconduct relating to an affair he was attempting to keep hidden from the public.[102] The Alabama constitution authorized impeachment of the governor for misconduct but provided no procedures to be followed in an impeachment.[103] The legislature scrambled to put together the requisite procedures. In the meantime, the state auditor filed an ethics complaint against Bentley with the State Ethics Commission.[104] On April 5, the Ethics Commission found probable cause that Bentley had committed four felonies.[105] Two days later, the special counsel authorized by the state House to investigate the matter released a 131-page report detailing Bentley's misconduct.[106] Shortly after his impeachment proceedings began on April 10, 2016, Bentley resigned from office.[107]

As the state of Alabama was wrestling with the misconduct of its governor and chief justice, Pennsylvania had its own widening scandal. It began with a bit of history, the election of Kathleen

Kane, who was the first female and the first Democrat to be elected Pennsylvania's attorney general.[108] The timeline of her demise tells a sordid story of corruption that ultimately challenged every branch of government and a variety of mechanisms for addressing public misconduct.

Kane was sworn into office as the state's attorney general on January 15, 2013.[109] As a candidate, she had campaigned not only as an outsider but also as a critic of Republican governor Tom Corbett for failing as the state's attorney general to bring child molestation charges against Jerry Sandusky, a retired assistant football coach at Penn State who worked under the legendary head coach Joe Paterno.[110] Though there was obviously friction between Cornett and Kane as they each entered office in early 2013, Kane garnered considerable national attention during her first year in office. One of her first acts was to launch an investigation into the Sandusky case, which did not cover any misconduct but uncovered thousands of emails sent by state officials with pornographic, racist, or misogynistic content.[111]

Also, in her few months of office, she rejected Cornett's plan to privatize the management of the state lottery, refused to defend the state's ban on gay marriage, and exposed corruption in the Pennsylvania Turnpike Commission.[112] Despite criticism, she also promoted her twin sister, who had already been working in the attorney general's office.[113] Also, during Corbett's first few months in office, she shut down a sting operation that he had begun when he was attorney general and had recorded four state legislators and a judge from Philadelphia—all Democrats—accepting illegal gifts.[114]

A year after Kane had shut down the sting operation, the *Philadelphia Inquirer* published an article revealing that the sting operation had taken place and Kane had shut it down.[115] In response to Republican leaders who condemned her for petty partisanship and favoritism, Kane claimed that the cases had been mismanaged and had been too weak for her office to bring prosecutions.[116]

Kane's actions led to a feud with Frank Fina, a former state prosecutor who had overseen the sting operation and the Sandusky case and who had joined the chorus of her critics. Among other things, she had challenged Fina's boss to take over the case built on the sting operation. Fina accepted the challenge, and his office eventually secured convictions of five of the six officials involved.[117] On

May 29, Montgomery County court judge William Carpenter appointed a special prosecutor to investigate the leaked grand jury materials.[118] Barely a week later, on June 6, 2014, the *Philadelphia Daily News* published reports from a grand jury investigation in which Fina had previously been involved. Fina cried foul again, claiming that Kane had leaked the information in violation of state laws (and an agreement she had signed) to keep grand jury deliberations and investigations confidential.[119] Though in fact she had leaked the information, Kane initially denied the charges and even testified falsely under oath that she had not done it.[120] As Fina pressed his case, Kane then, on September 25, released the emails she had uncovered in the Sandusky investigation.[121] They revealed, among other things, the names of one retired and two current Pennsylvania Supreme Court justices who had been among those emailing and receiving the offensive emails.[122] Two of the Pennsylvania Supreme Court justices resigned rather than face impeachment or other disciplinary proceedings.[123] In mid-November, Kane testified before the grand jury investigating the leak; a month later, on December 18, 2014, the grand jury recommended charging Kane with perjury, obstruction of justice, and contempt of court.[124]

Throughout the first few months of 2015, Kane tried but failed to stop the investigations into whether she had illegally leaked grand jury investigative material. On April 27, the grand jury report on Kane was made public.[125] On August 6, Montgomery County district attorney Risa Fetri Ferman charged Kane with perjury, obstruction of justice, official oppression, and false swearing.[126] Although Kane publicly attacked the charges made against her by Ferman's office, the Pennsylvania Supreme Court unanimously voted to suspend Kane's law license, the first time this had ever been done to a state attorney general.[127] Kane then claimed that another Pennsylvania Supreme Court justice had sent "racial, misogynistic pornography on state computers," and the Montgomery Country prosecutors added a second count of perjury against her for lying about whether she had signed an oath of secrecy not to reveal confidential investigative material.[128] Though she denied it, detectives discovered the signed oath.[129]

On November 9, 2015, a seven-member bipartisan committee of the state senate met to determine whether Kane could continue to serve as the state's attorney general even though her law license had been suspended.[130] On December 7, the panel unanimously voted to recommend that the full senate vote on Kane's possible removal from office.[131] She objected, asserting that impeachment was the only permissible way to remove her from office.[132] On December 16, Kane revealed that her sister too had sent inappropriate emails but said that her sister would not be disciplined as other lawyers in the office had been.[133]

On February 10, the state senate failed to muster a majority vote in favor of Kane's removal.[134] Six days later, she announced she would not seek re-election but asked the state's supreme court to reinstate her law license.[135] It refused.[136] On August 8, her criminal trial began.[137] A week later, she was convicted on all nine counts that she had been charged with.[138] The next day, she resigned from her position as state attorney general.[139] Kane was sentenced in October to 10–23 months in prison, ending her career in public office.[140]

How popular is the impeachment process around the world?

At the time of the drafting of the Constitution, the framers were aware—and even mentioned—that Parliament was just beginning a high-profile impeachment of Warren Hastings, who had been charged with various acts of corruption and misconduct during the time he was the first governor-general of India.[141] It took Edmund Burke four days to read the charges against Hastings in Parliament. Although the proceedings lasted seven years (because it was often interrupted by more pressing business), the House of Lords eventually acquitted Hastings of all charges.[142] Eventually, the British system of allowing impeachment to be used against anyone for any kind of misconduct proved unworkable, and it transformed into its present mode where Parliament may oust a prime minister on the basis of a vote of no confidence.

Elsewhere around the world, impeachment became popular as a mechanism for holding leaders accountable. Dozens of countries around the world have adopted constitutions or laws allowing for the impeachment of high-ranking officials. Many countries, including Norway and the Philippines, have adopted schemes similar to the one set forth in the federal Constitution, but some countries, like Germany and South Korea, vest their legislatures with the power to impeach but their constitutional courts with the authority to try impeachments. Countries differ further on the grounds for impeachment and removal, the officials who are impeachable, the requisite votes required to impeach and to convict and remove, and the available sanctions for impeachment and alternatives to or in addition to it, such as recalls, criminal proceedings, and votes of no confidence.

For different historical reasons, some countries, notably Canada and Poland, do not have provisions for impeaching their leaders; they allow for removal by other means—in Canada, the prime minister may be replaced in his party's convention or by a vote of no confidence (as in Great Britain), while in Poland investigations of misconduct in office can be done by the State Tribunal (if one of the highest-ranking officials are involved) or a special Parliament committee. In other places, the mechanisms for impeachment have yet to be used. For example, in England, Parliament has had the power of impeachment since 1600s, but the last person to be impeached in England was Henry Dundas, who was acquitted in 1806 after having been impeached for misappropriation of public money as secretary of state for war.[143] Parliament has also had the power of impeachment, dating back to the Settlement Act of 1701, to petition the queen for the removal of a judge of the High Court or the Court of Appeal, but no judge on either of those courts has ever been impeached, much less convicted and removed.[144]

What world leaders outside of the United States have been impeached in recent history?

Since 1981, there have been ten notable impeachments of the presidents of countries other than the United States. Two recent ones were the presidents of Brazil and South Korea.

In 2010, Dilma Rousseff was the first woman to be elected the president of Brazil.[145] She was narrowly re-elected in 2014.[146] Throughout her re-election campaign, she had to fend off charges of corruption both while she was president and beforehand, when she was president of the board of directors of the Brazilian petroleum company Petrobras.[147] More than twelve months into her second term as president, Rousseff was formally charged in an impeachment petition for criminal administrative misconduct, for violating federal budget laws, and for having engaged in misconduct as president of Petrobras.[148] On April 17, 2016, she was impeached based on the charges of her misconduct while Brazil's president, but the prosecutor-general successfully argued against including the charges based on her misconduct that occurred during her tenure as president of Petrobras on the ground that a sitting president could not be impeached for misconduct that occurred before she took office. On May 12, the Senate voted to suspend her powers as president for the duration of her impeachment trial, and Rousseff's vice president, Michael Temer, became acting president.[149] On August 31, the Senate voted 61–20 to find Rousseff guilty of violating Brazil's budget laws and to remove her from office.[150]

Although Temer was sworn in as the new president, he was accused of irregularities in funding the 2014 campaign he had run along with Rousseff. Both Rousseff and Temer faced a trial in the Superior Electoral Court on these new charges.[151] On June 9, 2017, the Electoral Court rejected, 4–3, the allegations of campaign finance violations by Rousseff and Temer and dismissed the charges.[152] As a result, Temer remained in office as president.

Meanwhile, in South Korea its first female president, Park Geun-hye, was also facing impeachment. After serving in the National Assembly and leading her political party, Park, whose father had once been president, assumed office in January 2013.[153] But, as a result of revelations in October 2016 of her conspiring with an aide to solicit funds in exchange for her help and advancement, her popularity plummeted to 4 percent, and more than 75 percent of the public supported her ouster from office.[154] Though she repeatedly apologized for her misconduct, the opposition party took control of the National Assembly in early December 2016.[155]

On December 9, the National Assembly voted 234–56 to impeach her, surpassing the two-thirds required for an impeachment.[156] She was immediately suspended from office, and the prime minister temporarily assumed the powers of her office.[157] According to South Korea's constitution, the South Korean Constitutional Court had to act on the impeachment within 180 days.[158] After a series of procedural delays and a brief hearing on the president's whereabouts in the immediate aftermath of the tragic Sewol Ferry accident that had killed more than three hundred people, the Constitutional

Court unanimously upheld the impeachment, formally terminating Park's presidency and making her the first leader of South Korea to be removed by impeachment.[159]

Have there been notable failed impeachment attempts outside of the United States in recent history?

Just as there have been the notable failures to convict and remove two American presidents for misconduct and a forced resignation of a third that preempted his impeachment, other countries have had leaders who were involved in scandals or faced corruption charges but were not impeached. One of the most unusual of these involved Boris Yeltsin, who became the president of the Russian Federation in 1991 after the dissolution of the Soviet Union. Over the next eight years, Yeltsin survived three impeachment attempts.

According to Article 93 of the Russian constitution, the State Duma (the lower legislative chamber) has the authority to impeach the president by a two-thirds majority vote, and the Federation Council has the authority to remove the president by a two-thirds majority vote of its own.[160] On March 28, 1993, Yeltsin was charged with violating the Russian constitution, but the vote of the deputies in the State Duma fell short of the requisite two-thirds majority for an impeachment.[161] Later that same year, on September 22, Yeltsin was charged again, and this time the Federation Council dismissed him and delegated the duties of the presidency to the vice president.[162] But Yeltsin refused to step down and instead dissolved the Supreme Soviet.[163]

The third and final effort to impeach and remove Yeltsin arose in 1999, when the State Duma formulated several charges against him, including responsibility for the collapse of the Soviet Union, responsibility for the 1993 constitutional crisis in Russia, the outbreak of war in Chechnya in 1994, destroying the armed forces by depriving them of sufficient funding, and the genocide of the Russian people by promoting reforms that impoverished them and raised the death rate.[164] Though the effort failed, it, along with the other impeachment attempts and Yeltsin's deteriorating popularity and political stature, led him to announce his resignation from office at the end of December 1999.[165] In the statement that he made at that time, he apologized to the Russian people for the many errors he had made as Russia's leader.[166] The prime minister, Vladimir Putin, became acting president and signed a decree guaranteeing Yeltsin immunity from prosecution for any crimes.[167]

A recent failed presidential impeachment was directed against Pedro Pablo Kuczynski, a well-respected economist who was elected Peru's president in 2016.[168] On December 15, 2017, the Congress of Peru initiated impeachment proceedings against President Kuczynski for lying about taking bribes from a Brazilian construction firm more than a decade earlier.[169] Initially, Kuczynski denied the allegations, but he later acknowledged that he received the payments, which he then claimed had been paid in exchange for advisory services, not political favors.[170] On December 21, a majority of the Congress voted to remove him from office.[171] Because the vote fell short of the minimum two-thirds required to support removal, Kuczynski remained in office. Three days later, Kuczynski pardoned former Peruvian president Alberto Fujimori, who had left office in 2000 and fled the country to Japan amid a major scandal involving corruption and human rights violations.[172] Kuczynski resigned under pressure on March 21, 2018.

Chapter 8

WILL DONALD TRUMP
BE IMPEACHED?

My concern in this chapter is the same as it has been throughout this book: it is not with questions of fact or with whether or not someone actually did something bad or not. Whether or not President Trump will ever be subject to the impeachment process is not something I or anyone else knows. It will of course depend on the facts—facts that will have to be developed through the different processes our legal and constitutional systems establish for holding people accountable for their misconduct in office. During the Senate hearings on Watergate, Howard Baker, a Republican senator from Tennessee, famously asked, "What did the president know, and when did he know it?" These are central questions in any impeachment hearing, but I cannot and do not attempt to answer them here with respect to the current president. Indeed, nothing I say here is about the facts or whether the President actually did something meriting ouster from office. For example, we should all be able to agree that obstruction of justice is an impeachable offense apart from whether any particular president (or any other impeachable official) engaged in that kind of misconduct. When discussing the possibility of impeaching President Trump, my focus is on the constitutional law applicable to the particular question or circumstances.

Will Donald Trump be impeached?

Anyone who tells you they already know the answer to this question is someone to whom you probably should not listen. Of course, no one can know that now, and it does not advance any understanding of the law of impeachment to profess otherwise. The same holds true for anyone who is confident that either the president has already committed a wide range of impeachable offenses or that he has done nothing wrong at all. It is important, for the sake of intellectual precision and honesty, not to get ahead of the evidence or the law.

As a candidate, President Trump promised that he would "shake things up."[1] And shaking things up is bound to be messy. It will look disruptive, and certainly not pretty. At the same time, even if the public that elected President Trump wanted him to shake things up, that does not mean he has a blank check to do whatever he wants, however he likes. The truth is that many, if not most, presidents push the boundaries of their job. Indeed, the job itself demands that presidents do something other than stand pat, and, as some political scientists have suggested, there are ways in which to understand presidents in terms of their successes and failures to reshape the powers of their office and the constitutional order more generally.[2] Pushing boundaries basically comes with the job, especially when Congress cannot respond as quickly as the president does to the exigencies he is asked to address when in office. The question is, When do presidents' pushing or extending of boundaries go too far, or at what point do their efforts to do so—and go beyond those boundaries even as they are attempting to redefine them—provide a basis for impeachment?

Of course, there are many related questions about President Trump, including the possible relevance of alternatives to impeachment, notably the Twenty-fifth Amendment.[3] In fact, the kinds of issues that relate to the possibility of his (or any other president's) impeachment are relatively clear. The objective here is to fit the charges that could or might be made against President Trump into the framework of impeachment law.

What are the most serious charges made against the president?

There are at least six different kinds of misconduct that President Trump could conceivably be charged with or that pundits, scholars, or some members of Congress allege against him, though there is some overlap among these charges.

The first involves the president's finances, which have largely been kept private from the public and the media.[4] Finance-related questions encompass possible problems not only with financial arrangements that Trump failed to disclose as a candidate but also with whether, to what extent, or in what ways he or his companies have benefited, or could benefit, financially while he was president. One of the many concerns about his finances relates to possible conflicts of interest that he has not acknowledged or has disregarded after he entered office.[5] Other concerns regarding the president's finances are possible violations of the emoluments clause, committing fraud, or otherwise attempting through inappropriate means to hide his financial arrangements with or connections to businesses or governments with which he is interacting as president. In the Teapot Dome scandal during Warren Harding's administration and during the Watergate affair, journalists and other investigators adopted the strategy of "following the money" in order to identify who was benefiting from or encouraging criminal misbehavior.[6] The same principle applies to President Trump; that is, they attempt to follow the ways in which he has made money either as president or in business but never disclosed while he was a candidate.

The second major area of concern has to do with possible obstruction of justice. Obstruction of justice entails trying to impede an official investigation.[7] The president has been accused of obstructing justice through such means as firing James Comey as the head of the Federal Bureau of Investigation,[8] or through taking actions or making false statements to impede Special Prosecutor Robert Mueller's investigation into possible connections between the president or his campaign with the Russian government.[9]

The third area of concern has to do with so-called collusion with the Russian government. This is a concern apart from any possible obstruction or financial interest pertaining to Russia. The collusion and coordination itself is a problem: if it happened before the election, it would have violated federal laws; and if it has happened after the election, it presents a serious problem. Depending on what an investigation would show, that could amount to treason (if American interests were compromised or jeopardized in any way), bribery (if anything was given to the president in exchange for favors), or breaking federal criminal laws.

The fourth area of concern involves possible abuses of power. One of the grounds for impeaching President Nixon was his ordering officials within his administration to harass his political enemies. A similar concern has been expressed with respect to President Trump, having to do with whether he has abused particular powers, such as his pardon and removal powers.[10]

Yet another charge made against the president has to do with the extent to which he has engaged in misconduct that degrades his office. The question here is the extent to which his conduct has damaged the office of the presidency in sufficiently serious ways to warrant consideration in impeachment or some other process. For example, concerns about his mental competence might lead to a consideration of the mechanisms set forth in the Twenty-fifth Amendment for addressing a president's mental or physical incapacity.

Moreover, there are many pending lawsuits that were filed against President Trump before his election, and more than one hundred lawsuits have been filed against him since he was elected president.[11] The overwhelming majority of the cases filed against him as a private citizen, well before he became a presidential candidate, have been resolved. Of the remaining lawsuits filed against him in his private capacity (which would have extended until his inauguration in January 2017), perhaps the most significant claim that the president should be liable for libel, fraud, and sexual harassment.[12] Besides the charges made in the cases themselves, it is relevant that President Clinton ended up in impeachment trouble because he lied under oath. As a result, members of Congress, journalists, and others will be watching what the president himself does in any of these cases, particularly whether he testifies truthfully under oath and what he may do to try to avoid liability.

How many lawsuits were filed against Donald Trump prior to his election as president?

Prior to Donald Trump's election as president, more than four thousand lawsuits were filed against him or his business interests.[13] These cases extend back over several decades. No other president comes anywhere close to the total of lawsuits Trump has had filed against him before winning the presidency. The subject matters of these lawsuits varied, including allegations of nonpayment of bills and of fraud, but the vast majority have been disposed of.

As of President Trump's inauguration, there were about 75 cases pending against him.[14] Since his inauguration in January 2017, more than 100 additional lawsuits have been filed against him.[15]

What is the relevance of any of the lawsuits pending against the president at the time of his inauguration or filed against him since then?

Generally, we do not know. The more notable lawsuits filed against the president after he assumed office allege that he has violated the emoluments clause,[16] that his tweets are covered by the Presidential Records Act requiring the preservation or maintenance of all written records produced by the president,[17] and that he violated the First Amendment by blocking some people or press from being able to follow his Twitter account.[18]

The public has been made aware of all the lawsuits filed against President Trump both before and after his election. So there is no credible claim that he was hiding the fact of any of these lawsuits from the public. But, since the president has denied any wrongdoing alleged in any of the pending cases that pertain to pre-presidential conduct, there is a question about the possible relevance of any findings of liability in any of these cases. To be sure, the president might settle some of these lawsuits (and he has already done so in some of these cases); otherwise, it might take years for these cases to be fully litigated, including the disposition of all motions, discovery, and appeals.

The fact that the president might be found liable in any of these cases is not necessarily a problem of impeachment proportions. He can dispute the rulings if any do not go his way. More important, the nature of the misconduct for which he might be found liable (assuming he is found liable) could conceivably become a problem. Nonpayment of bills, for example, might be considered poor judgment and bad form and could be found to be the result of breaches of contract, among other things. Because the public knows about the claims in the cases, it would be difficult to argue that these judgments have any impeachment-related significance.

Nonetheless, if President Trump denies the charges or judgments, as Bill Clinton did in response to Paula Jones's claims of sexual harassment, questions could arise about whether the president lied in public or under oath and whether his denials should be considered an effort to defraud the American public about the offending conduct in question.

And because sexual harassment and fraud are serious kinds of misconduct, any finding that the president engaged in such misconduct could be used against him in any re-election campaign as well as in an impeachment hearing that is focusing on both the misconduct and the veracity of his claims about it. If Bill Clinton's lies under oath and efforts to hide his relationship with Monica Lewinsky from the public were serious enough to provide a basis for his impeachment, then the same could be said about any similar misconduct in which President Trump—or any other chief executive—engaged.

Just to be clear, I am now talking about the relevance of pre-presidential misconduct to an impeachment proceeding. If we assume for the sake of argument that President Trump lied under oath while he has been president or attempted to destroy or otherwise keep hidden from the public important, pertinent information about his misconduct, then any impeachment based on that kind of misconduct would not be an attempt to undo an election. Obviously, impeachment should not be used to undo an election or relitigate issues that were raised in an election. But, if we assume that Donald Trump lied under oath while he has been president, then the misconduct would be analogous to the misconduct for which the House impeached President Clinton in 1998. The facts would have to support any such claim, and it is easy to predict that the president and his supporters in Congress, the media, and the public will likely deny that he lied under oath.

Which constitutional clauses pertaining to emoluments might have relevance to the question of whether President Trump has possibly committed any impeachable offense?

There are two constitutional clauses, which come up often in discussions about whether President Trump has committed an impeachable offense. The first is Article I, Section 9, Clause 8, which is commonly called the foreign emoluments clause and which provides that "No Title of Nobility shall be granted by the United States: And no Person holding any Office of Profit or Trust under them, shall, without the consent of the Congress, accept of any present, Emolument, Office, or Title, of any kind whatever, from any King, Prince, or foreign State." The other clause, which comes up in discussions about whether President Trump has committed any impeachable offenses, is the compensation clause, set forth in Article II, Section 1, Clause 7: "The President shall, at stated Times, receive for his Services, a Compensation, which shall neither be increased nor diminished during the Period for which he shall have been elected, and he shall not receive within that Period any other Emolument from the United States, or any of them."

Would violating either the foreign emoluments or the compensation clause be an impeachable offense?

Whether a violation of the foreign emoluments clause or the compensation clause constitutes a legitimate basis for impeachment depends on the answers to several questions. First, we know by its very language that the compensation clause applies to the president, but does the foreign emoluments clause apply to him? Professors Tillman and Blackmun argue that the clause does not apply to the president, but most presidents (admittedly not the earliest ones, including Washington and Jefferson), the Congressional Research Service (which advises members of Congress on legal and constitutional questions), and the Justice Department's Office of Legal Counsel have concluded that the clause does apply to the president. If the clause does not apply to the president, then we do not need to consider any other questions; however, if the foreign emoluments clause does apply to the president, there are several other questions we have to answer in order to determine whether a violation of that clause, or the compensation clause, is serious enough to constitute a legitimate basis for impeachment.

Second, both clauses raise the question of what exactly are emoluments? Emoluments are the "profit derived from a discharge of the duties of office," or so Professors Blackmun and Tillman maintain in their commentaries on the subject.[19] In the literature, emoluments include payments, gifts, or benefits given to the president from foreign powers.[20] Thus we have to determine the nature of the payment, benefit, or gift to the president and particularly whether it came from a foreign power. A payment from a private source, including a citizen, group, or business from another country, might not satisfy this clause's express concern with a benefit given to the president by a foreign power.

Third, has Congress approved the receipt of the emolument? What we call the emoluments clause allows Congress to authorize the president to receive the emolument from a foreign power. If Congress were to authorize the payment or gift (presumably for a legitimate reason), then the emoluments clause analysis ends.

However, the compensation clause still bars the President's receipt of any "emolument" from the United States besides his official salary.[21] If, for example, it could be shown that the president received benefits of some kind from the US government beyond his salary, that could be a problem. Without President Trump's financial statements or tax returns, we do not know if this has happened or, even if it has happened, to what extent. Even then, he might argue that the American people might have ratified (i.e., consented to) his benefiting from the presidency in some financial way. An obvious response is that Article II, Section 1, Clause 7, recognizes no exceptions to its restrictions on presidential salaries.[22] It is therefore immaterial that the American people have permitted this, assuming they ever did.

In response, President Trump or those supporting him in Congress (or elsewhere) could still try to make a different argument. They could claim that, even if he somehow violated the foreign emoluments clause, voters determined that any such violation would be the price to be paid to have this successful businessman elected to the presidency. Indeed, they might assert that any such violations might be a small price to pay to have a successful businessperson elected to the presidency. In the great scheme of things, this problem would be outweighed by all the good that the president can achieve, including, in the case of Donald Trump, making America great again. A fourth question is how significant or substantial is the gift, payment, or benefit to the president. It could be inconsequential or relatively trivial. Indeed, one reason that may explain why Washington and Jefferson did not report the gifts given to them is the possibility they might have concluded they were minor, that is, unimportant. If a foreign power takes the president to dinner, we do not consider that to pose an emoluments problem. But, if the gift is substantial, say, a house or yacht, then it more clearly might qualify as an emolument for purposes of this clause.

Last but not least, has President Trump breached the foreign emoluments clause in bad faith? The size, magnitude, or substantiality of the gift or payment to the president is one thing, but it is reasonable to ask did the president inadvertently fail to report it to Congress or was it perhaps even something he was not aware of? An inadvertent error will not likely count as a violation of this clause, but a deliberate effort to circumvent the clause's applicability and deceive Congress or the American public about the receipt of a substantial benefit, gift, or payment is likely to violate the emoluments clause *and/or* the compensation clause of the Constitution. The seriousness of breaching one or both clauses should be obvious; any such breaches would undermine the president's integrity, reflect bad judgment and perhaps something worse such as cravenness, degrade the office (and its standing around the world), and injure the Republic. The flouting of the Constitution or the law is always a matter of grave concern.

What if the payment, gift, or benefit given to the president came from a source other than a foreign power?

The source of a payment, gift, or benefit to the president (assuming it is substantial in size) could provide a legitimate basis for impeachment, but we need to know more. To be sure, even if the receipt of the benefit, gift, or payment is not a violation of a statute or the foreign emoluments clause, the possibility of impeachment is not out of the question. Something does not have to be technically illegal—that is, forbidden expressly by civil or criminal law—in order for it to constitute an impeachable offense. The test for determining whether something constitutes an impeachable offense has to do with whether there was bad faith and a bad act. At one extreme, if we assume the president was bribed, then we know with certainty that his misconduct is impeachable, since the Constitution expressly provides bribery as an impeachable offense. Even if the president did not commit bribery, there could still be a problem if the argument can be persuasively made that the receipt of the gift, payment, or benefit corrupted the presidency or caused the republic serious injury.

Consider the following hypothetical: assume that, before he became president, Donald Trump's business had licensed a hotel that is located in Moscow. Assume further that war or armed hostilities break out between the United States and Russia, and, as the president considers possible bombing targets, he makes clear that he wants his hotel to be off-limits for bombing. Perhaps he even allows targeting of other hotels that are competitors of his. Is there a problem with his decision, and if so does it rise to the level of an impeachable offense?

It could, and the reason why should be obvious: we do not want the president's judgment or actions to be tainted or corrupted by his financial interests. One of the basic things we know from the origins and design of the federal impeachment process is that curbing presidential corruption was a major objective for the framers. If a link could be established between a presidential directive, decision, or action and his own financial interest, then it seems an inquiry, at the very least, is justified to explore the nature of that connection.

There is, however, an additional wrinkle to keep in mind. Let's assume that the benefit, payment, or gift goes not to the president but rather to his family or his friends. Is that a problem? In all likelihood, the answer is yes. In this scenario, the president is not receiving an emolument in violation of the Constitution, but he is using his powers or his office for the personal gain of his family or friends. It is not hard to imagine that a federal official's corruption need not be purely for his own gain in order for it to be an impeachable offense; it could be done to benefit friends, political allies, business associates, or family. (Indeed, Walter Nixon was impeached, convicted, and removed from office for making false statements to a grand jury that helped the son of a former business partner.) Surely, that is a kind of corruption that easily fits within the scope of the impeachable offenses that were of concern to the framers and architects of our Constitution.

Let's change the hypothetical to make the problem easier to understand. Assume that someone is blackmailing the president or that the president wants to return a favor done for him (before or after becoming president); may he use his powers as president to do so? In one sense, the answer is yes. Presidents appoint their friends and allies to federal offices all the time. For instance, it is commonly supposed that ambassadorships go to the friends and even the benefactors (i.e., campaign contributors) of a president. But, in another sense, this can be a problem. What may be appropriate in some circumstances might not be in others. If the president is lining his pocket as a result of some official action he has undertaken, then it appears the quid pro quo is different from giving an office to someone as a favor or payback. The appointment is not likely to be a secret, and the person given the office or appointment still has to do the job to which they were appointed. If, however, the president's action benefits him financially, then the quid pro quo appears to be in the form of "pay to play," which the criminal law disfavors and, perhaps more important for purposes of impeachment, is serious misconduct. This is true for any president, not just this one.

Is it a problem that the president has never disclosed his tax returns or the sources of his income and the degree of his indebtedness?

The answer is yes, but we need to understand why. First, let's rule out some things as possible grounds for impeachment. As a candidate and later as president, the president decided not to release his tax returns. Presidents starting with President Carter have voluntarily released their tax returns, but the practice of releasing the returns is a norm—that is, it is an informal arrangement or practice that people follow but is not required by the law. While the violation of a norm will likely provoke some backlash, the backlash is informal and the law does not require either the disclosure or the backlash. Many norms are relatively trivial, but it is not clear how the norm of disclosure of tax returns is, especially given that everyone knows the president broke the norm in public and still won the election.

Second, the president might have had benign reasons for breaking the norm. He might have been concerned that people might not understand his finances, he did not want his competitors to know about his finances, or he was concerned that the media and his opponents would distort the data to hurt him politically. Indeed, during the presidential campaign, one of the president's tax returns was leaked to the media. It appeared he had substantial losses that he used to offset the taxes he owed and he ended up not having to pay taxes for the year in question. True, the losses were substantial (nearly a million dollars), but tax lawyers generally agreed that what he had done on his taxes was perfectly legal, and the president deftly turned the issue to his advantage in a presidential debate when, in response to a question as to what the tax return showed about him, he said it showed he was "smart."

Third, it is possible that either the president's tax returns or his financial statements could reveal embarrassing or damaging information about the president. We do not know this for a fact. But another way to express this problem is that the president's finances could be a ripe area of concern to Congress, the American people, and the special counsel, Robert Mueller. We can only speculate on what if any damaging or embarrassing information his financial statements or tax returns might reveal, but it is not hard to imagine circumstances that might justifiably concern the country and members of Congress. Say the returns or financial statements revealed that President Trump was heavily indebted to foreign interests or powers for whom he is now, as president, trying to do favors. Being indebted in this way might not be illegal, but it would look bad. It suggests the possibility that the president's judgment has been corrupted, and one major reason for the impeachment process is to address the corruption of our president. Presidents doing favors for foreign interests or delivering benefits to them because they owe money to these foreign interests is a matter that is at the heart of the impeachment process.

Fourth, the IRS routinely audits presidents' tax returns. Under such circumstances, it might turn out that there is a problem only if the auditors find one. If they do not, then the president can no doubt argue that there is no basis for concern, much less with an impeachment inquiry. Nevertheless, the concern is that his tax reporting could be in order but reveal something that could be pertinent to a different problem, one that might go beyond the routine audit—namely, that the president has a conflict of interest because of an investment or financial assistance or arrangements. To be sure, auditors pay attention to the credibility and veracity of claims made on income tax forms, but sometimes things are not discovered in tax returns if the auditors are not looking for them. So, one question many citizens and journalists will ask is what were the auditors searching for.

How do we know where to draw the line on what
is impeachable and what is not when it comes to a
president's receipt of foreign or other financial gifts?

This all comes down to drawing the right lines. A good way to understand the scope of impeachable offenses is to imagine a spectrum of misconduct. At one end is misconduct that everyone agrees is impeachable, such as treason and bribery. At the other end is the misconduct that everyone agrees is not impeachable, such as jaywalking or a moving violation. Whenever we are considering whether the bad acts under consideration are "other high crimes and misdemeanors," we have to figure out to which end of the spectrum they are closest. Gerald Ford's answer, for which he got much grief, captured this dynamic when he suggested that a majority of the House would make the appropriate determination. It will do so, and its determination will turn on many factors, including the composition of the Congress, the magnitude of the harm or damage, a president's mindset or attitude, whether the electorate has had a chance to weigh in on the subject, and the connection or link between the misconduct and the president's duties. In some cases, these factors will point, sometimes clearly, in one direction, as they did in Richard Nixon's case, whereas in others they may cut against impeachment (John Tyler's case) or against conviction and removal (Andrew Johnson's and Bill Clinton's cases).

Questions of fact are ultimately up to the Congress to decide. The president might contest each and every one of the characterizations or assumptions about misbehavior made by his opponents. His denials are important, both in determining what happened and for determining his credibility.

What about Hillary Clinton's emails? Didn't she break
the law, and should she face criminal liability and
perhaps impeachment because of her misconduct?

After Hillary Clinton left office as President Obama's secretary of state in 2013, both the FBI and Congress investigated her handling of her official emails, including the extent to which her emails (which might have been damaging or embarrassing to her) were deliberately lost or destroyed. On January 4, 2018, the Justice Department, with President Trump's appointee Jefferson Sessions at the helm as attorney general, reopened its investigation into her use of a private server and her handling of classified material while she was secretary of state. The basic legal issue here is whether she engaged in misconduct, such as allowing classified information to fall into the hands of our enemies. Assuming that she either broke laws or acted inappropriately with respect to the classified information that came into her possession because she was secretary of state, there are at least two basic issues we should consider that pertain to impeachment.

The first question is whether Hillary Clinton may be subject to the impeachment process. This is a question about whether a former official, or someone who has left office, may be impeached for misconduct in that office. In all likelihood, the answer is yes. To be sure, the Constitution speaks only of particular officials as being subject to the impeachment process, perhaps raising the inference that only people who are currently president, vice president, or civil officers of the United States may be impeached for certain misconduct. Indeed, we also know that the impeachment process should not be used against private citizens. Perhaps we therefore could conclude that Hillary Clinton, having left office, is no longer subject to the impeachment process.

The counterargument has to do with when the misconduct was discovered and what the misconduct entailed. True, a person who has returned to private life may be subject to criminal or civil liability for the misconduct in question. Yet there are two sanctions for impeachment. One is removal, which by definition no longer applies to Clinton. But the other is disqualification. Perhaps she could then be subject to the impeachment process for the purpose of disqualifying her from future government service or pensions. A complication is that the constitutional language speaks of people who, upon conviction, are removed from office. That language could be read with the other text to reinforce the conclusion that a former official is not subject to impeachment.

Moreover, the argument could be made that Congress has never subjected any former officials to impeachment. Indeed, it has a record, including the cases of Blount, Belknap, and Kent, of not continuing with an impeachment once someone has left office. The fact that Congress has never done this does not necessarily mean it lacks the power to do it. Congress exercises discretion as to whether to initiate impeachments, just as it has discretion when determining whether to exercise any power. There are no historical practices supporting the impeachment of a former official, but their absence might simply be the result of the House's or the Senate's decision at a particular moment in time not to go further with an impeachment. That is different from saying that each concluded it lacked the power to go ahead. In any event, even if the House or the Senate ever reached that conclusion, it is not binding on a future House or Senate.

The second question is whether the deliberate destruction (or ordering the deliberate destruction) of Secretary Clinton's emails is an impeachable offense. In order to be an impeachable offense, her conduct does not have to be criminal. If it were, that would no doubt heighten the seriousness of her offense. For example, if it could be shown she had broken particular federal laws, then those violations are likely to be felonies, which are the most serious offenses in the criminal code. But in an impeachment proceeding, the prosecution does not have to show that a federal statute has been violated. Something can be serious without being technically illegal or demonstrably violating some federal criminal law. With impeachment, we are concerned with bad faith (not just the inadvertent use of a private server) and bad conduct (not just an inconsequential disclosure but a breach of national security). The facts become important, because they go to whether she had the requisite bad faith *and* had done the requisite bad act, which would become the basis for impeachment.

President Trump's lawyer has said that the president is immune in the civil cases that have been filed against him. Is the president's lawyer right?

Of course not. Since the US Supreme Court's unanimous opinion in *Clinton v. Jones*, it has been well settled that the president is not immune from a civil action for damages based on pre-presidential conduct. There are no exceptions to that ruling, nor has it been overruled. It remains good law.

What is collusion?

The word "collusion" has no meaning in the law or the Constitution. There is no federal statute that uses the word "collusion." Nor does the Constitution use the term.

Why do people keep talking about "collusion" if the term has no meaning in the law?

People might use the word "collusion" for at least two reasons. First, they might use it because they know that collusion is not a crime (because it does not appear in any federal criminal statutes). So, some defenders of the president might be able to argue that even if he somehow engaged in "collusion," it was not illegal, because no federal statute forbids it. True, no federal statute actually outlaws collusion per se, but the law does outlaw "coordination" between a private citizen and a foreign power to influence the outcome of an election. Indeed, Special Counsel Robert Mueller has been specifically authorized to investigate any "coordination" along those lines during the 2016 presidential election.

The second reason people might use the term "collusion" is as a catch-all to reach any kind of inappropriate activity between the Trump campaign and the Russian government. As such, it could become the basis for an impeachment, because, as we know, impeachment does not have to be based on a statutory crime.

Who is Robert Mueller, and what is his role in investigating President Trump?

On May 17, 2017, Deputy Attorney General Rod Rosenstein, who had been appointed by President Trump, appointed Robert Mueller to serve as special counsel for the US Justice Department. News reports about possible contacts between Trump campaign officials and the Russian government and the demands of Democratic lawmakers to ensure an impartial investigation into any such contacts put pressure on Trump's Justice Department to look into the nature of any such contacts. Because of reports that Jeff Sessions, as a campaign surrogate for President Trump, had met twice with the Russian ambassador, Sessions recused himself from any involvement with or oversight of the Justice Department's investigation in order to ensure public confidence in the impartiality of the investigation. Sessions' recusal made Deputy Attorney General Rosenstein the acting attorney general for purposes of making the appointment and overseeing the work of the special counsel charged with investigating possible collusion between the Trump campaign and Russia.

Prior to this appointment, Mueller had had a distinguished career in government and private practice. After serving as a platoon leader in the Vietnam War, for which he earned a Bronze Star, Mueller worked for a major law firm in San Francisco for three years, followed by twelve years as a prosecutor in the US Attorney's office for San Francisco, several years as a partner in a prestigious law firm in Boston, several years in different positions within the Justice Department, including leading its criminal division, several years as the US Attorney for San Francisco, and more than a decade as the head of the FBI. Though President George W. Bush had appointed Mueller to a ten-year term as the head of the FBI, President Obama asked him to extend his term for two additional years.[23]

If Mueller is not looking at collusion, what exactly is he investigating?

Rosenstein asked Mueller (and his team) to investigate "any links and/or coordination between" the Russian government and the Trump presidential campaign and "any matters that arose or may arise directly from the investigation." There is no deadline for Mueller to complete the investigation. By early 2018, his office had secured guilty pleas from at least three people associated with the campaign (including Michael Flynn, who served briefly as President Trump's national security adviser) and criminal indictments of Paul Manafort, who was chairman of Trump's presidential campaign from May 19 to August 19, 2016, and his deputy for money laundering, conspiracy, and other charges.

Who is James Comey, and why is he relevant to Mueller's investigation?

In 2013, President Obama appointed James Comey to succeed Mueller as the director of the FBI. Mueller returned to private practice.[24] Previously, Comey had served as the US attorney for the Southern District of New York and deputy attorney general as well as general counsel for Lockheed Martin, a global aerospace, defense, and advanced technologies company that is the US Defense Department's largest contractor.[25] In late June 2016, then Attorney General Loretta Lynch recused herself from the administration's investigation into Hillary Clinton's use of a private email server while she had been secretary of state. She made the announcement after she had been criticized for meeting with Bill Clinton after he boarded her plane while both her plane and his were parked near each other on the tarmac at Phoenix's Sky Harbor International Airport. Lynch announced she would defer to the FBI's recommendations regarding the probe.[26]

On July 5, 2016, Comey announced the FBI's recommendation that no criminal charges be brought against Clinton, though his report criticized her handling of her emails while secretary of state.[27] But, two weeks before the 2016 presidential election, Comey announced the FBI was reopening the investigation to review previously undiscovered emails that had been found on the computer of the estranged husband of Clinton's chief of staff. On November 6, 2016, just two days before the election, Comey wrote to Congress to say that their review of the new emails did not lead the FBI to change its recommendation not to proceed with any criminal charges against Clinton. In early May 2017, Comey asked the Justice Department for an increase in funding and personnel to assist the Russian probe.[28]

On May 9, President Trump dismissed Comey as the director of the FBI.[29] Initially, the president explained that he fired Comey based on the recommendations of his attorney general, Jeff Sessions, and deputy attorney general, Rosenstein.[30] But, on May 11, Trump said in an interview on NBC News that he would have dismissed Comey at least in part because "Russia is a made up story" that he wanted to put to rest.[31] In congressional testimony, Comey testified that the president had asked him for a personal pledge of loyalty and that on three occasions, in response to the president's questions, Comey told Trump that he was not under investigation.[32] Concerns about the possibility that the president discharged Comey to stymie the investigation helped to intensify pressure within the Justice Department to appoint a special prosecutor to look into any possible criminal conduct relating to possible collusion between the Trump campaign and Russia.

Are any of the things Mueller is investigating impeachable offenses?

It is too soon to know for sure, particularly with respect to President Trump. Mueller might uncover some illegal interactions between campaign officials and Russian nationals or the Russian government, but we have no idea what Mueller knows about what the president knew and when he knew about any such interactions, much less authorizing or encouraging any of them. Nor do we know what Mueller might be investigating with respect to the president's own conduct or involvement. It is not hard to imagine that a president's actual involvement with foreign interests' efforts to influence the outcome of an election is sufficiently serious to rise to the level of an impeachable offense. Such interactions would not only break federal criminal laws but could also constitute treasonous behavior. The president denies any such involvement, and it remains to be seen what evidence actually comes forward to support claims that the president was personally involved in the "collusion" he vigorously denies.

There are also questions about whether the president might have used his presidential powers to thwart the investigation into any connections between his campaign and Russian nationals or the Russian government. For example, one concern commonly expressed among Democratic voters and some members of Congress is that the president's dismissal of Comey might have been an effort to obstruct justice.[33] It is unlikely that Mueller is investigating any issues relating to the president's abuse of power, since many of them might not involve violations of federal criminal laws but rather violations of the Constitution that can be more properly addressed through congressional oversight or impeachment inquiries.

Indeed, in early December 2017 six Democratic members of the House introduced a resolution to initiate an impeachment inquiry against President Trump based on his failure to quickly and clearly denounce white nationalist marchers in Charlottesville, Virginia, tweeting an anti-Muslim video not based on fact, and public acts and statements denigrating different groups and individuals.[34] On

December 5, the House voted 364–58 to table the proposed resolution, with fewer than a third of the Democrats in the House opposing the motion to table.[35]

Does the president have the power to fire the special counsel, Robert Mueller?

Federal regulations governing removal of a special prosecutor, such as Robert Mueller, vests the attorney general with the authority to dismiss the special prosecutor for misconduct or some kind of wrongdoing.[36] Because of Sessions's decision to recuse himself from the department's investigation of any possible collusion between the Russian government and the Trump campaign, Rod Rosenstein, the second-ranking official in the department, became acting attorney general for the purpose of making the special prosecutor appointment and for dismissing Mueller.

Though many Republican members of Congress have complained that Mueller and his staff have overly close ties with James Comey and Democratic candidates, Deputy Attorney General Rosenstein has indicated no intention to dismiss Mueller.[37] Instead, he has expressed confidence in Mueller on more than one occasion.[38]

Nevertheless, the president could conceivably get Mueller removed through two ways. The first is he could direct the deputy attorney general to remove Mueller and fire the deputy attorney general if he fails to do as the president requests. The president could then seek to replace the deputy attorney general with someone more amenable to the president's suggestion. Alternatively, the president could consider bypassing the regulatory scheme for dismissing Mueller and instead act on his own claimed inherent authority to fire Mueller. The president's argument would be that, because Mueller is an executive branch official, the president has the authority, by virtue of being the head of that branch, to dismiss Mueller on whatever basis he deems appropriate. This argument follows from what scholars sometimes refer to as the robust theory of the unitary executive, a theory that posits that *all* executive power is consolidated in the president and therefore he must be able to dismiss anyone not exercising executive power as he sees fit.[39] Otherwise, the argument goes, the president is not able to control the exercise of executive power even within his own branch.

It came to light in January 2018 that President Trump ordered the firing of Robert Mueller in June 2017.[40] White House counsel Donald McGahn refused to pass the order on to the Department of Justice, and he threatened to resign if the president persisted in firing Mueller over his objection.[41] After McGahn's threatened resignation, the president decided against his initial order firing Mueller.[42] When the story was reported in late January 2018, the president dismissed it as "fake news."[43]

Both the president's order to fire Mueller and his denial of the story raise at least two possible concerns pertinent to impeachment. First, there is a possible concern pertaining to whether the order to fire Mueller strengthens a charge against the president for obstruction of justice. If the motivation for the order was to stop the investigation into possible Russian collusion in the election, then the order itself could pose a problem for the president. The fact that it did not succeed is irrelevant to whether there was obstruction of justice, which includes attempts that failed. It could be argued that the president's order reflects his bad intent and fits into a pattern of misbehavior, including the dismissal of Comey. Second, the president's public denial could be construed as a lie. If so, it could be understood as an effort to obstruct justice. It is often said that the cover-up can be worse than the crime, and the efforts to hide incriminating information that would impede or interfere with any official investigations into collusion support a claim of obstruction of justice.

Richard Nixon fired the special prosecutor who was investigating Watergate, Archibald Cox. Why wasn't he impeached for that?

In fact, Richard Nixon was not the person who fired Special Prosecutor Archibald Cox, who had been investigating the Watergate affair and had subpoenaed the president to turn over the taped White House conversations in his possession. Cox lost his position during an episode called the Saturday Night Massacre.

The attorney general at the time was Elliot Richardson, who was sometimes called Mr. Clean because he had been an outstanding public official with an impeccable reputation for honesty.[44] When

Richardson took over the position of attorney general, he promised the House Judiciary Committee that he would appoint a special prosecutor to look into the Watergate affair. Richardson asked his former mentor at Harvard Law School, Archibald Cox, to take the position.[45] Cox agreed.[46] In October 1973, Cox subpoenaed President Nixon to turn over the taped conversations from the White House that he had in his possession.[47] On October 20, Nixon ordered Richardson to fire Cox, but Richardson refused and then resigned in protest.[48] Nixon then ordered the deputy attorney general, William Ruckelshaus, to fire Cox, but he too refused and resigned in protest.[49] That left the third-ranking official within the Justice Department, Solicitor General Robert Bork, in charge of the department and in the position of having the authority to fire Cox. Bork wanted to resign, too, but Richardson and Ruckelshaus persuaded him to remain for the sake of maintaining morale within the department.[50] Bork, reluctantly, acquiesced and fired Cox.[51]

Nixon's order to dismiss Cox was one of the many things that the House Judiciary Committee considered when it drafted impeachment articles against Nixon. In fact, Gerhard Gesell, a widely respected federal district judge in the District of Columbia, ruled on November 14, 1973, that firing Cox was illegal absent a finding (by the attorney general or deputy attorney general) of extraordinary impropriety, as required in the regulation establishing the special prosecutor's office.[52] The government made no such showing. The committee eventually chose not to use the firing of Cox as a basis for impeachment. Nor did it approve an article based on income tax fraud. Instead, the committee went with what its members thought were the three strongest articles of impeachment against the president—abusing his powers by ordering the IRS and the FBI to harass his political enemies, obstructing justice, and refusing to comply with a legislative subpoena to turn over the White House tapes.[53]

Is firing the special counsel an impeachable offense?

The facts will be important to the answer. True, the House Judiciary Committee did not approve an impeachment article against Nixon for firing Cox, but the judicial ruling that the termination was illegal supports a claim of an abuse of power. The president or his counsel might argue, as they have with respect to the firing of James Comey, that the president's power of removal is plenary, meaning that he can fire anyone in his cabinet or another executive office for any reason he likes. But this argument goes too far. Surely not every reason for a dismissal is legitimate. If the president fired someone for being black, Jewish, or a woman, it would be a serious problem. If he fired someone to stop their legitimate investigation of some wrongdoing, that too is a serious problem; it undermines the integrity of the investigative process.

The president or his defenders might argue as well that President Grant fired a special prosecutor investigating corruption in his administration and he, like Nixon, did not face impeachment for that decision.[54] This is true, but the dismissals of Cox and of the special prosecutor investigating corruption in the Grant administration hurt Presidents Nixon and Grant politically. Those decisions undermined their public support, and, in both cases, the decisions to terminate the special prosecutors were construed at the time and by historians since as supporting or reinforcing the perception that the presidents had engaged in some wrongdoing.

In Nixon's case, the firing of the special prosecutor was one of several acts of misconduct that the House Judiciary Committee later weighed in determining which would make the strongest grounds for impeachment articles. Its decision not to include the firing of the special prosecutor may not mean very much when one recalls that one of those articles of impeachment charged Nixon with obstructing justice. If Nixon broke the law to discharge Cox in an effort to obstruct justice (and that certainly seems to have been the basic reason he did so), the House Judiciary Committee did not let him get away with it; the misconduct was a principal concern of the House Judiciary Committee and the basis for the impeachment articles it approved against Nixon.

But what if the firing of the special prosecutor is the only misconduct? Does this misconduct, standing alone, constitute an impeachable offense? It is still an abuse of power. If the president discharges someone for the wrong reason, then it can easily form the basis for an impeachment for the simple reason that the Congress could conclude that the exercise of power was done for illicit reasons. The discharge does not have to be technically illegal; it just has to be considered a bad act that was done in bad faith.

The decision to discharge Mueller, if it should come to pass, would come at a steep cost. The Supreme Court in *Nixon v. Fitzgerald* recognized several ways to hold presidents accountable for their misconduct in office. Impeachment was one way, but the other ways of holding the president accountable for his misconduct (or what many in the media or the Congress will argue was misconduct) remain in effect. These other ways include congressional oversight (there would likely be hearings to investigate the legitimacy of the grounds for the dismissal); the judgment of history (presidents care about their legacies even if this means that the repercussions for the president's action come later); popular support and re-election (the dismissal might hurt the president's chances for reelection if the firing occurred before his re-election campaign); and the media (the decision would likely inundate the president with bad press).

President Trump's lawyer has said the president cannot obstruct justice. Is he right?

It depends on what John Dowd meant by this statement. If Dowd meant that, because the president is the head of the executive branch and as such can oversee the administration of executive or prosecutorial power in any way he sees fit, he was wrong. This claim would mean that the president is above the law, and there is nothing in our constitutional history, design, and traditions to suggest that the president is above the law.

In *Marbury v. Madison*, the great Chief Justice John Marshall recognized for a unanimous Supreme Court that when courts are considering whether there is a remedy to redress the failure of a political actor, such as the president or secretary of state, to do something, courts must appreciate that there are two different kinds of actions these officials can make. One kind entails decision-making on a matter over which the political actor has complete discretion. If the law imposes no constraint on the discretion to be exercised, courts have no role to play in second-guessing or overturning the decision.[55] The political actor has the final say.[56] For example, the president can nominate anyone he likes to the Supreme Court. If he chooses to nominate someone without legal training, he can do that. The constitution does not bind or constrain his discretion in any way. The same can be said for the Senate when it decides whether or not to confirm this individual.

But, if the law does constrain the discretion, then, Chief Justice Marshall said, the actor has no discretion to avoid compliance with the law.[57] So, if the law says the president may not discriminate against someone on the basis of race (the Supreme Court has interpreted the Fifth Amendment as barring government from disadvantaging people because of their race, unless the government has a compelling justification), then the president cannot discharge an employee because she is African American.[58] The Supreme Court has also interpreted the Fifth Amendment as prohibiting sex discrimination, so the president could also not fire someone for being a woman.[59] While it might be difficult to prove that a president discriminated against someone because of his or her race, the principle still stands that he may not discriminate against someone because of their race. So, if the president fired someone for the wrong reason, it could be illegal.

Even if an action is not illegal per se, impeachment is not restricted to the specific kinds of misconduct that are codified in the criminal code. Members of Congress could decide, based on the evidence, that a president used his power for an illicit purpose. Hence, a president's pardoning someone as payback for their campaign contributions or pardoning a co-conspirator to protect himself would be an abuse of power. Trying to impede an investigation to protect himself or his family is an equally bad act. Indeed, we expect the president to follow the law, like everyone else, in filing taxes, not committing murder, or not committing sexual assault. If the president seeks to mount an attack on the integrity of the courts or the administration of the criminal justice system, it would be a bad act for which impeachment is a perfectly well-suited response.

Indeed, the House of Representatives has twice claimed that a president may be impeached for obstruction of justice. It did this in Nixon's case, and it approved an article of impeachment against President Clinton for obstruction of justice.[60] Indeed, in the proceedings on both of these presidents in the House, no one seriously argued that the president was not capable of obstructing justice.

But, if President Trump's lawyer meant that President Trump could not be criminally prosecuted for obstruction of justice while he is president, then Dowd may have had a point. The special prosecutors who investigated Watergate and Whitewater and many scholars have concluded that a sitting president is immune from criminal prosecution while he is president. The argument is that any such prosecution would paralyze not just the president by distracting him from his duties but also the entire executive branch that he is charged with overseeing. The remedy or solution to this problem is impeachment; a president can be subject to impeachment for having done something criminal (such as obstruction of justice) and then, once he has been convicted and removed from office, he will be subject to the criminal process.

Some people may worry that this argument may go too far. It is based on the belief that no criminal process may go forward against the president as long as he is president. There would be no crime, not even treason or murder, for which a sitting president could be tried. If he can be criminally prosecuted only after leaving office, the president has an incentive not to resign or leave office, and if impeachment does not work the American people (and the world) are stuck with a president who stays in office under a great cloud of misconduct and crime. Under such circumstances, we find ourselves again falling back on the different ways to hold a president accountable for misconduct apart from criminal prosecution and impeachment—the judgment of history, popularity, media scrutiny, and congressional oversight. Given these different checks, it is possible that a president operating under these circumstances would not be able to wield much influence or power. The pressure to resign would be intense, and the pressure on the American people to direct their leaders to take action would be even more intense.

It is sometimes said that if we ever find ourselves in some outrageous situation, such as members of Congress deciding legislative matters on the basis of coin flips, or Congress allowing presidents who have engaged in egregious misconduct to remain in office, then it is too late to expect the law to make some difference. The principal actors, who have the ultimate authority to keep their leaders in check, are the American people. How voters react and use their vote—what kinds of behavior they accept or do not accept from their leaders—is a function of many different things, including our culture. Culture shapes and is shaped by the values of the general public. The public may not be to blame for the misdeeds of the leaders they elect, but the public's tolerance, acceptance, or condemnation of those misdeeds significantly influences the extent to which their leaders' misconduct is checked or ignored. For example, had the American public merely shrugged its collective shoulders in indifference when confronted with Richard Nixon's misbehavior, Nixon might have been able to remain in office. Similarly, when much of the public had that reaction to Clinton's misconduct, he was allowed to finish his term. The public's support for or opposition to impeachment is an important factor, which can influence its exercise.

Why is sexual harassment an impeachable offense?

Both our civil and criminal laws proscribe sexual harassment or misbehavior. Sexual harassment is a form of gender discrimination that violates Title VII of the 1964 Civil Rights Act when it occurs in a workplace.[61] Specifically, Title VII prohibits employers from discriminating on the basis of sex and several other conditions, including race.[62] Sexual harassment is one kind of prohibited form of discrimination; it involves unwanted sexual advances, requests for sexual favors, and other verbal or physical conduct of a sexual nature when submission to such conduct is made a condition of employment or made the basis of employment decisions or has the purpose or effect of unreasonably interfering with an individual's work performance or creating an intimidating, hostile, or offensive working environment.[63] Rape, sexual abuse or assault, or an unwanted touching can all be criminal offenses.[64]

Any sexual misbehavior of this kind can become the basis for an impeachment because it can be an abuse of power, breach of duty, or serious injury to the administration of justice, the rule of law, or the integrity of our judicial system. The impeachment charges against Samuel Kent in 2009 included unwanted sexual contact and his lying about his sexual misconduct.[65] Kent's misbehavior included sexual assault.[66] It should not be hard to imagine that any impeachable official, including the president, could be subject to impeachment for similar sexual misconduct.

Again, the fact that an impeachable offense does not have to be an actual crime suggests that a broader or a different range of sexual misconduct could become the basis for impeachment. The question is what kind of sexual misconduct is inappropriate for someone who is president, vice president, or another civil officer of the United States. There is a spectrum of sexual misbehavior. At one end is rape, which is clearly and unquestionably serious enough to form the basis for an impeachment, and at the other might be an innocent mistake, such as trying to hold the hand of a person who did not want her hand held. To state what should be obvious, sexual harassment is much closer to the end of the spectrum that encompasses impeachable misconduct. It breaches a duty that we expect people in high office to abide by, degrades their office, and reflects the kind of bad judgment and bad conduct that provides the legitimate basis for impeachment.

Could President Trump be impeached for doing any of the things he claimed in an Access Hollywood interview that was aired during the presidential campaign?

In the infamous *Access Hollywood* recording (a conversation that was recorded during an interview between Trump and the television show's host, Billy Bush, in September 2005), Donald Trump said that he grabbed women "by the pussy."[67] Immediately after the taped comments became public, Trump said that his comments were merely "locker room talk."[68] The question is whether he actually did what he said he did. (The president later denied that he had said the things that were recorded and broadcast.) If it can be shown that Trump did what he said he did, the problem then is whether he may be impeached for lying during the presidential campaign and for having engaged in this kind of misconduct. The presumption is that, if he engaged in this kind of misconduct, it was unwanted, that is, it was sexual assault.

When we consider whether something is impeachable, we are not asking whether Congress would actually impeach someone for that kind of misconduct. We do not know whether Congress in 2018 would impeach the president for the misconduct (assuming it could be proved at that time). We never know whether Congress would impeach someone for some kind of misconduct until it actually does.

The question that is pertinent is whether it would be legitimate for Congress to treat as an impeachable offense a presidential candidate's having lied about sexual assault and having engaged in that kind of misconduct before his election as president. I hope the answer is yes. I say I hope because I do not know what an actual Congress would do, but I know that this kind of misconduct is serious and completely out of order for someone who occupies the highest office in our government. If someone lied about this kind of misconduct during a campaign, it could be argued that he basically defrauded the people during the election about something important.

The tougher question is whether people voted for the president in spite of or even because of this information. If people thought the president was lying and voted for him anyway, then the issue becomes whether they effectively ratified his misbehavior. This is arguably what happened when Bill Clinton ran for president the first time (when he acknowledged in an interview he had "caused pain" in his marriage and after several women had claimed he had assaulted them) and when he ran for re-election (when many voters might have believed he had continued to be unfaithful to his wife or continued to lie about his prior misconduct). Perhaps there were many people who voted for President Trump in spite of whatever sexual misconduct he might have committed before becoming president.

The question becomes whether Congress should disregard misbehavior when the American people have effectively accepted it. I am not sure there is a clear yes or no to this question. I have taken the position that the decision whether something is an impeachable offense turns on a variety of factors. One factor might be that the American people have accepted some misconduct from their president. Another factor might be the damage that the misconduct has done to the rule of law and to the office. With certain misconduct, such as murder or sexual harassment, there is no question that the conduct is unquestionably bad. Even if the public or members of Congress are indifferent, their indifference does not change the fact that some misconduct is just bad. At the very least, the judgment of history will be harsh.

How is the case of Alex Kozinski relevant to our understanding of whether sexual harassment may constitute an impeachable offense?

In 1985, President Reagan appointed Alex Kozinski to the prestigious US Court of Appeals for the Ninth Circuit.[69] Kozinski was thirty-five at the time, becoming one of the youngest federal appellate judges in American history. Over the next thirty-two years, he became widely known for colorful, often quirky, irreverent opinions, and as a judge whose law clerks were often selected to clerk on the US Supreme Court. In 2008, he invited an investigation of himself by his fellow judges because he had maintained a publicly accessible website featuring sexually explicit photographs and videos.[70] Kozinski's apology and deletion of the website helped to conclude the matter.

Over the course of several months in 2017, an even darker side of Kozinski became apparent as a result of revelations from six former female clerks and junior staffers that Kozinski often talked to them about or showed them pornography, asked sexually suggestive questions, and spoke about his sexual history.[71] Several other women anonymously complained that he acted improperly toward them.[72] Kozinski initially ignored the revelations but then issued a public statement apologizing for any offense he had caused, insisting he had treated his male and female clerks the same, and attributing the possibility of any offense to have been caused by his unusual sense of humor.[73] Nine more women, including a professor and a judge, came forward to complain of inappropriate sexual behavior, including unwanted touching and fondling, that spanned nearly the entire time he had been a federal appellate judge.[74] When the furor over his misbehavior intensified and the chief judge of the US Court of Appeals ordered an investigation, Kozinski abruptly resigned.[75]

Throughout the weeks preceding Kozinski's resignation, some legal scholars and others wondered if his misconduct constituted an impeachable offense.[76] The fact that Kozinski voluntarily subjected himself to an investigation within his circuit suggests, not surprisingly, that he was not worried about the possible sanction or did not think his actions were serious. Indeed, one possible reason he had so quickly asked for such an investigation might have been that he knew an internal investigation by the court was likely to be focused on conduct that was bad but fell short of an impeachable offense. The Judicial Discipline and Disability Act vests judges with some disciplinary authority over other judges because it does not regard any proceedings or sanctions imposed under the act as substitutes for impeachment. In practice, the proceedings often are; they can resolve the matters under investigation in the absence of an impeachment proceeding. Because the act does not authorize judges to remove other judges, much less disqualify them from further service, Kozinski might have expected that he would not be subject to the harshest possible treatment under the act and its proceedings could take the wind out of the sails of any movement toward impeachment.

But, at the same time, invoking the statutory procedures for discipline under the act does not prevent impeachment. In the right case, impeachment could still be available, as it was with each of the judges whom the House impeached and the Senate removed from office in the 1980s.

Would Kozinski's misconduct have been a legitimate basis for impeachment?

The answer is absolutely yes. Assuming that the charges made against Kozinski were all true, his misconduct occurred nearly throughout the entirety of his time on the bench as a federal appellate judge. His behavior was reprehensible, degrading the integrity of the judiciary, damaging to the administration of justice, and eroding the moral authority he required in order to perform the important functions of a judge. His misconduct broke laws that as a judge he had the authority to administer. To the extent he lied about his misconduct, he trashed the integrity of his court.

In 1936, the House impeached and the Senate convicted and removed Halsted Ritter from a federal district judgeship because he had engaged in a series of inappropriate transactions with litigants that degraded the judiciary.[77] The fact that Ritter was convicted and removed on the sole basis of bringing the judiciary into disrepute might be cause for some concern, since that basis is arguably too vague. The vagueness of the grounds could conceivably be used against anyone. Except, as it turns out, the House and the Senate have not overused this as a basis for impeachment and removal. And Ritter's problem was the underlying misconduct that the Congress found to have brought the federal judiciary into disrepute.

Kozinski unquestionably engaged in misconduct that brought the federal judiciary into disrepute. Here, just as in Ritter's case, the underlying misconduct was offensive and reprehensible. The fact that Kozinski had previously been investigated by his own court for misbehavior simply made it worse for him. It showed that he had a history of commingling his peculiar proclivities and private life with his public responsibilities as a judge.

How might the Kozinski case help us better understand impeachment?

The Kozinski case is important because it enables us to recognize another, useful way to consider whether official misconduct rises to the level of an impeachable offense. There are the traditional tests that the framers and members of Congress have used for identifying impeachable misconduct—namely, whether the misconduct is a breach of duty, abuse of power, or injures the Republic. Another way to get at the same thing is to ask these questions differently. We could ask, for example: is the misconduct incompatible with the office, does it rob the targeted official of the moral authority he or she needs to function in that office, or does the misconduct effectively disable the targeted official from exercising the responsibilities of that office? If the answers to these questions are all yes, then we can have confidence that the misconduct at issue is an impeachable offense. In Richard Nixon's case, the answers were all yes, and they were all yes in Ritter's case, too. In Kozinski's case, the answers to all these questions are clearly yes. His resignation may thus be understood, much like Nixon's, as recognition of the inevitability of his impeachment, conviction, and removal from office. By the time Kozinski resigned, it was clear to everyone that he had no business remaining a federal judge any longer.

May the president use his pardon power to stop the Congress from attempting to impeach him or anyone else close to him?

Previously, we noted that Article II, Section 2, of the Constitution provides that the president "shall have the power to grant reprieves and pardons for offences against the United States, except in cases of impeachment." This provision plainly makes a presidential pardon inapplicable to an impeachment. Otherwise, this language contains no apparent limitation other than the fact that the pardon power may extend only to federal offenses, not state ones. The absence of any other limitation raises the question about where the boundaries or limits of the pardon power may be, including whether the president may use the pardon power to shield himself, his friends, or his allies from federal criminal investigations.

Was President Trump's pardon of Sheriff Joe an abuse of power?

On August 25, 2017, President Trump pardoned Sheriff Joe Arpaio of Maricopa County, Arizona, of criminal contempt charges for refusing to obey a federal court order that barred him from racial profiling in detaining individuals suspected of being in the United States illegally. The question is whether this pardon, the first one granted by President Trump, was an impeachable offense because it had not followed the usual procedures for pardons, including the practice of waiting at least five years after a conviction to determine the merits of the request for presidential mercy; appeared to be a political payoff to Arpaio, who had supported Trump during the presidential campaign; undermined the court's authority; and left the victims of Arpaio's civil rights violations without meaningful remedy.

There is a credible case to be made that the president had the authority to grant a full pardon to Arpaio in spite of Arpaio's unappealing attributes and obvious disregard for the court's order. To begin with, the text of the Constitution expressly posits no limitations on the pardon power except for its applying only to federal crimes and its not applying "in cases of impeachment." Indeed, in its 1866 decision in *Ex parte Garland*, the Supreme Court declared that the president's pardon power was "unlimited."[78] The Court further held that "This power of the president is not subject to legislative control."[79] The Court explained that "Congress can neither limit the effect of his pardon nor exclude from its exercise any class of offenders. The benign prerogative of mercy reposed"[80] in the president "cannot be fettered by any legislative restrictions."[81]

The pardon of Arpaio might well have been a contemptible act, but the "unlimited" nature of the pardon power—and the absence of any text limiting the conditions for presidential pardons—and historical practices in this realm argue in favor of the legitimacy of the Arpaio pardon. This pardon is perhaps not unlike many other pardons, such as the pardons of friends, as President George H. W. Bush did with his 1992 pardon of Caspar Weinberger (who served in his cabinet) for any involvement with the Iran-Contra affair, or as President Bill Clinton did with the pardon of Marc Rich, a major campaign donor who had fled the country to avoid criminal prosecution after he had been indicted for tax evasion, wire fraud, and other criminal acts, including trading with Iran at a time when Iranian revolutionaries were holding American hostages. Presidents have pardoned people who did horrible things, as President Carter did when he used the pardon power to restore full citizenship to Jefferson Davis, the leader of the Confederacy during the Civil War.

In the absence of any textual constraint on President Trump's determination to give a pardon to Arpaio, it nonetheless remains subject to popular approval, congressional oversight, and the judgment of history. On the one hand, the pardon played well with the president's base but confirmed Trump's cravenness to the substantial portion of the public that holds him in contempt. On the other hand, the pardon is part of President Trump's legacy, reflecting both his penchant for rewarding his friends and disdain for the law, particularly the civil rights of minorities that the president does not count among his constituents.

May the president pardon himself and, if he does, is that an abuse of power and therefore an impeachable offense?

The Constitution does not allow the president to use his pardon power to shield himself from impeachment or accountability for misconduct, and therefore a president who attempts to use the pardon power in that way has, in all likelihood, committed an impeachable offense. To understand why, we need to consider the problems with the argument that he has such power and why the counterargument is more compelling.

The argument that the president may pardon himself is based on the constitutional provision granting him this power. While it limits the pardon power to federal crimes, it does not limit, in any way, the people whom the president may pardon. The absence of any such limitation plainly raises the inference that the president may pardon anyone, including himself.

There are, however, several other factors cutting against this construction of the Constitution and instead barring a president from pardoning himself. To begin with, no power is absolute. There is nothing in our constitutional history or tradition indicating that any authority was somehow above the law or beyond the mechanisms in the Constitution designed to ensure accountability even for the president.

Just as with any other power, the pardon power is susceptible to abuse. If President Trump used the pardon power to block Mueller's criminal investigations (by pardoning friends and family who might have information that could have incriminated Trump or his campaign), Congress retains the authority to inquire into whether the president had used this power in good faith. Indeed, this is exactly what Congress did when, after President Ford pardoned Richard Nixon to put the American nightmare of Watergate behind it, the House Judiciary Committee requested Ford to appear before it to answer questions about why he pardoned Nixon. To his credit, President Ford appeared and answered questions, allaying concerns about why he had pardoned Nixon.

While the Supreme Court has said that the pardon power is "unlimited," it has recognized impeachment as a possible check against it. In *Ex parte Grossman*, the Supreme Court in 1922 alluded to this in the course of its decision upholding the pardon of an individual whom a court had held in contempt for violating Prohibition. The Court recognized that the pardon power was a check on the judiciary "to ameliorate or avoid particular criminal judgments."[82] The Court suggested that "To exercise [this power] to the extent of destroying the deterrent effect of judicial punishment would be to pervert it; but whoever is to make it useful must have full discretion to exercise it."[83] The Court recognized that the prospect of a president's "successive pardons of constantly recurring contempts" to "deprive a court of power to enforce its orders" was "so improbable as to furnish but little basis for argument."[84] "Exceptional cases like this," the Court said, "if to be imagined at all, would suggest resort to impeachment rather than to a narrow and strained construction of the general powers of the President."[85]

The fact that the Constitution says the pardon power may not be used "in cases of impeachment" raises an interesting inference that perhaps impeachment is a suitable check against a president's using the pardon power to protect his own interests, not those of the nation or even his office. The other language in the constitutional provision vesting the president with the power to pardon further cuts against a presidential self-pardon. For example, the Constitution uses the word "grant" in its provision on pardons, a word that ordinarily means giving to someone else, not to one's self. Moreover, the framers were modeling this power on how it had been employed by English monarchs, who conceived of it as an act of mercy. Giving mercy to oneself is not consistent with the wording or purpose of the power. Nor is it consistent with the widely held view of the framers and the public at the time of the Constitution's ratification that no one should be a judge in his own case, a principle that Chief Justice Marshall repeated in *Marbury v. Madison* and that has been a bedrock of American jurisprudence throughout the nation's history.

The excesses of the pardon power are ripe for consideration, as would be the abuse of any power, in an impeachment inquiry. Impeachment is an essential check against a president's use of that power to undermine the Constitution's carefully calibrated checks and balances.

What if members of Congress and the public cannot agree on the severity of the misconduct or the damage that the misconduct caused?

The Constitution makes impeachment difficult if not unlikely. If there is a divergence of opinion on whether the misconduct did not occur, was bad enough to justify impeachment, or caused sufficient damage to the Republic or the Constitution, it is likely that there would be no ensuing impeachment, conviction, and removal. The odds are that, without the public and members of Congress being in agreement on the seriousness of an offense and the need for an impeachment, members of Congress might lack the resolve to take a strong stand on the matter. It is true that the Senate failed to do this when it acquitted Andrew Johnson, but that was a time when senators were not directly elected by the voters. With senators now subject to re-election by the people of their respective states, the question becomes to what extent are they likely to risk losing re-election because of their vote in a presidential impeachment trial? No senator lost his or her seat in the aftermath of Bill Clinton's trial.

Yet the trial was not the end of the matter. Clinton was held accountable in other venues, including the trial court that found him guilty of misconduct and the state bar that suspended his license. The judgment of history here, too, is likely to be harsh, since there is no longer any question he lied under oath and took advantage of a woman who was powerless under the circumstances. Bill Clinton's misconduct is not a secret but instead a taint on his presidency and a continuing problem for the Democratic Party, which sacrificed its long-standing commitment of championing women's rights for the sake of allowing one of its own to retain power.

What are norms, and why are they relevant to this discussion?

Norms are informal social customs or arrangements, which do not have the force of law but whose violations will trigger some kinds of sanctions. A basic ramification of President Trump's promise to shake things up is that he would be violating many norms pertaining to the presidency. It is upsetting to many people to see the president do just that.

Norms may be pertinent to a discussion of President Trump and impeachment in that his violations or breaches of norms may not be grounds for impeachment. We may appreciate, even respect, some norms associated with the presidency, such as the fact that when the president enters a room people stand or the president salutes soldiers who greet him upon his departure from Air Force One or arrival at certain locales. Violating these norms might show bad taste (or perhaps, to some people, good judgment), but they are not the serious breaches of duty or trust that comprise "treason, bribery, and other high crimes or misdemeanors."

In analyzing whether President Trump, or any other president, has committed an impeachable offense, we should try to filter through the claims to separate out the more serious kinds of misconduct from behavior that might be boorish or inconsistent with certain norms that we have come to expect presidents to follow. For example, the president's use of Twitter is a new and different way for him to communicate with the American people. The reluctance or failure of some prior presidents to communicate as often and as directly through Twitter with the American people could reflect an evolving norm for presidents to be more careful and cautious in speaking their minds to the American people. If there were a norm developing along these lines (consistent with how presidents have used their office as a bully pulpit), President Trump has obviously discarded it. The fact that he has does not mean, however, that he has engaged in some kind of misconduct. What he says might be a problem, but the choice of doing it in a new and different way falls well within the president's discretion.

The trickier question is whether violating norms might, when considered in the aggregate, degrade the presidency or demonstrate a general lack of competence and, if so, whether the misconduct may serve as the legitimate basis for an impeachment. In Trump's case, the vulgarities or systematic breaches or norms might be exactly the kinds of things that people who voted for him want to see, but the degradation of the presidency and incompetency in office are matters whose constitutional significance still must be ascertained.

If President Trump is incompetent, may he be impeached for that?

One defense that President Trump's defenders sometimes make against charges that he has done something wrong is that he is new to the office and learning as he goes.[86] Another way to think about this is that sometimes he seems incompetent in office, a perception perhaps reflected in his numerous contradictory statements on issues, misstatements of fact, or misunderstandings of his powers. One question that follows from such conduct is whether the president may be impeached simply for being incompetent. In the framers' day and in the debates at the constitutional convention, the framers included such incompetence in the term "maladministration."[87] It is clear from the records of the constitutional convention that the framers meant to exclude this as a basis for impeachment. As in the case of IRS commissioner John Koskinen, the narrowing of impeachable offenses to "Treason, bribery, and other high crimes and misdemeanors" excluded "maladministration" as a basis for impeachment, conviction, and removal.

The fact that both Alexander Hamilton and Joseph Story made reference to "maladministration" as a legitimate basis for impeachment has been cited to support efforts to ground impeachments on gross incompetence. Hamilton's reference to "maladministration" could, however, be understood as a sop to those people in the ratifying conventions who were worried that the new Constitution's president would be too powerful and thus assure them of the possibility of ousting a president who was bad for the Republic. Indeed, the fact that Hamilton personally favored a stronger presidency (who would serve for life) than the convention approved suggests that he might not have believed everything he was writing on behalf of the Constitution to secure its ratification. Story's commentaries on impeachment are authoritative, though it is possible he had a narrower conception of what "maladministration" might have meant to some of the framers. Story also emphasized that the actual scope of impeachable misconduct would be worked out by Congress over time, and Congress has not yet accepted "maladministration" as an appropriate or legitimate basis for impeachment.

The Pickering impeachment could be a counterexample. The House impeached and the Senate convicted and removed him from office based on charges that he was mishandling his job because of drunkenness and insanity.[88] A concern with the Pickering impeachment, or with allowing incompetence to serve as a basis for impeachment, is that it widens the scope of impeachment. Incompetence is a harder line to define than degrading the judiciary, abusing power, or breaching official duties. Based on these and other concerns, Congress in the years since Pickering's impeachment has not pursued impeachment in similar circumstances, and Congress enacted the Judicial Discipline and Disability Act to provide alternatives to impeachment for a judge's inability to do his job, which presumably might extend to incompetence.

True, there is no statutory mechanism for presidents analogous to the Judicial Discipline and Removal Act. Indeed, there is a general expectation that most issues pertaining to a president's performance in office are to be dealt with through the electoral process (if the president runs for re-election) and the other checks we have recognized as applying to presidential conduct, such as popularity, the press, the judgment of history, and congressional oversight. Impeachment is a last resort for handling misconduct that cannot be dealt with by other means and that involves misconduct sufficiently serious to constitute "treason, bribery, or other high crimes and misdemeanors."

Instead of being subject to a statutory mechanism like the Judicial Discipline and Disability Act, presidents are subject to the Twenty-fifth Amendment, which was ratified in 1967. It provides a mechanism for handling a president's becoming subject to some disability that prevents him from doing his job, such as a major stroke or serious mental illness. This mechanism seems better suited than impeachment for dealing with incompetence resulting from some mental or physical disability, and so we turn next to how it is supposed to work in practice.

How does the Twenty-fifth Amendment work?

The Twenty-fifth Amendment has four sections. The first section codifies the precedent set by John Tyler, which clarified who became president when a president died in office. Tyler claimed that the president's death automatically elevated him from the vice presidency to the presidency.[89] The Twenty-fifth Amendment's first section now makes that practice a constitutional directive.

Section 2 of the Twenty-fifth Amendment provides a procedure for replacing a vice president who resigns, dies, or is incapable of further performing the duties of his office. If any of those things happens, the president is empowered to nominate a replacement, who has to be approved by a majority of each chamber of Congress.

Section 3 of the Twenty-fifth Amendment provides a procedure for temporarily empowering the vice president to take over the responsibilities and duties of the presidency. It provides that when a president transmits a written declaration to the president pro tempore of the Senate and the speaker of the House that he is unable to perform his duties, the vice president assumes those duties until the president sends another written communication to the same officials declaring that he is capable of resuming his duties.[90]

The fourth section of the Twenty-fifth Amendment provides a procedure to be followed if the president becomes disabled but is unable to produce the written communications required in Section 3. This procedure allows the vice president, together "with a majority of either the principal officers of the executive departments or of such body as Congress may by law provide," to declare the president "unable to discharge the powers and duties of his office" through a written declaration submitted to the speaker of the House and the president pro tempore of the Senate.[91]

Section 4 is the only section of the Twenty-fifth Amendment that has never been invoked. Sections 1 and 2 were invoked three times during the Watergate scandal—Nixon's appointment of Gerald Ford to replace Vice President Spiro Agnew, Ford's ascending to the presidency as a result of Nixon's resignation, and Ford's appointment of Nelson Rockefeller to replace himself as the vice president.[92] Section 3 has been invoked three times to appoint vice presidents as acting presidents, once by President Reagan and twice by President George W. Bush, all for medical reasons.[93] Twice officials within the Reagan administration considered possibly invoking Section 4, once immediately after President Reagan had been shot and once in 1987 when senior staff were encouraged to consider whether—and later convinced themselves that—the president was fully in command of his mental faculties.[94]

Could President Trump have a problem with the Twenty-fifth Amendment?

The short answer is that it depends on the facts, but the media have given a lot of attention to the possible ways in which Section 4 of the Twenty-fifth Amendment could be invoked.[95] As we know from the plain language of this section, it comes into play if the vice president and a majority of the cabinet (or some other authority that the Congress has designated by statute) determine that the president has become disabled because of some mental illness or other problem.

This analysis cannot be a substitute for the kind of fact-finding that would have to be undertaken if this portion of the Twenty-fifth Amendment was ever invoked. However, we do know some of the things that this section requires to be invoked, so we know what to look for. We know, for example, from the congressional debates on the Twenty-fifth Amendment that these provisions were intended to address mental or physical incapacitation, as well as situations where a president might be out of reliable communication or kidnapped.[96] We know as well that the purpose of this section is not to provide a means for a "no-confidence" vote in the administration or the Congress. This amendment is designed to provide clarity and therefore some safeguards on circumstances when presidential incapacity requires putting his second in command in charge of the government, at least temporarily. The requirements themselves suggest a high threshold for its implementation, depending on the president's own allies and appointees to come together to a significant degree for the sake of the country to make the difficult determination that the president has become incapacitated to such an extent that his vice president should become the acting commander-in-chief.

Under any president, Section 4 is likely to be used cautiously, and its use will turn on a range of factors, including the president's condition, its likely duration, its likely severity, the extent to which domestic and international events call for presidential response or readiness, the president's attitude toward the disability provisions prior to the circumstances under consideration happened, the extent to which the public is aware of the president's condition, the vice president's capacity to lead, and many other factors. Yet another consideration is the fact that the rapidity with which events unfold might not allow for the time for none of the safeguards in the amendment to be invoked, leaving the president's staff, the cabinet, and the vice president to make expedient, but significant judgments about how to handle any crisis that unfolded while the president was somehow out of touch. Indeed, after President Reagan was shot, this is what happened. He was moved immediately into surgery and thus never had the chance to write the letters required in Section 3, and the vice president was in the air during the time when he was in surgery and unable to invoke Section 4.[97]

If Congress has to determine a Section 4 dispute between the vice president and the president, the Constitution makes it highly likely that the president will win (as he should, given the likelihood that he is the one who has been elected to the office). The requirements (1) for the acting president and a majority of the cabinet to send a second declaration that the president is incapacitated in response to the president's issuing a challenge within four days of their initial declaration *and* (2) for two-thirds of each chamber of Congress within twenty-one days to express their agreement with the second declaration of the president's incapacity (as a prerequisite for the vice president's continuing to serve as acting president) are powerful checks on the vice president and cabinet stealing the office from the president. The act's high thresholds create a default rule that the president remains in office unless they can be met.

Whether that two-thirds support actually exists would of course depend on the facts and public perception at the time as well as the congressional and public perceptions of the vice president and the cabinet. If, for example, the vice president and the majority of the cabinet were widely considered to be acting out of the best motives and perceived to have been loyal and credible, the public and members of Congress, particularly the president's partisan allies, might be more receptive to the determination of the need to replace the president temporarily. The presumption underlying the structure is that if the two-thirds threshold were met there must be compelling or strong evidence to declare the president incapacitated and thus unable to perform his duties.

This understanding of the Twenty-fifth Amendment provides the essential backdrop or framework for understanding how the amendment might be applied to President Trump or any other president. To begin with, it is clear that this amendment, like impeachment, does not exist to provide an alternative to a presidential election whose outcome many people might not like. If the American people elect someone as president who is a bully and who is boorish, arrogant, rude, and racist, it is their prerogative, and neither the impeachment process nor the Twenty-fifth Amendment is designed to permit the forced removal of the president for those reasons. Indeed, many of the people claiming Trump is disabled (and thus that the Twenty-fifth Amendment could apply) opposed his election and merely claim evidence to support judgments they had already made when they cast for their votes for his opponent. Nor is this amendment a substitute for impeachment, that is, it does not exist as a mechanism for handling misconduct that the Congress should have but failed to handle properly in the impeachment process. This process exists for a special kind of disability, one that is beyond the president's control and that must command an unusual degree of bipartisan consensus as debilitating and, even then, allows a vice president only a temporary opportunity to exercise the duties and powers of the presidency. If the threshold can be met—for example, through actual and verifiable mental deterioration or massive, disabling stroke—then this constitutional mechanism could come into play. Even then, the president's own allies and partisans would have to agree to a significant degree in order for any action to be taken.

Would it be wrong to take into account the fact that Mike Pence would become president if President Trump were either removed or resigned from office?

No, it would not be wrong to take that into consideration, no more wrong than it was for the House, then under the control of the Democrats, to consider impeaching George W. Bush to be foolish because it would have elevated his vice president, Dick Cheney, to the presidency. Vesting the impeachment authority in politically accountable leaders necessarily meant their deliberations would take many factors into account, including political considerations such as whether the vice president was someone they could tolerate or accept as president. Indeed, one reason some Republican senators voted to acquit Johnson was their opposition to elevating the next person in line of succession, Benjamin Wade, to the presidency.

Are the president's tweets in any way impeachable offenses?

President Trump's tweeting angers many people and pleases many others. The tweeting itself is not a problem. Through his tweeting, the president has expressed himself on a wide range of issues and found a new way to use the bully pulpit. Generally, presidents have wide latitude for expressing their opinions. Tweeting is just one vehicle, and the president's controversial comments are not made solely through tweets. For President Trump, the question is whether in tweeting or other communications he has gone too far. The White House has acknowledged that his tweets are official presidential statements. Consequently, there are several ways that his official statements have gone far enough to raise concerns that may relate to impeachment.

The first is that the president's encouraging prosecution of political enemies could be a problem. One impeachment article that the House Judiciary Committee approved against Richard Nixon was that he had abused power by ordering the IRS and FBI to harass his political enemies. One question will be whether President Trump's encouraging the Justice Department and FBI to investigate Hillary Clinton or any other political enemies is any different. One answer is that the tweets are just talk, while another has to do with the fervent belief of the president and his ardent supporters that evidence pertaining to Clinton's or others' misbehavior has not been properly handled by the authorities.

The threat to investigate Clinton was not mere words. Had it been, it could have been dismissed as political hyperbole or a president's entitlement to speak his mind or express an opinion. But in apparent response to the president's tweet, the Justice Department reopened its investigation of Hillary Clinton, and members of Congress followed the president's lead in insisting that Clinton and her foundation should be investigated for fraud and other illegal activities and that she and her campaign should be investigated for their own illegal contacts with Russia during the campaign.[98] While it could be argued that the drive to investigate Clinton and her associates seems to have been politically motivated, evidence came forward after the election indicating that the Justice Department, upon the order of Attorney General Loretta Lynch, might have tried to stifle or weaken the effort to investigate Clinton's mishandling of her emails.[99]

The revelation likely makes it harder to claim that the reopening of the investigation was purely politically motivated. The department can respond to new information or evidence. At the same time, it remains to be seen what difference this new information or evidence might make. If the reopening of an investigation against a political enemy can be traced to purely political motives (such as deflecting attention from the investigation into the president's legal troubles), it becomes more suspect. If, however, the investigation by the Justice Department can show that there was an abuse of power under President Obama, then President Trump and his administration can claim they are protecting, not undermining, the rule of law. They can make the same claim depending on how an investigation of the Clinton Foundation turns out.

The congressional investigation into Russian influence over the 2016 presidential election is more complicated. If it shows collusion (as the Trump administration's allies understand it) between the Clinton campaign and Russia, that collusion is of course legally and politically significant. Yet the fact that one campaign does something bad does not necessarily mean that another campaign is innocent of any wrongdoing. When congressional leaders argue that the Clinton campaign might have had a role in arranging for the development and use of a dossier with arguably damaging information about the connections between Trump and the Russian government, those claims do nothing to discredit the dossier. Nor do they take the Trump campaign off the hook; regardless of whether the claims have any merit, they do not establish that the Trump campaign is innocent of all charges made against it.

A second issue arising from the president's tweets and other public statements is his persistent attacks on the press, claims of fake news, and deriding the press as "the enemy of the people."[100] The fact is that most presidents have had issues with the press coverage of their administrations, and President Trump's attacks on the media appear to differ more in degree than in kind from other presidents' questioning of the motives or accuracy of press reports on the administration. Here, we must recognize that the media itself have changed over time; the proliferation of the twenty-four-hour news cycle has increased dramatically the extent to which the media reports "soft news," which merely consists mainly of speculation and commentary, more than it does the "hard news," which are the facts and figures relating to different events. With the proliferation of soft news, it stands to reason that a president will likely be confronted more often with the need to push back against the hurtful speculation and commentary that passes for news on cable and radio. If the president's words were coupled with actions that hurt the press, then there is greater concern that he has injured the "freedom of the press" and thus caused the country harm in some way. Without overt acts following upon the president's rhetoric, the president can credibly be said to be merely defending his administration, his image, and policies. People can differ with him about the substantive content of his attacks, but as long as they remain free to do so the problem seems to be well suited to be worked out in public debate.

A third set of issues arising from the president's tweets and other communications involve his rude, offensive, and false comments. Being rude and offensive is not new for a president. More important, Trump is pushing the boundaries of public discourse. His breaking norms in doing so can be disruptive and upsetting, including in making derogatory comments about other nations' leaders or policies.[101] But breaking the norms of rhetoric can be defended as making the presidency more transparent, candid, valiantly keeping the press in check, and strengthening public discourse—making it more robust. If we take seriously that impeachment is a last resort for handling misconduct (of a certain order and severity), we cannot ignore how there are many checks on the president's rhetoric, including pushback from the media, interest groups, fellow Republicans, the Democratic Party and its leaders, and experts of various kinds. These others can try to keep the president honest.

Spreading false information or making false statements about other people may, however, be different. As far as civil liability for defamation goes, the president is immune from any civil damages for his official acts and statements. Claiming that his statements are official might be enough to bar any civil actions. But could there be a problem in the area of impeachment? It is likely there is not, because the corrective actions allowed by the Constitution—congressional oversight, public approval, and the judgment of history—are equally available in this context. Moreover, if some statements are considered to be unofficial actions, they may be treated like pre-presidential misconduct, for which a president is not civilly immune from damages. Lord Acton referred to impeachment as the "one-hundred-ton" gun that the government can use against the misconduct of public officials.[102] It seems to be overkill to turn that weaponry on something that can be, and has been, addressed through other less disruptive means, including the president's facing re-election.

A tougher issue arises with respect to the extent to which the president's tweets and public comments degrade the presidency itself. This is especially true for comments and tweets that are racist. The corrective measures for much of his rhetoric might not ameliorate the possible damage done to the institution of the presidency itself, to the morale of the country, and to its standing abroad. One response to this charge, apart from denials that the president made certain comments or that they might have been justified or did no harm, is that other presidents have said or done worse things for which they were not impeached.

What about —?

No doubt, in the course of this discussion of President Trump, many people who have read this far wonder about the significance of other presidents who might have done or said something worse than President Trump has said or done but who were never subject to impeachment for their arguable misconduct. Should we attribute any significance to the failure to impeach any of these other presidents who engaged in worse misconduct than President Trump has so far?

Professor Adrian Vermuele of Harvard Law School has asked this question in a provocative way. He has asked whether we think a president who has unilaterally suspended habeas corpus, waged war without congressional approval, and encouraged and supported the prosecution of his political enemies may be impeached. We could add to the list of misconduct the president's telling lies to the American public, making or encouraging racist statements, and engaging in sexual escapades. Most people might be tempted to say yes, but the presidents who did these things were not Trump but rather Abraham Lincoln, Woodrow Wilson, Franklin Roosevelt, and John F. Kennedy. What about these presidents, and why should Trump get a pass if Congress failed to impeach these presidents for their misconduct?

To answer this final question, we need to answer several other questions. The first is whether the failure to impeach these other presidents should be counted as historical practices that have shaped understanding of the impeachment power. Does the failure to impeach these presidents mean that no presidents may ever be subject to impeachment for similar misconduct? If the failures actually reflected an understanding shared by Congress that its failures to impeach meant that impeachment would be inappropriate for the misconduct in question, then I might say that the answer to the latter question could be yes. However, these failures reflected something else; they were not judgments that impeachment was inappropriate for the misconduct in question. That is what has happened with respect to the impeachment of senators, something that the

Senate once decided was inappropriate and subsequent congresses have chosen to follow. The failure to impeach presidents for various sorts of misconduct reflected how judgments regarding impeachment turns, at any given time, on a variety of factors. These factors include but are not limited to the composition of the Congress, the president's popularity, the public's knowledge and attitudes about the misconduct, the severity of the misconduct, the damage done by the misconduct, and the extent to which the misconduct in question was handled or addressed by other means.

Justice Antonin Scalia used to argue, in a different context, that the failure of Congress to do something had no legal significance. In his judgment, it was a non-event that could be attributable to many different things, which would be difficult to verify but none of which took the form of law. In the context of impeachment, the failure to impeach in any of these circumstances mentioned above could be dismissed simply as non-events.

The second question is about estoppel, that is, should we regard the failure to have impeached in any of these circumstances to have estopped Congress from ever doing so? Congress itself has rejected the notion that it should be estopped from doing something because a prior Congress either did or did not do it. The doctrine that the Congress is following here is called the doctrine against entrenchment, which posits that a current majority in the legislature may not bind the hands of a future majority. This principle means that a prior majority in a legislature may not bind a current majority in the same legislature from reaching a different conclusion on the matter. To put the point differently, even assuming that the failure to impeach in these prior instances was in each case a deliberate decision that was made, the Constitution allows Congress to change its mind.

Third, as we think through these difficult questions, we can better understand the severity of misconduct and whether certain misconduct, such as degrading the presidency, is an impeachable offense, by asking about it in different ways. Does this misconduct effectively disable the president from doing his job? Many people would answer this question negatively, though many of the people who might say no are people who support the president. This leads us to ask the question about whether certain misconduct is impeachable in an entirely different way—whether you would consider this same misconduct impeachable if it were done by a different president?

Say, if we replace Trump in this hypothetical with Hillary Clinton? We can test ourselves and our own approach to and attitudes about impeachment by asking, for any given misconduct, whether we think the same misconduct done by a different president provides a legitimate basis for impeachment. If you like President Trump and resist thinking that degrading the presidency could ever be a legitimate basis for impeaching him, what if we assume that a different president has done the same thing. Should the answer be different? What if we ask this question about Bill Clinton—or Barack Obama? If we think a president we like should not be impeached for certain misconduct but a president we dislike should be impeached for the same misconduct, what does that say about our judgment?

This is likely what Professor Vermuele is challenging us to come to terms with. Wilson, like Adams, launched prosecutions of the critics of his administration and particularly the war effort underway. But neither man was ever impeached. Should they have been? The press was complicit in keeping President Kennedy's sexual escapades private, but should he have been impeached for them? What about the charges that Bill Clinton was a moral degenerate? Clinton even lied under oath (which was later judged to be perjury), but the Senate did not convict him for this. If Trump lies under oath or shrugs off his racist comments, what happens then? How much degradation of the presidency is too much? At what point do we draw a line?

Part of the answer is that, even if Congress has never done something like this before, that should not matter much if at all. One could argue that there is a first time for everything, including impeaching a judge or president for obstruction of justice. Perhaps the time has come for a moral reckoning, whether it is one for the president, Congress, or both.

In the final analysis, we come back to the question of whether a president may be impeached for degrading the presidency. This is not a hard question. I think a president may be impeached for degrading the presidency or, to put this in terms similar to the basis for Ritter's conviction and removal as a judge, for bringing the presidency into disrepute. In his book on the Clinton impeachment trial, Judge Richard Posner argued that Bill Clinton should also have been considered impeachable for his degrading the presidential office.[103] I agree with Judge Posner, and I agree with the emerging number of Democratic senators who insist, at least now, that his sexual harassment or misbehavior, like that of former judge Alex Kozinski, went far enough to justify impeachment, conviction, and removal.[104]

The question is whether the multiplicity of factors taken into consideration drive toward impeachment, rather than against it. One insensitive remark, one racist comment, or one hateful, false statement about a political foe might be one thing, but the aggregation of a pattern or practice of degrading behavior or comments can take a toll, even on the presidency itself. A president's moral character or leadership is not out of bounds for consideration, at least to the extent to which it becomes seriously questioned, based on his violation of the standards that Congress and the American people regard as the minimal qualifications to remain in office. Such a problem may justify the deployment of the "one-hundred-ton gun" of impeachment.

CONCLUSION

In this book, we have covered a lot of ground. We have reviewed the history and practice of impeachment. We have asked and tried to answer every conceivable question about impeachment, and considered the extent to which public figures, such as the president, may be subject to the impeachment process. It is not, however, intended to be a how-to manual for impeaching President Trump, but something bigger than that. Understanding impeachment requires more than merely understanding the scope of impeachable offenses, which is admittedly a difficult subject. But there are other difficult questions that have to be understood to figure out not just what may be possible with respect to the impeachment of the current chief executive, but also other chief executives or other high-ranking officials, for their misconduct in office. These issues involve the procedures and sanctions that may be used in the impeachment process as well as the alternatives to impeachment as a mechanism for addressing "the misconduct of public men," in Hamilton's cramped phrasing in the Federalist Papers.

Understanding impeachment as a check on official misconduct requires understanding the constitutional checks on impeachment. When Congress fails to impeach public officials that many people might think warranted impeachment, it might reflect a limitation of the impeachment process, in which the responsible authorities are subject to political pressure, time constraints, and their own moral or political foibles. It is not just the people responsible for making the big decisions on impeachment that are imperfect; the process itself is not perfect. The pressures on the party in power to keep a president of its own are enormous. In cases involving obscure political officials, the time expenditures are costly, requiring the members of Congress willing to take a leadership role to devote their attention and energies to matters that their constituents are unlikely to care about or reward. The concerns about establishing a precedent that could come back to haunt the party in power further counsel cautious deployment of the potent weapon of impeachment.

At the same time, the boundaries of impeachment are not so clear that everyone can agree on them, and the common law in this area developed by Congress over time is not so voluminous that it can provide clear guidance to the people who are subject to, or responsible for the exercise of, impeachment. Nor is it entirely clear how the alternatives to impeachment fit together. Where one ends and another begins or may overlap is a question that is perennially debated within the Congress and the academy.

Reassurances on the scope of impeachment may be hard to come by, but that is all right. It means that the present generation has been left with the difficult work of figuring out the meaning of the Constitution in an important area. Aside from the usual challenges of clarifying constitutional meaning (e.g., where should we look for its meaning and how should we interpret that particular source), there is a bigger challenge in figuring out who is in charge of the process. When Congress fails to do something that we think it should have done, who is to blame? And when it succeeds, who should get the credit? The conventional answer is often said to be the public, but that is too simplistic.

The framers of our Constitution did not trust the public; they created a system of checks and balances that are overwhelmingly counter-majoritarian—that is, they are designed to frustrate the popular will, not empower or vindicate it. The framers created a democratic republic, which means a government in which the key decision makers are not the people but are elected by the people. This is nowhere truer than in the impeachment process.

A number of factors influence those impeachment decision makers, including presidential popularity. It stands to reason that a popular president will be difficult to impeach and remove from office, but it has been equally difficult with regard to unpopular presidents. Andrew Johnson was as unpopular a president as we have had, and he was at least as crude and profane as the current occupant of the White House. But his crudeness was not used as a basis for his impeachment, though it increased the disposition of the members of Congress whom he derided to consider ousting him from office. If, historically, neither an unpopular president nor a popular one could be removed (Clinton's popularity remained strong throughout his impeachment proceedings in spite of his misconduct), what does that tell us about the utility of the impeachment process?

Another way to think about the effectiveness of impeachment as a check on presidential misconduct is to consider what the history of impeachment tells us about the Constitution, the Congress, and the American people. In the few critical instances in which high-profile public figures were the subject of impeachment proceedings, strengths and weaknesses of the impeachment process were evident. Perhaps the high threshold required for conviction and removal is the price that must be paid to avoid the overzealous use of the impeachment process. The system is designed, in other words, to err on the side of acquitting, not convicting, people.

Congress has fallen prey to sharp partisan divides that make the possibility of reaching consensus on impeachment difficult, though not impossible—as in the case of Thomas Porteous, who was unanimously impeached by the House in 2010 and convicted, removed, and disqualified from office by the Senate in the same year.[1] As for the American people, they do not wield direct power in the process, but impeachments ultimately reflect the values and standards of their time. In some cases, the standards change, as in the case of sexual misconduct. But in other regards the standards do not change, as we as a populace expect certain levels of honesty and integrity from the highest-ranking officials in our government.

The point is that culture matters. Our culture provides the framework for the construction of the Constitution. The language of the Constitution and its history do not change, but the social, political, and legal environments in which the standards of impeachment are applied do change. Sexual mores, for example, have evolved, and the political and social reaction to a president's philandering might change. With Bill Clinton, for example, there was shock and outrage, at least in some quarters, about the revelations of his sexual escapades in the White House. The disgust over Clinton's conduct set the stage for his impeachment, but the willingness to accept it as not a problem in itself and to allow room for him to lie about it were factors in his acquittal. A related factor was the public's attitude about Clinton. His sexual misconduct was, in the opinion of many people, fully in character and not pertinent to his public leadership. For others, his misconduct entailed damaging the rule of law and the presidency.

By contrast, when a news report broke in January 2018 that President Trump's lawyer had apparently paid more than $100,000 to silence a porn star with whom he allegedly had a tryst (which was consensual, by her account), his supporters barely blinked, while the opposition understood there was no chance it would change people's attitudes about Trump.[2] How misbehavior is understood in society at any given time makes a big difference as to whether it may serve as the basis for an impeachment.

Though the constitutional standards pertaining to impeachment do not change, we cannot ignore that they are applied at given moments and to specific contexts. The standards are traceable to the Constitution, but whether they are satisfied and maintained by the people in high-ranking office is a challenge for every generation to meet. If Congress fails, its members can and must look themselves in the mirror and know who was at fault. But the American people also must know that, if their leaders cannot maintain the standards of behavior the Constitution demands from them, they have the power to do something about it. And when future generations look back upon what the Congress did or did not do in a particular case involving presidential misconduct, they will know that the outcome says a lot about Americans, and America, at the time.

Appendix

TABLE OF US IMPEACHMENTS

William Blount (US Senator, Tennessee)

Impeached 41–30 by the House of Representatives (July 7, 1797) for a single article charging him with "a high misdemeanor, entirely inconsistent with his public duty and trust as a Senator"; impeachment trial dismissed (January 14, 1799) 14–11 by the Senate for want of jurisdiction because he had previously been expelled by the Senate.

John Pickering (US District Judge)

Impeached 45–8 by the House of Representatives (March 2, 1803) on the basis of four articles of impeachment charging him with abuses of authority and intoxication on the bench; convicted and removed from office (March 12, 1804) by the Senate by a vote of 19–7 on all four articles.

Samuel Chase (Associate Justice, US Supreme Court)

Impeached 73–32 (March 12, 1804) on the basis of eight articles of impeachment charging him with various abuses of power and misconduct during trials; acquitted by a vote of 21–22 on all eight articles (March 1, 1805).

James H. Peck (US District Judge)

Impeached 123–49 (April 24, 1830) by the House of Representatives for abuse of contempt power; acquitted (January 31, 1831) by the Senate by a vote of 21–22.

West Humphreys (US District Judge)

Impeached "without division" (May 6, 1862) on the basis of seven articles of impeachment charging him with various abuses of power and crimes for abandoning his judgeship to join the Confederacy; convicted and removed from office and disqualified from future office by the Senate (June 3, 1862) by votes of 39–0 (Art. I), 36–1 (Art. II), 33–4 (Art. III), 28–10 (Art. IV), 39–0 (Art. V), 36–1 (Art. VI, specification 1), 35–1 (Art. VI, specification 3), 35–1 (Art. VII), and 27–10 (disqualification).

Andrew Johnson (President of the United States)

Impeached 126–47 by the House of Representatives (February 24, 1868) on the basis of eleven articles of impeachment charging him with violating the Tenure of Office Act, showing contempt for Congress, and interfering with Reconstruction policy; acquitted (May 26, 1868) by the Senate by votes of

35–19 (Art. II), 35–19 (Art. III), and 35–19 (Art. XI). The Senate chose to vote on only three articles of impeachment.

Mark Delahey (US District Judge)

Impeached "without division" by the House of Representatives (February 28, 1893) for a single article of impeachment charging intoxication on the bench and unfitness for office; resigned prior to Senate impeachment trial.

William Belknap (Secretary of War)

Impeached unanimously (March 2, 1876) by the House of Representatives on the basis of five articles of impeachment for bribery; acquitted (August 1, 1786) after he had resigned from office but before his Senate impeachment trial could begin.

Charles Swayne (US District Judge)

Impeached by the House of Representatives (December 13, 1904) on the basis of thirteen articles of impeachment, including one voted unanimously, for various abuses of power; acquitted by the Senate (February 27, 1905) by votes of 33 (guilty) to 49 (not guilty), 32–50, 32–50, 13–69, 13–69, 31–51, 19–63, 31–51, 31–51, 31–51, 31–51, and 35–47.

Robert Archbald (US Commerce Court Judge)

Impeached (July 11, 1912) 223–1 by the House of Representatives on the basis of thirteen articles of impeachment charging him with receiving inappropriate payments and gifts from litigants; convicted in the Senate by votes of 68–5 (Art. I), 60–11 (Art. III), 52–20 (Art. IV), 66–6 (Art. V), 42–20 (Art. XIII), removed, and disqualified from future office by a vote of 39–35 (January 13, 1913).

George W. English (US District Judge)

Impeached (April 1, 1926) by the House of Representatives 306–62 on the basis of five impeachment articles charging him with various abuses of power; resigned from office (November 4, 1926) and Senate proceedings dismissed (December 13, 1926).

Harold Louderback (US District Judge)

Impeached 183–142 by the House of Representatives (February 24, 1933) on the basis of five impeachment articles charging misbehavior in office; acquitted (May 24, 1933) by the Senate by votes of 34–42, 23–47, 11–63, 30–47, and 45–34.

Halsted Ritter (US District Judge)

Impeached 181–146 by the House of Representatives (March 2, 1936) on the basis of seven articles of impeachment charging corruption and bringing the judiciary into disrepute; convicted (April 17, 1936) in the Senate on a single impeachment article and removed from office.

Harry Claiborne (US District Judge)

Impeached 406–0 by the House of Representatives (July 22, 1986) on the basis of four impeachment articles charging tax fraud; convicted and removed from office (October 9, 1936) on three of the articles, by Senate votes of 87–10 (Art. I), 90–7 (Art. II), and 89–8 (Art. IV).

Alcee Hastings (US District Judge)

Impeached by the House of Representatives (August 3, 1988) 413–3 on the basis of seventeen impeachment articles charging bribery and perjury; convicted in the Senate on eight of the articles and removed from office by votes of 69–26 (Art. I), 68–27 (Art. II), 69–26 (Art. III), 67–28 (Art. IV), 67–28 (Art. V), 69–26 (Art. VI), 68–27 (Art. VIII), and 70–25 (Art. IX) (October 20, 1989).

Walter Nixon (US District Judge)

Impeached 417–0 by the House of Representatives (May 10, 1989) on the basis of three impeachment articles for making false statements to a grand jury; convicted in the Senate on two articles and removed from office (November 3, 1989) on the basis of two impeachment articles charging obstruction of justice and perjury, by votes of 89–8 (Art. I) and 78–19 (Art. II).

William Jefferson Clinton (President of the United States)

Impeached by the House of Representatives (December 19, 1998) on charges of perjury and obstruction of justice; acquitted on both articles by the Senate (February 12, 1999) by votes of 55–45 (Art. I) and 50–50 (Art. II).

Samuel Kent (US District Judge)

Impeached by the House of Representatives (June 19, 2009) by votes of 389–0, 385–0, 381–0, and 372–0 on the basis of four impeachment articles charging sexual assault and perjury; resigned from office (June 30, 2009) before the end of Senate impeachment trial.

Thomas Porteous (US District Judge)

Impeached by the House of Representatives (March 11, 2010) unanimously on the basis of four impeachment articles charging corruption and perjury; convicted and removed from office and disqualified from future office (December 8, 2010) by the Senate in votes of 96–0 (Art. I), 69–27 (Art. II), 88–8 (Art. III), and 90–6 (Art. IV).

NOTES

Introduction

1 James C. Nelson and John Bonifaz, "Legal Scholars: Why Congress Should Impeach Donald Trump," TIME, Feb. 6, 2017, http://time.com/4658633/impeach-donald-trump-congress/.

2 Jason Le Miere, "Trump Colluded with Russia and Will Be Impeached, Says Maxine Waters," NEWSWEEK, Sep. 23, 2017, http://www.newsweek.com/trump-russia-collusion-impeachment-waters-669866.

3 Barry H. Berke, Noah Bookbinder, and Norman Eisen, *Presidential Obstruction of Justice: The Case of Donald J. Trump*, BROOKINGS INSTITUTION, Oct. 10, 2017, https://www.brookings.edu/research/presidential-obstruction-of-justice-the-case-of-donald-j-trump/.

4 Conor Friedersdorf, "Donald Trump's Impeachable Offense," THE ATLANTIC, Oct. 13, 2017, https://www.theatlantic.com/politics/archive/2017/10/impeach-donald-trump-article-one/542841/.

5 Frank Bowman, "President Trump Committed another Impeachable Offense on Friday," SLATE, Nov. 3, 2017, http://www.slate.com/articles/news_and_politics/jurisprudence/2017/11/president_trump_committed_another_impeachable_offense_on_friday.html.

6 Ezra Klein, " 'Unfit to Be President': 58 House Democrats Want to Start Debating the Impeachment of Donald Trump," Vox, Dec. 6, 2017, https://www.vox.com/policy-and-politics/2017/12/6/16743162/impeach-trump-impeachment-al-green-democrats.

7 Joseph Isenbergh, "Impeachment and Presidential Immunity from Judicial Process" (last modified Dec. 31, 1998) ("In my view, all the essential constitutional elements at issue in these [impeachment] events are misconceived by the participants and most academic commentators."), http://chicagounbound.uchicago.edu/cgi/viewcontent.cgi?article=1012&context=occasional_papers.

8 Senate Historical Office, *The Impeachment of Andrew Johnson (1868)*, UNITED STATES SENATE (last visited Dec. 19, 2017) ("By mid-1867, Johnson's enemies in Congress were repeatedly promoting impeachment."), https://www.

senate.gov/artandhistory/history/common/briefing/Impeachment_ Johnson.htm.

9 Senate Historical Office, *Senate Censures President*, UNITED STATES SENATE (last visited Dec. 17, 2017), https://www.senate.gov/artandhistory/ history/minute/Senate_Censures_President.htm.

10 *Id.*

11 Senate Historical Office, *The Impeachment of Andrew Johnson (1868)*, UNITED STATES SENATE (last visited Dec. 17, 2017), https://www.senate.gov/ artandhistory/history/common/briefing/Impeachment_Johnson.htm.

12 Carl Bernstein and Bob Woodward, "Woodward and Bernstein: 40 Years after Watergate, Nixon Was Far Worse Than We Thought," WASH. POST, Jun. 8, 2012, https://www.washingtonpost.com/opinions/woodward-and-bernstein-40-years-after-watergate-nixon-was-far-worse-than-we-thought/ 2012/06/08/gJQAlsi0NV_story.html?utm_term=.bd2c071b193b.

13 "Support for Ford Declines Sharply," N.Y. TIMES, Sep. 12, 1974, http:// www.nytimes.com/1974/09/12/archives/support-for-ford-declines-sharply-a-poll-links-drop-to-pardon-and.html.

14 "Texan Acts for Impeachment," N.Y. TIMES, Mar. 6, 1987, http://www. nytimes.com/1987/03/06/us/texan-acts-for-impeachment.html.

15 Anthony Lewis, "Abroad at Home; Clinton and His Enemies," N.Y. TIMES, Dec. 29, 1997 (Opinion), http://www.nytimes.com/1997/12/29/opinion/ abroad-at-home-clinton-and-his-enemies.html; Erik Eckholm, "From Right, a Rain of Anti-Clinton Salvos," N.Y. TIMES, Jun. 26, 1994, http://www. nytimes.com/1994/06/26/us/from-right-a-rain-of-anti-clinton-salvos. html?pagewanted=all.

16 Francis X. Clines, "A 'Dreadful Day' Unfolds on and off House Floor," N.Y. TIMES, Dec. 19, 1998, http://www.nytimes.com/1998/12/19/us/ impeachment-capitol-sketchbook-a-dreadful-day-unfolds-on-and-off-house-floor.html.

17 Chris Suellentrop, "The Left Debates Impeachment," N.Y. TIMES, Mar. 9, 2006 (Opinion), https://opinionator.blogs.nytimes.com/2006/03/ 09/the-left-debates-impeachment/; Charles Babington, "Democrats Won't Try to Impeach President," WASH. POST, May 12, 2006, http:// www.washingtonpost.com/wp-dyn/content/article/2006/05/11/ AR2006051101950.html.

18 *See* Chris Edelson, "The Curious Case of GOP Objections to Executive Action," THE HILL, Nov. 20, 2014, http://thehill.com/blogs/pundits-blog/ immigration/224887-the-curious-case-of-gop-objections-to-executive-action.

19 *See,* e.g., Jonathan Ashbach, "The GOP Needs to Elect Trump, then Impeach Him," THE FEDERALIST, Oct. 25, 2016, http://thefederalist.com/2016/10/ 25/gop-needs-elect-trump-impeach/; Darren Samuelson, "Could Trump Be Impeached Shortly after He Takes Office," POLITICO, https://www.politico. com/magazine/story/2016/04/donald-trump-2016-impeachment-213817.

20 Taylor Link, "Donald Trump Is Never Going to Release His Tax Returns," SALON, Oct. 23, 2017, https://www.salon.com/2017/10/23/donald-trump-is-never-going-to-release-his-tax-returns/.

21 *See,* e.g., Elizabeth Drew, "The Case for Impeaching Donald Trump Is Real and Serious. Here's Why," DAILY

BEAST, Oct. 10, 2017, https://www.thedailybeast.com/
the-case-for-impeaching-donald-trump-is-real-and-serious-heres-why.

22 Jeet Heer, "The Democrats' Dangerous Obsession with Impeachment,"
    NEW REPUBLIC, Dec. 5, 2017, https://newrepublic.com/article/146098/
    democrats-dangerous-obsession-impeachment.

23 *Id.*

Chapter 1

1 *See* "Impeach," DICTIONARY.COM (last visited Jan. 24, 2018), http://www.
   dictionary.com/browse/impeach?s=t.

2 U.S. Constit. art. I, § 2, cl. 5.

3 Tuan Samahon, "Impeachment as Judicial Selection?" 18 WM. & MARY
   BILL RTS. J. 595, 623 (referring to the clauses pertaining to impeachment,
   impeachment trial, impeachment judgment, and impeachment grounds as
   "the impeachment clauses").

4 U.S. Const. art. I, § 2, cl. 5.

5 *Id.*, art. I, § 3, cl. 6.

6 Buckner F. Melton, Jr., "Federal Impeachment and Criminal Procedure: The
   Framers' Intent," 52 MD. L. REV. 437 (1993).

7 Mark R. Slusar, "The Confusion Defined: Questions and Problems of
   Process in the Aftermath of the Clinton Impeachment," 49 CASE W. RES.
   L. REV. 869, 889–92 ("Among the most troubling aspects of the variance in
   interpretations is the confusion over whether the Constitution mandates
   removal for the commission of treason, bribery, or other high crimes and
   misdemeanors.").

8 U.S. Constit. art. I, § 3, cl. 7.

9 *Id.*, art. II, § 2, cl. 1.

10 *Id.*, art. III, § 1.

11 *Id.*, amend. V.

12 *Id.*, art. I, § 6, cl. 2.

13 *Id.*, art. I, § 9, cl. 8.

14 *Id.*, art. II, § 1, cl. 7.

15 Richard T. Haley, "The Impeachment of Federal Officers in United
    States History," 10 THE HISTORIAN 135, 135 (1948) ("The framers of the
    Constitution were familiar with the power of impeachment because of its
    long practice in England, where it served as a judicial method of removing
    guilty officials from office.").

16 Peter Charles Hoffer and N. E. H. Hull, *Impeachment in America, 1635–1805*
    (New Haven: Yale University Press, 1984), 3.

17 Hoffer, 3–4.

18 Hoffer, 45.

19 Hoffer, 3.

20 Hoffer, 5.

21 Raoul Berger, *Impeachment: The Constitutional Problems*, 64.

22 Dave Lindorff and Barbara Olshansky, *The Case for Impeachment*, 40
    ("History shows that the English concept of impeachment as a device
    intended to remedy momentous political offenses or serious injuries
    to the state made its way across the ocean with the Founders and was
    incorporated by the Framers into the laws of the new republic.").

23 Joseph D. Jamail, Jr., "The Jury System," Houston Lawyer, Sep. 2005. ("William Blackstone [was] the Framers' accepted authority on English law and the English Constitution[.]").

24 *See* Bestor, "Impeachment," quoting Blackstone, "Commentaries on the Laws of England," 75. Blackstone commented that "Treason . . . in its very name (which is borrowed from the French) imports a betraying, treachery, or breach of faith . . . [T]reason is . . . a general appellation, made use of by the law, to denote . . . that accumulation of guilt which arises whenever a superior reposes a confidence in a subject or inferior, . . . and the inferior . . . so forgets the obligations of duty, subjection, and allegiance, as to destroy the life of any such superior or lord. . . . [T]herefore for a wife to kill her lord or husband, a servant his lord or master, and an ecclesiastic his lord or ordinary; these, being breaches of the lower allegiance, of private and domestic faith, are denominated *petit* treasons. But when disloyalty so rears it's [*sic*] crest, as to attack even majesty itself, it is called by way of eminent distinction *high* treason, *alta proditio*; being equivalent to the *crimen laesae majestatis* of the Romans."

25 Hoffer, 10–12.

26 *Id.* at 62, 63, 67.

27 *Id.* at 68.

28 Peter Charles Hoffer and N. E. H. Hull, *Impeachment in America, 1635–1805*, xiii (New Haven: Yale University Press, 1984).

29 Hoffer, 96.

30 *Id.* at 96.

31 Charles Doyle, "Impeachment Grounds: Part 2: Selected Constitutional Convention Materials," CRS Report for Congress (1998), 1.

32 *Id.* at 1–2.

33 Farrand's Records, V.1, 244.

34 *Id.*

35 *Id.* at V.1, 252.

36 *Id.* at V.1, 252–69.

37 *Id.* at V.1, 289.

38 *Id.* at V.1, 291–93.

39 *Id.* at V.1, 292–93.

40 *Id.* at V.2, 136.

41 *Id.* at V.2, 178–79, 186.

42 *Id.* at V.2, 186.

43 *Id.* at V.2, 427.

44 *Id.* at V.2, 428.

45 *Id.*

46 *Id.*

47 *Id.*

48 *Id.* at V.2, 429.

49 *Id.*

50 *Id.*

51 *Id.*

52 *Id.* at V.2, 493.

53 *Id.* at V.2, 493–95.

54   *Id.* at V.2, 551.
55   *Id.*
56   *Id.*
57   *Id.*
58   *Id.*
59   *Id.*
60   *Id.*
61   Hoffer and Hull, 100; Farrand's Records, V.2, 64–70.
62   Farrand's Records, V.2, 66.
63   *Id.* at V.2, 64–66.
64   *Id.* at V.2, 64.
65   *Id.* at V.2, 65.
66   *Id.*
67   *Id.* at V.2, 65–66.
68   *Id.* at V.2, 67.
69   *Id.* at V.2, 68.
70   *Id.* at V.2, 64, 69.
71   *Id.* at V.2, 116.
72   *Id.* at V.2, 69.
73   *Id.* at V.2, 550.
74   *Id.* at V.2, 65–66.
75   *Id.* at V.1, 78.
76   *Id.* at V.2, 112–13.
77   *Id.* at V.2, 337.
78   *Id.* at V.2, 499.
79   *Id.*
80   *Id.* at V.2, 550.
81   *Id.*
82   *Id.*
83   Carter, *The Confirmation Mess*, 146. "The Senate, responsive to public will but also sharing some of the distance of the courts, has the ability, if it chooses, to give voice not simply to the passions of the moment but to the enduring and fundamental values that shape the specialness of the American people. The institutional design of bicameralism makes this balance possible: what the House votes in its haste, the Senate may reconsider at its leisure."
84   U.S. Constit. art. II, § 4.
85   *Id.*, art. I, § 3, cl. 9.
86   *Id.*, art. I, § 3, cl. 8.
87   *Id.*, art. III, § 3. cl. 1.
88   18 U.S.C. 201 (2012).
89   *See,* e.g., Alice O'Connor, *"During Good Behavior": Judicial Independence and Accountability: A Guide for Discussion of Proposals to Establish Terms of Office for the Federal Judiciary* (Jefferson Foundation, 1984); Raoul Berger, *Impeachment: The Constitutional Problems* (Harvard University Press, 1974).
90   *See* United States v. Hatter, 532 U.S. 557, 567 (2001); Vicki C. Jackson "Packages of Judicial Independence: The Selection and Tenure of Article III Judges," 95 GEO. L.J. 965, 987 ("The traditional understanding, expressed recently by the Supreme Court, is that 'the Clause securing federal judges

appointments 'during good Behaviour,' is the practical equivalent of life tenure.").

91 *See,* e.g., Peter M. Shane, "Who May Discipline or Remove Federal Judges? A Constitutional Analysis," 142 Univ. of Penn. L.R. 209, 210 (1993) ("No feature of our public institutional life, however, is likely more essential to preserving a government of laws than an honorable and independent judiciary.").

92 Indeed, "[t]he old Canons of Judicial Ethics contained a requirement that judges' conduct, both on and off the bend, be 'beyond reproach.' " Steven Lubet, "Judicial Ethics and Private Lives," 79 Nw. U.L. Rev. 983, 990 (1984).

93 Bestor, *Impeachment,* 263–64.

94 U.S. Constit. art. II, § 2, cl. 1.

95 Story's Commentaries on the Constitution, Book III, Ch. X, pg. 217 § 744.

96 *Id.*

97 Charles Black, *Impeachment: A Handbook* 56–57 (1974).

98 Berger, 59.

99 Berger, 59–61.

100 Bruce Ackerman, "Constitutional Politics/Constitutional Law," 99 Yale L.J. 453 (1989).

101 *Id.* at 455.

102 List of Individuals Impeached by the House of Representatives, United States House of Representatives (last visited Dec. 16, 2017), http://history.house.gov/Institution/Impeachment/Impeachment-List/.

103 Impeachment, Complete List of Senate Impeachment Trials, United States Senate (last visited Dec. 17, 2017), https://www.senate.gov/artandhistory/history/common/briefing/Senate_Impeachment_Role.htm#4.

104 *Id.*

105 Impeachment, Complete List of Senate Impeachment Trials, United States Senate (last visited Dec. 17, 2017), https://www.senate.gov/artandhistory/history/common/briefing/Senate_Impeachment_Role.htm#4; *see also* CRS Report, *Former Presidents: Federal Pension and Retirement* Benefits, 2008, 2. https://www.senate.gov/reference/resources/pdf/98-249.pdf; *but see* Preble Stolz, "Disciplining Federal Judges: Is Impeachment Hopeless," 57 Calif. L. Rev. 659, 670 fn. 43 (1969) ("Conversely, unless a pension could be described as an 'office of . . . profit' it seems doubtful that Congress could make a judgment of impeachment without more grounds for removal of retirement rights.").

Chapter 2

1 List of Individuals Impeached by the House of Representatives, United States House of Representatives (last visited Dec. 18, 2017), http://history.house.gov/Institution/Impeachment/Impeachment-List/.

2 *Id.*

3 *Id.*

4 *Id.*

5 *Id.*

6 *Id.*

7 *Id.*

8 *Id.*

9 *Id.*

10   *Id.*
11   *Id.*
12   *Id.*
13   *Id.*
14   *Id.*
15   *Id.*
16   *Id.*
17   *Id.*
18   *Id.*
19   *Id.*
20   *Id.*
21   *Id.*
22   *Id.*
23   T. J. Halstead, "An Overview of the Impeachment Process," CRS Report for Congress, CRS-6.
24   "Impeachment," UNITED STATES SENATE (last visited Dec. 26, 2017), https:// www.senate.gov/artandhistory/history/common/briefing/Senate_ Impeachment_Role.htm.
25   Mary Louise Hinsdale, "A History of the President's Cabinet," 206.
26   "War Secretary's Impeachment Trial," UNITED STATES SENATE (last visited Dec. 29, 2017), https://www.senate.gov/artandhistory/history/minute/ War_Secretarys_Impeachment_Trial.htm.
27   *Id.*
28   Hind's Precedents, V.3, "The Impeachment and Trial of William W. Belknap," Chapter 77, 904–05.
29   "War Secretary's Impeachment Trial," UNITED STATES SENATE (last visited Dec. 29, 2017), https://www.senate.gov/artandhistory/history/minute/ War_Secretarys_Impeachment_Trial.htm.
30   Hind's Precedent's, V.3, "The Impeachment and Trial of William W. Belknap," Chapter 77, 934.
31   *Id.* at 945.
32   *Id.* at 946.
33   *Id.*
34   *Id.*
35   For a discussion of Belknap's potential acquittal, *see* Brian C. Kalt, "The Constitutional Case for the Impeachability of Former Federal Officials: An Analysis of the Law, History, and Practice of Late Impeachment," 6 TEX. REV. L. & POL. 13, 94–102.
36   Deschler's Precedents, Vol. 3, Ch. 14, § 16, https://www. gpo.gov/fdsys/pkg/GPO-HPREC-DESCHLERS-V3/pdf/ GPO-HPREC-DESCHLERS-V3-5-5-3.pdf.
37   *Id.*
38   Department of Justice, "U.S. District Court Judge Sentenced to 33 Months in Prison for Obstruction of Justice," May 11, 2009 (updated Sep. 15, 2014), https://www.justice.gov/opa/pr/ us-district-court-judge-sentenced-33-months-prison-obstruction-justice.
39   Letter from Judge Samuel B. Kent to the Impeachment Task Force, Jun. 1, 2009, https://judiciary.house.gov/_files/hearings/pdf/Kent090603.pdf.

40 H. Rept. 111–59, Jun. 17, 2009, https://www.congress.gov/congressional-report/111th-congress/house-report/159/1?q=%7B%22search%22%3A%5B%22kent%22%5D%7D.

41 Associated Press, "Texas: Convicted Judge Submits Resignation," N.Y. TIMES, Jun. 2, 2009, http://www.nytimes.com/2009/06/03/us/03brfs-CONVICTEDJUD_BRF.html.

42 H. Res. 661 (Jul. 20, 2009).

43 "Impeachment Articles against Judge Dismissed," N.Y. TIMES, Jul. 22, 2009, http://www.nytimes.com/2009/07/23/us/23brfs-IMPEACHMENTA_BRF.html.

44 List of Individuals Impeached by the House of Representatives, UNITED STATES HOUSE OF REPRESENTATIVES (last visited Dec. 18, 2017), http://history.house.gov/Institution/Impeachment/Impeachment-List/.

45 "William Blount," Biographical Directory of the United States Congress (last visited Dec. 30, 2017), http://bioguide.congress.gov/scripts/biodisplay.pl?index=b000570.

46 Brian C. Kalt, "The Constitutional Case for the Impeachability of Former Federal Officials: An Analysis of the Law, History, and Practice of Late Impeachment," 6 TEX. REV. L. & POL. 13, 86.

47 *Id.*

48 Milton M. Klein, "The First Impeachment," 35 TENN. B.J. 11, 12 (1999).

49 Brian C. Kalt, "The Constitutional Case for the Impeachability of Former Federal Officials: An Analysis of the Law, History, and Practice of Late Impeachment," 6 TEX. REV. L. & POL. 13, 86.

50 Jonathan Turley, "Senate Trials and Factional Disputes: Impeachment as a Madisonian Device," 49 DUKE L.J. 1, 47 n. 196.

51 "Senate Adopts First Impeachment Rules," UNITED STATES SENATE (last visited Jan. 1, 2018), https://www.senate.gov/artandhistory/history/minute/Senate_Adopts_First_Impeachment_Rules.htm.

52 *Id.* at 48.

53 Hoffer and Hull at 155.

54 Buckner F. Melton, Jr., *The First Impeachment: The Constitution's Framers and the Case of Senate William Blount*, 232 (1998).

55 Berger, at 214–15.

56 *Id.* at 215–23.

57 *See id.* at 222–23.

58 For an in-depth discussion of this event, *see* Kirsten E. Wood, " 'One Woman so Dangerous to Public Morals': Gender and Power in the Eaton Affair," 17 J. OF THE EARLY REPUBLIC 237 (1997).

59 For an in-depth discussion, *see* Joseph C. Burke, "The Cherokee Cases: A Study in Law, Politics, and Morality," 21 STAN. L. REV. 500 (1969).

60 *See* Jerry L. Mashaw, "Administration and 'The Democracy': Administrative Law from Jackson to Lincoln, 1829–1861," 117 YALE L.J. 1568, 1589–91 (2008).

61 *Id.* at 1590.

62 *Id.*

63 "Party Division," UNITED STATES SENATE (last visited Jan. 1, 2018), https://www.senate.gov/history/partydiv.htm.

64 Cong. Debates, 23 Cong., 1 Sess., 1813 (March 28, 1834).

65 Gerard N. Magliocca, "Veto! The Jacksonian Revolution in Constitutional Law," 78 NEB. L. REV. 205, 238–39 (1999).

66 *Id.*

67 13 Cong. Deb. 504 (1837).

68 Norma Lois Peterson, *The Presidencies of William Henry Harrison & John Tyler* (1989), 26–27.

69 *Id.* at 41.

70 *Id.* at 100, 104–6.

71 *Id.* at 102.

72 *Id.*

73 *Id.* at 102–03.

74 *Id.* at 66, 103.

75 *Id.* at 101–07.

76 Cong. Globe., 27th Cong., 2d Sess. 894–96 (1842) (quoting the select committee's report).

77 *Id.* at 896.

78 *Id.*

79 Peterson at 105.

80 Peterson at 106.

81 Peterson at 169.

82 *Id.*

83 *See* Michael J. Gerhardt, "Constitutional Construction and Departmentalism: A Case Study of the Demise of the Whig Presidency," 12 U. PA. J. CONST. L 425, 444 (2009–2010).

84 List of Individuals Impeached by the House of Representatives, UNITED STATES HOUSE OF REPRESENTATIVES (last visited Dec. 18, 2017), http://history.house.gov/Institution/Impeachment/Impeachment-List/.

85 *Id.*

86 Impeachment, Complete List of Senate Impeachment Trials, UNITED STATES SENATE (last visited Dec. 18, 2017), https://www.senate.gov/artandhistory/history/common/briefing/Senate_Impeachment_Role.htm#4.

87 "Andrew Johnson," THE WHITE HOUSE (last visited Jan. 1, 2018), https://www.whitehouse.gov/about-the-white-house/presidents/andrew-johnson/.

88 "Andrew Johnson," Biographical Directory of the United States Congress (last visited Dec. 29, 2017), http://bioguide.congress.gov/scripts/biodisplay.pl?index=j000116.

89 George S. Sirgiovanni, "Dumping the Vice President: An Historical Overview and Analysis," 24 PRES. STUDIES QUARTERLY 765, 768–69.

90 "Andrew Johnson," Biographical Directory of the United States Congress (last visited Dec. 29, 2017), http://bioguide.congress.gov/scripts/biodisplay.pl?index=j000116.

91 Keith E. Whittington, "Bill Clinton Was No Andrew Johnson," 2 U. PA. J. CONST. L., 422, 426 (2000).

92 Statutes at Large, Sess. II, Chap. 154, Mar. 2, 1867. "An Act Regulating the Tenure of Certain Civil Offices," https://www.senate.gov/artandhistory/history/resources/pdf/Johnson_TenureofOfficeAct.pdf.

93 Whittington, at 430.

94 "The Impeachment of President Andrew Johnson," History, Art & Archives of the United States House of Representatives (last visited Jan. 1, 2018), http://history.house.gov/Historical-Highlights/1851-1900/The-impeachment-of-President-Andrew-Johnson/.

95 "The Articles of Impeachment," Andrew Johnson, National Park Service (last updated Apr. 14, 2015).

96 "Congress Profiles: 40th Congress," History, Art & Archives for the United States House of Representatives (last visited Jan. 1, 2018), http://history.house.gov/Congressional-Overview/Profiles/40th/; "Party Division," UNITED STATES SENATE (last visited Jan. 1, 2018), https://www.senate.gov/history/partydiv.htm.

97 "The Impeachment of Andrew Johnson (1868)," UNITED STATES SENATE (last visited Jan. 1, 2018), https://www.senate.gov/artandhistory/history/common/briefing/Impeachment_Johnson.htm.

98 Michael Les Benedict, *The Impeachment and Trial of Andrew Johnson*, 168 (1973).

99 *See* id. at 283.

100 Kennedy, *Profiles in Courage*, 126–51 (1956).

101 Gene Smith, *High Crimes and Misdemeanors: The Impeachment and Trial of Andrew Johnson*, 284 (1985).

102 Benedict, at 171 n. 7.

103 Davis, at 266–67, 290–91.

104 Historical Election Results, National Archives and Records Administration, https://www.archives.gov/federal-register/electoral-college/scores.html.

105 John Herbers, "The 37th President Is First to Quit Post," N.Y. TIMES, Aug. 9, 2017, http://www.nytimes.com/1974/08/09/archives/the-37th-president-is-first-to-quit-post-speaks-of-pain-at-yielding.html?_r=0.

106 Bill Kovach, "Charges Against Nixon Called Justified by 79% in Poll of Impeachment Reaction; 2,000 Persons Surveyed," N.Y. TIMES, Jan. 6, 1974.

107 Roger Wilkins, "The Power Misused," N.Y. TIMES, Aug. 11, 1974.

108 R. W. Apple, Jr., "In 2 Years, Watergate Scandal Brought Down President Who Had Wide Mandate," N.Y. TIMES, Aug. 9, 1974; "The Agreed Articles," N.Y. TIMES, Aug. 1, 1974.

109 John Herbers, "The 37th President Is First to Quit Post," N.Y. TIMES, Aug. 9, 1974, http://www.nytimes.com/1974/08/09/archives/the-37th-president-is-first-to-quit-post-speaks-of-pain-at-yielding.html?_r=0.

110 Fred H. Alshuier, "Comparing the Nixon and Clinton Impeachments," 51 HASTINGS L.J. 745, 747 (2000).

111 James M. Naughton, "Nixon Slide from Power: Backers Gave Final Push," N.Y. TIMES, AUG. 11, 1974.

112 *Id.*

113 The Starr Report, 3–4.

114 *Id.* at 2.

115 Clinton v. Jones, 520 U.S. 681, 687 (1997).

116 *Id.* at 687–88.

117 Clinton v. Jones, 520 U.S. 681 (1997).

118 The Starr Report, at 3.

119 *Id.*

120 *Id.*

121 *Id.* at 8.

122 *See* The Starr Report, generally.

123 "Impeachment of William Jefferson Clinton, President of the United States; Report of the Committee on the Judiciary House of Representatives," H. Res. 611, 1, https://www.gpo.gov/fdsys/pkg/CRPT-105hrpt830/pdf/CRPT-105hrpt830.pdf.

124 Kevin Merida, "It's Come to This: A Nickname That's Proven Hard to Slip," WASH. POST, Dec. 20, 1998 (last visited Dec. 30, 2017), https://www.washingtonpost.com/wp-srv/politics/special/clinton/stories/slick122098.htm.

125 "Impeachment of William Jefferson Clinton, President of the United States; Report of the Committee on the Judiciary House of Representatives," H. Res. 611, 126, https://www.gpo.gov/fdsys/pkg/CRPT-105hrpt830/pdf/CRPT-105hrpt830.pdf.

126 "Trial Memorandum of President William Jefferson Clinton," Jan. 13, 1999 ("The House Judiciary Committee held a total of four hearings and called but one witness."), http://www.cnn.com/ALLPOLITICS/stories/1999/01/13/clinton.memorandum/.

127 John King, "House Impeaches Clinton," CNN, Dec. 19, 1998 (last visited Dec. 30, 2017), http://www.cnn.com/ALLPOLITICS/stories/1998/12/19/impeachment.01/.

128 List of Individuals Impeached by the House of Representatives, UNITED STATES HOUSE OF REPRESENTATIVES (last visited Dec. 18, 2017), http://history.house.gov/Institution/Impeachment/Impeachment-List/.

129 Peter Baker and Helen Dewar, "The Senate Acquits President Clinton," WASH. POST, Feb. 13, 1999 (last visited Dec. 29, 2017), https://www.washingtonpost.com/wp-srv/politics/special/clinton/stories/impeach021399.htm.

130 *Id.*

131 *Id.*

132 "Proceedings of the United States Senate in the Impeachment Trial of President William Jefferson Clinton, Volume IV: Statements of Senators Regarding the Impeachment Trial of President William Jefferson Clinton," Feb. 12, 1999, https://www.gpo.gov/fdsys/pkg/CDOC-106sdoc4/pdf/CDOC-106sdoc4-vol4.pdf.
These senators were: Senators Feingold, Murray, Johnson, Biden, Mikulski, Breaux, Sarbanes, Kerrey, Lautenberg, Robb, Boxer, Cleland, Durbin, Levin, Kohl, Moynihan, Graham, Kennedy, Harkin, Reid, Edwards, Akaka, Leahy, Dodd, Wellstone, Lieberman, Bryan, Dorgan, Kerry, Lincoln, Hollings, Wyden, Rockefeller, Byrd, Landrieu, Bingaman, Reed, and Daschle (listed in order of their statements in the Senate report).

133 "Proceedings of the United States Senate in the Impeachment Trial of President William Jefferson Clinton, Volume IV: Statements of Senators Regarding the Impeachment Trial of President William Jefferson Clinton," Feb. 12, 1999, https://www.gpo.gov/fdsys/pkg/CDOC-106sdoc4/pdf/CDOC-106sdoc4-vol4.pdf.

134 *Id.*

135 *Id.*

136 *Id.*

137 Fred Thompson, "Senate Trial of Clinton Is Over, and It's Time to Move On," Knoxville News-Sentinel, Feb. 15, 1999.

138 John M. Broder with Neil A. Lewis, "Clinton Is Found to Be in Contempt in Jones Lawsuit," N.Y. Times, Apr. 13, 1999, http://www.nytimes.com/1999/04/13/us/clinton-is-found-to-be-in-contempt-on-jones-lawsuit.html.

139 Roberto Suro and Joan Biskupic, "Judge Finds Clinton in Contempt of Court," Wash. Post, Apr. 13, 1999, https://www.washingtonpost.com/wp-srv/politics/special/clinton/stories/contempt041399.htm.

140 "Clinton Disbarred from Practice before Supreme Court," N.Y. Times, Oct. 1, 2001, http://www.nytimes.com/2001/10/01/national/clinton-disbarred-from-practice-before-supreme-court.html.

141 "George W. Bush," The White House (last visited Dec. 26, 2017), https://www.whitehouse.gov/about-the-white-house/presidents/george-w-bush/.

142 S.J. Res. 23, Sep. 14, 2001—Authorization for Use of Military Force.

143 David E. Sanger, "Bush to Formalize a Defense Policy of Hitting First," N.Y. Times, Jun. 17, 2002, http://www.nytimes.com/2002/06/17/world/bush-to-formalize-a-defense-policy-of-hitting-first.html.

144 David E. Sanger, "Threats and Responses: The President's Speech; Bush Sees 'Urgent Duty' to Pre-empt Attack by Iraq," N.Y. Times, Oct. 8, 2002, http://www.nytimes.com/2002/10/08/us/threats-responses-president-s-speech-bush-sees-urgent-duty-pre-empt-attack-iraq.html.

145 David C. Gombert, Hans Binnendijk, and Bonny Lin, "The Iraq War: Bush's Biggest Blunder," Newsweek, Dec. 25, 2014, http://www.newsweek.com/iraq-war-bushs-biggest-blunder-294411.

146 Elizabeth Holtzman, "The Impeachment of George W. Bush," The Nation, Jan. 11, 2006, https://www.thenation.com/article/impeachment-george-w-bush/.

147 Joseph Carroll, "Americans' Ratings of Dick Cheney Reach New Lows," Gallup News, Jul. 18, 2007, http://news.gallup.com/poll/28159/americans-ratings-dick-cheney-reach-new-lows.aspx.

148 Ilya Shapiro, "President Obama's Top 10 Constitutional Violations of 2013," Forbes (Opinion), Dec. 23, 2013, https://www.forbes.com/sites/realspin/2013/12/23/president-obamas-top-10-constitutional-violations-of-2013/#7dd7c4c57667.

149 "The Lie Used to Sell Obamacare to America #TBT" GOP.com, Mar. 16, 2017, https://www.gop.com/the-lie-used-to-sell-obamacare-to-america-tbt/.

150 Kate Martin, "Are US Drone Strikes Legal?" Cen. for Am. Progress, Apr. 1, 2016, https://www.americanprogress.org/issues/security/reports/2016/04/01/134494/are-u-s-drone-strikes-legal/.

151 Andrew C. McCarthy, "Explosive Revelation of Obama Administration Illegal Surveillance of Americans," Nat'l Rev. May 25, 2017, http://www.nationalreview.com/article/447973/nsa-illegal-surveillance-americans-obama-administration-abuse-fisa-court-response.

152 Micah Zenko, "Obama's Embrace of Drone Strikes Will Be a Lasting Legacy," N.Y. Times (Opinion), Jan. 12, 2016, https://www.nytimes.

com/roomfordebate/2016/01/12/reflecting-on-obamas-presidency/
obamas-embrace-of-drone-strikes-will-be-a-lasting-legacy.

153 Adam Liptak and Michael D. Shear, "Supreme Court Tie Blocks Obama
Immigration Plan," N.Y. TIMES, Jun. 23, 2016, https://www.nytimes.com/
2016/06/24/us/supreme-court-immigration-obama-dapa.html; Robert
Barnes, "Supreme Court Rebukes Obama On Recess Appointments," WASH.
POST, Jun. 26, 2014, https://www.washingtonpost.com/politics/supreme-
court-rebukes-obama-on-recess-appointments/2014/06/26/e5e4fefa-e831-
11e3-a86b-362fd5443d19_story.html?utm_term=.0be01c917cd4.

154 King v. Burwell, 135 S.Ct. 2480 (2015).

155 Jon Swaine, "Barack Obama 'Has Authority to Use Drone Strikes to Kill
Americans on US Soil," THE TELEGRAPH, Mar. 6, 2013, http://www.
telegraph.co.uk/news/worldnews/barackobama/9913615/Barack-Obama-
has-authority-to-use-drone-strikes-to-kill-Americans-on-US-soil.html.

156 "Presidential Approval Ratings—Barack Obama," GALLUP NEWS, http://
news.gallup.com/poll/116479/barack-obama-presidential-job-approval.
aspx.

Chapter 3

1 U.S. Constit. art. II, § 4.

2 Wharton, Francis, *State Trials of the United States*, 1849, at 251–52.

3 *Id.* at 316.

4 U.S. Constit. art. I, § 5, cl. 2.

5 "Blount Expulsion," UNITED STATES SENATE (last visited Jan. 3, 2018),
https://www.senate.gov/artandhistory/history/common/expulsion_
cases/Blount_expulsion.htm; "List of Individuals Impeached by the House
of Representatives," History, Art & Archives of the United States House
of Representatives (last visited Jan. 3, 2018), http://history.house.gov/
Institution/Impeachment/Impeachment-List/.

6 Senate Historical Office, "United States Senate Election, Expulsion and
Censure Cases" (last visited Jan. 3, 2018), https://www.senate.gov/
reference/reference_item/election_book.htm.

7 United States Senate, "Expulsion and Censure" (last visited Jan. 3, 2018),
https://www.senate.gov/artandhistory/history/common/briefing/
Expulsion_Censure.htm.

8 "Code of Official Conduct," Rules of the House of Representatives (last
visited Jan. 5, 2018), https://ethics.house.gov/publication/code-official-
conduct; "Senate Code of Official Conduct," US Senate Select Committee
on Ethics (last visited Jan. 5, 2018), https://www.ethics.senate.gov/public/
index.cfm/files/serve?File_id=EFA7BF74-4A50-46A5-BB6F-B8D26B9755BF.

9 Kevin Hopkins, "The Politics of Misconduct: Rethinking How We Regulate
Lawyer-Politicians," 57 RUTGERS L. REV. 839, 903 (2005); Josh Chafetz,
*Democracy's Privileged Few: Legislative Privilege and Democratic Norms in the
British and American Constitutions*, 280 n. 68 (Yale University Press, 2007).

10 U.S. Constit. art. II, § 2.

11 *Id.* at art. I, § 6.

12 *Id.* at art. II, § 2.

13 United States v. Mouat, 124 U.S. 303, 307 (1888); Free Enterprise Fund
v. Public Co. Accounting Oversight Board, 561 U.S. 477, 497–98 (2010).

14 Office of Legal Counsel, "Whether a Former President May Be Indicted and Tried for the Same Offenses for Which He was Impeached by the House and Acquitted by the Senate," 122, n. 34.

15 Raoul Berger, *Impeachment* (Harvard University Press, 1974).

16 *Id.* at 216–17.

17 *Id.* at 218.

18 Seth Barrett Tillman and Josh Blackman, "Yes, Trump Can Accept Gifts" N.Y. Times (Opinion), Jul. 13, 2017, https://www.nytimes.com/2017/07/13/opinion/trump-france-bastille-emoluments.html?_r=0.

19 Seth Barrett Tillman, *Citizens United and the Scope of Professor Teachout's Anti-Corruption Principle*, 107 Nw. U.L. Rev. Colloquy 1, 12 (2012).

20 *Id.*

21 1 Journal of the Senate of the United States of America 441 (Washington, Gales & Seaton 1820) (May 7, 1792 entry).

22 Seth Barrett Tillman, *Citizens United and the Scope of Professor Teachout's Anti-Corruption Principle*, 107 Nw. U.L. Rev. Colloquy 1, 16 (2012) ("Simply put, Hamilton's reply included all *appointed* officers *from each of the three branches* of the federal government, but no *elected* officials *from any branch*.").

23 *Id.* at n. 54.

24 *See,* e.g., Farrand's Records, V.2, 68.

25 U.S. Constit. art. I, § 9, cl. 8.

26 Farrand's Records, V.3, 327.

27 Jonathan Elliott, ed. *The Debates in the Several State Conventions on the Adoption of the Federal Constitution as Recommended by the General Convention at Philadelphia in 1787*, v. 3, 515.

28 *Id.*

29 Zephyr Teachout, "The Foreign Emoluments Clause," National Constitution Center (last visited Jan. 6, 2018) ("[W]hen the Emoluments Clause alone is considered in the broader context of the Constitution, it becomes evident the constitution contains within it a structural commitment to fighting corruption."), https://constitutioncenter.org/interactive-constitution/articles/article-i/the-foreign-emoluments-clause-by-zephyr-teachout/clause/34.

30 *Id.*

31 "President Jackson's Veto Message Regarding the Bank of the United States," Jul. 10, 1832, The Avalon Project (last visited Jan. 6, 2018), http://avalon.law.yale.edu/19th_century/ajveto01.asp.

32 Frank Bowman, *Foreign Emoluments, the President & Professor Tillman*, Impeachable Offenses (Oct. 27, 2017), https://impeachableoffenses.net/tag/gouverneur-morris/.

33 Farrand's Records, V.2, 68–69.

34 U.S. Constit. art. I, § 2, 3; art. III, § 1.

35 The Federalist, no. 78.

36 Declaration of Independence ("He has made Judges dependent on his Will along, for the Tenure of their Offices, and the Amount and Payment of their Salaries.").

37 Berger, at 150–53.

38 The Federalist, no. 79, at 532–33.

39 Nixon v. United States, 113 S.Ct. 732, 738 (1993) ("In our constitutional system, impeachment was designed to be the *only* check on the Judicial Branch by the Legislature."); Northern Pipeline Construction Co. v. Marathon Pipe Line Co. 458 U.S. 50, 59 ("The 'good behaviour' Clause guarantees that Art. III judges shall enjoy life tenure, subject only to removal by impeachment.").

40 28 U.S.C. § 351 (2002).

41 28 U.S.C. § 354(a)(2) (2002).

42 28 U.S.C. § 354(b)(2) (2002).

43 Benjamin F. Westhoff, "Judges Bound by the Law: A Case Study of the Unconstitutional Misapplication of the Judical Conduct and Disability Act of 1980 and a Proposal to Prevent Future Misapplications," 21 St. Louis U. Pub. L. Rev. 231 (2002); Lynn A. Baker, "Unnecessary and Improper: The Judicial Councils Reform and Judicial Conduct and Disability Act of 1980," 94 Yale. L.J. 1117 (1985).

44 "Impeachment," United States Senate (last visited Jan. 4, 2018), https://www.senate.gov/artandhistory/history/common/briefing/Senate_Impeachment_Role.htm.

45 "The Impeachment and Trial of John Pickering," *Precedents of the House of Representatives*, § 2319, p. 681.

46 Jonathan Turley, "Senate Trials and Factional Disputes: Impeachment as a Madisonian Device," 49 Duke L.J. 1, 58–60 (1999).

47 H. Res. 1030, 111th Cong., 2d Sess. 1 (2010).

48 *Id*. at 2.

49 Potentially a part of his answer to Art. II, Fourth Affirmative Defense?

50 *Id*. at 6–8.

51 *Id*. at 68.

52 H. Rep. 111–427, 111th Cong. 2d Sess. 14447 (2010); Cong. Rec. Dec. 8, 2010, s8611.

53 Niraj Chokshi, "Federal Judge Alex Kozinski Retires Abruptly after Sexual Harassment Allegations," N.Y. Times, Dec. 18, 2017, https://www.nytimes.com/2017/12/18/us/alex-kozinski-retires.html?_r=0; *see also* Matt Zapotesky, "Nine More Women Say Judge Subjected Them to Inappropriate Behavior, Including Four Who Say He Touched or Kissed Them," Wash. Post, Dec. 15, 2017, https://www.washingtonpost.com/world/national-security/nine-more-women-say-judge-subjected-them-to-inappropriate-behavior-including-four-who-say-he-touched-or-kissed-them/2017/12/15/8729b736-e105-11e7-8679-a9728984779c_story.html?utm_term=.6a015827f4df.

Chapter 4

1 "Articles of Impeachment Exhibited by the House of Representatives of the United States of America in the Name of Itself and of all of the People of the United States of America, Against Richard M. Nixon, President of the United States of America, in Maintenance and Supports of its Impeachment Against Him for High Crimes and Misdemeanors." The American Presidency Project (last visited Jan. 8, 2018), http://www.presidency.ucsb.edu/ws/?pid=76082.

2 Elliott's Debates, v.3, 240.

3 The Federalist, no. 65.

4 *Id.*

5 James Wilson, *Collected Works of James Wilson*, V.2, 862.

6 Bestor, "Impeachment," 263, quoting Story, *Commentaries*, § 788, 256.

7 Story, *Commentaries*, § 405, 28788 (citations omitted).

8 "Impeachment," UNITED STATES SENATE (last visited Jan. 7, 2018), https://www.senate.gov/artandhistory/history/common/briefing/Senate_Impeachment_Role.htm.

9 *See* Berger at 53–54; *see also* Bob Barr, "High Crimes and Misdemeanors: The Clinton-Gore Scandals and the Question of Impeachment," 2 TEX. REV. L & POL. 1, 10 (1997).

10 Michael J. Gerhardt, "Chancellor Kent and the Search for the Elements of Impeachable Offenses," 74 CHI. KENT L.R. 91, 108 (1998).

11 *Id.*

12 For an excellent discussion of this, *see* Hoffer and Hull, at 206–20.

13 Deschler's Precedents, Ch. 14 § 18, 2244 ("So the Senate convicted Judge Ritter on the seventh article of impeachment, charging general misbehavior and conduct that brought his count into scandal and disrepute.").

14 "List of Individuals Impeached by the House of Representatives," History, Art & Archives of the United States House of Representatives (last visited Jan. 7, 2018), http://history.house.gov/Institution/Impeachment/Impeachment-List/.

15 "Impeachment," UNITED STATES SENATE (last visited Jan. 7, 2018), https://www.senate.gov/artandhistory/history/common/briefing/Senate_Impeachment_Role.htm.

16 *Id.*

17 "Submission by Counsel for President Clinton to the Committee on the Judiciary of the United States House of Representatives," § 2, available at http://www.nytimes.com/library/politics/120998clinton-text-2.html.

18 "The Impeachment Trial of Harry E. Claiborne (1986)," UNITED STATES SENATE (last visited Jan. 8, 2018), https://www.senate.gov/artandhistory/history/common/briefing/Impeachment_Claiborne.htm; Neil A. Lewis, "Senate Convicts US Judge, Removing Him from Bench," N.Y. TIMES, Nov. 4, 1989.

19 "The Impeachment Trial of Harry E. Claiborne (1986)," UNITED STATES SENATE (last visited Jan. 8, 2018), https://www.senate.gov/artandhistory/history/common/briefing/Impeachment_Claiborne.htm; Neil A. Lewis, "Senate Convicts US Judge, Removing Him from Bench," N.Y. TIMES, Nov. 4, 1989.

20 Mike DeBonis, "IRS Commissioner Faces GOP Critics Seeking His Impeachment," WASH. POST, Sep. 21, 2016.

21 114th Cong. 2d sess. Serial No. 114–74, "Examining the Allegations of Misconduct Against IRS Commissioner John Koskinen" (Part I), 25.

22 *Id.* at 2, 51.

23 David S. Joachim, "Examining a Scandal within a Scandal about Emails at the I.R.S.," N.Y. TIMES (Q&A), Jun. 23, 2014, https://www.nytimes.com/2014/06/24/us/questions-and-answers-on-lois-lerners-lost-emails-in-irs-scandal.html?_r=0.

24 "Written Testimony of John A. Koskinen Commissioner Internal Revenue Service Before the House Oversight and Government Reform Committee on IRS Operations," Mar. 26, 2014, https://oversight.house.gov/wp-content/uploads/2014/03/Koskinen-Testimony.pdf.

25 David M. Herszenhorn and Jackie Calmes, "House to Consider I.R.S. Commissioner's Impeachment," N.Y. Times, May 23, 2016.

26 114th Cong. 2d sess. Serial No. 114–74, Examining the Allegations of Misconduct against IRS Commissioner John Koskinen (Part I), 9.

27 *Id.*

28 *Id.* at Part II, 46.

29 *Id.* at 89.

30 *Id.* at 89.

31 Joseph Isenberg, *The Scope of the Power to Impeach*, 84 Yale L.J. 1316 (1975).

32 Joseph Isenberg, *Impeachment and Presidential Immunity from Judicial Process*, 18 Yale L. Policy Review 53 (1999).

33 *Id.* at 63.

34 U.S. Constit. art. II, § 4.

35 Isenberg, at 75.

36 McCulloch v. Maryland, 17 U.S. 316, 353 (1819).

Chapter 5

1 Hoffer and Hull, at 206–20.

2 George Lardner Jr., "White House Strategy: It's Bad, but It's Not Watergate," Wash. Post, Dec. 9, 1998.

3 The Starr Report, 129–204.

4 Grimes, *Research Papers*, 50; Gerhardt, *The Federal Impeachment Process*, at 176.

5 Richard K. Neumann Jr., "The Revival of Impeachment as a Partisan Political Weapon," 34 Hastings Const. L.Q. 161, 251 (2007).

6 U.S. Constit. art. I, § 2, cl. 7.

7 "Impeachment," History, Art & Archives of the United States House of Representatives (last visited Jan. 12, 2018), http://history.house.gov/Institution/Origins-Development/Impeachment/.

8 *Id.*

9 U.S. Constit. art. 1, § 5.

10 William Rehnquist, *Grand Inquests*, 215–17.

11 Gerhardt, *The Federal Impeachment Process*, at 177.

12 *Id.* at 176.

13 Michael Gerhardt, "The Historical and Constitutional Significance of the Impeachment and Trial of President Clinton," 28 Hofstra L. Rev. 349, 370 (1999).

14 U.S. Constit. art. I, § 5, cl. 2.

15 "The Impeachment of Andrew Johnson (1868)," United States Senate (last visited Jan. 12, 2018), https://www.senate.gov/artandhistory/history/common/briefing/Impeachment_Johnson.htm.

16 *Id.*

17 Gerhardt, *The Federal Impeachment Process*, 48.

18 "Rules of Procedure and Practice in the Senate When Sitting on Impeachment Trials," United States Senate, Rule XI.

19 *Id.* Rule VI.

20 Susan Navarro Smelcer, Cong. Research Service, *The Role of the Senate in Judicial Impeachment Proceedings: Procedure, Practice, and Data* 10 (2010).

21 Gerhardt, *The Federal Impeachment Process*, 43–46.

22 *Id.*

23 Nixon v. United States, 506 U.S. 224, 226 (1993).

24 Stewart, "Commentary," 54.

25 David O. Stewart, "Impeachment by Ignorance," 76 ABA J. 52 (1990).

26 *Id.*

27 Joan Biskupic, "Familiar Words—Nixon, Impeach—But Unusual Test of Power," Wash. Post, Oct. 11, 1992.

28 Nixon v. United States, 506 U.S. 224 (1993).

29 Nixon v. United States, 506 U.S. 224, 238 (1993).

30 William Rehnquist, *Grand Inquests: The Historic Impeachments of Justice Samuel Chase and President Andrew Johnson* (1992).

31 Nixon v. United States, 506 U.S. 224, 229–32 (1993).

32 Nixon v. United States, 506 U.S. 224, 233 (1993).

33 U.S. Const. art. I, § 3, cl. 6.

34 *Id.*

35 *Id.* at art. I, § 3, cl. 7.

36 *Id.* at art. I, § 3, cl. 6.

37 *Id.* at art. I, § 5, cl. 2. *But see* United States v. Ballin, 144 U.S. 1, 5 (1892), observing that "each house . . . may not by its rules ignore constitutional restraints or violate fundamental rights, and there should be a reasonable relation between the mode or method of proceeding established by the rule and the result which is sought to be attained. But within these limitations all matters of method are open to the determination of the house, and it is no impeachment of the rule to say that some other way would be better, more accurate or even more just. . . . [This rulemaking power is] within the limitations suggested, absolute and beyond the challenge of any other body or tribunal."

38 Jefferson, *Jefferson's Manual of Parliamentary Practice*, noting that the Senate's impeachment rules are in part derived from English parliamentary practice and the latter including using evidentiary committees in conducting impeachment trials and noting further that "the [English] practice is to swear the witnesses in open House, and then examine them there; or a committee may be named, who shall examine them in committee, either on interrogatories agreed on in the House, or such as the committee in their discretion shall demand."

39 *See*, e.g., Hamilton, The Federalist, no. 65, 440, 442.

40 Prior to the constitutional convention, the states had sometimes used legislative committees to investigate whether to draw up articles of impeachment. *See* Hoffer and Hull, *Impeachment in America*, 29, 33. In addition, in colonial governments and state legislatures, the subjects of impeachment proceedings often appeared before committees to answer the charges against them. *See* Walter Nixon v. United States, 113 S.Ct. 732, 746 (1993) (Justice White concurring).

41 *See* generally Williams, "Historical and Constitutional Bases," 512, 523–32, reviewing English precedent relating to impeachment in detail and

concluding that it "shows beyond doubt that the House of Lords used committees to hear evidence during impeachment trials in the early 17th century. . . . It is clear . . . that, unlike other practices which were outlawed by affirmative action of the House of Lords, the use of committees to take evidence and examine witnesses has never been banned or disavowed as precedent—as were other impeachment procedures considered to have been wrongly invoked" (footnotes omitted).

42 *Id.* at 520, 537–39, 543–44. *See also* Nixon v. United States, F.2d 239, 259–65 (D.C. Cir. 1993; Justice Edwards dissenting in part and concurring in judgment).

43 Wright, *The Law of Federal Courts,* § 109, 771.

44 Ex parte Peterson, 253 U.S. 300, 312 (1920). *See also id.,* recognizing this authority as part of a federal court's "inherent power." The power of federal courts to appoint special masters is now embodied in Rule 53 of the Federal Rules of Civil Procedure. That rule permits the master broad powers in receiving evidence and taking testimony for use by the court. *Id,* 53 (c).

45 U.S. Const. art. I, § 5.

46 Barry v. United States ex rel. Cunningham, 279 U.S. 597, 616 (1929).

47 Nixon, 113 S.Ct. 736.

48 *Id.*

49 369 U.S. 186, 217 (1962).

50 *Id.* at 736.

51 U.S. Const. art. I, § 3, cl. 6.

52 Nixon, 113 S.Ct., 739.

53 395 U.S. 486 (1969).

54 U.S. Const. art. I, § 5.

55 Nixon, 113 S.Ct., 739–40.

56 *Id.* at 740 (emphasis in original).

57 *Id.*

58 *Id.* at 741 (Justice White concurring in the judgment).

59 *Id.* at 743.

60 *Id.* at 744.

61 *Id.* at 748 (Justice Souter concurring in the judgment).

62 U.S. Constit. art. I, § 3, cl. 9.

63 Richard W. Stevenson, "The President's Acquittal: The Chief Justice; Rehnquist Goes with the Senate Flow, 'Wiser but Not a Sadder Man'," N.Y. Times, Feb. 13, 1999, http://www.nytimes.com/1999/02/13/us/president-s-acquittal-chief-justice-rehnquist-goes-with-senate-flow-wiser-but.html.

64 Akhil Reed Amar, "An(other) Afterword on the Bill of Rights," 87 Geo. L.J. 2347, 2358 (1999).

65 U.S. Constit. art. I, § 5, cl. 2.

66 James Wilson, *The Works of James Wilson, Associate Justice of the Supreme Court, v. 1,* 425–26.

67 *Id.* at 408.

68 Charles Black, *Impeachment: A Handbook* 17 (1974).

69 *Id.* at 18.

70 U.S. Constit. amend. V.

71 U.S. Constit. art. I, § 3, cl. 9.

72 *See*, e.g., Imbler v. Pachtman, 424 U.S. 409, 429 (1976) ("[J]udges [are] cloaked with absolute civil immunity.").

73 Neil A. Lewis, "Senate Convicts U.S. Judge, Removing Him from Bench," N.Y. TIMES, Nov. 4, 1989; "The Impeachment Trial of Harry E. Claiborne," UNITED STATES SENATE, https://www.senate.gov/artandhistory/history/common/briefing/Impeachment_Claiborne.htm.

74 U.S. Constit. art. III, § 1, cl. 2.

75 Ch. 9, § 21, 1 Stat. 117 (April 30, 1790).

76 The Supreme Court has recognized that the actions of the First Congress illuminate the original understanding of the Constitution because twenty of its members had also been delegates at the constitutional convention. *See, e.g.*, Bowsher v. Synar, 478 U.S. 714, 724n.3 (1986); Marsh v. Chambers, 463 U.S. 783, 790–91 (1983); J.W. Hampton, Jr. and Co. v. United States, 276 U.S. 394, 411–12 (1928); McCulloch v. Maryland, 17 U.S. (4 Wheat.) 316, 424 (1819).

77 Burbank, "Alternative Career Resolution," 643, 668–69.

78 *See* United States v. Isaacs, 493 F.2d 1124 (7th Cir.), *cert. denied*, 417 U.S. 976 (1974); United States v. Claiborne, 727 F.2d 842 (9th Cir.), *cert. denied*, 469 U.S. 829 (1984).

79 *See* Claiborne at 845–46.

80 493 F.2d 1124 (7th Cir.), *cert. denied*, 417 U.S. 976 (1974).

81 *Id.* at 1142.

82 *Id.* at 1144.

83 765 F.2d 784 (9th Cir. 1985), *appeal denied*, 781 F.2d 1327 (9th Cir.), *stay of execution denied*, 790 F.2d 1355 (9th Cir. 1986).

84 United States v. Claiborne, 727 F.2d 842, 846 (9th Cir.), *cert. denied*, 469 U.S. 829 (1984).

85 Claiborne, 727 F.2d, 845–46.

86 *Id.* at 845–46.

87 *See* generally Baker, *Conflicting Loyalties*.

88 *See*, e.g., United States v. Claiborne, 727 F.2d 842, 847–48 (9th Cir.), *cert. denied*, 469 U.S. 829 (1984); United States v. Hastings, 681 F.2d 706, 710–11 (11th Cir. 1982), *cert. denied*, 459 U.S. 1203 (1983).

89 *See* generally Peterson, "The Role of the Executive Branch in the Discipline and Removal of Judges," 243, 277–318.

90 Claiborne, 727 F.2d, 846.

91 Claiborne, 790 F.2d, 1360 (Justice Kozinski dissenting).

92 Catz, "Removal of Federal Judges by Imprisonment," 103, 109.

93 *Claiborne*, 727 F.2d, 846–47.

94 *Id.* at 846.

95 *See*, e.g., Maxman, Note, "In Defense of the Constitution's Judicial Impeachment Standard," 420, 457.

96 U.S. Const. art. I, § 6, cl. 1, provides in pertinent part that "The Senators and Representatives shall . . . in all cases, except treason, felony, and breach of peace, be privileged from arrest during their attendance at the session of their respective Houses, and in going to and returning from the same; and for any speech or debate in either House they shall not be questioned in any other place."

97　United States v. Lee, 106 U.S. 196, 220 (1882), holding that "[a]ll officers of the government, from the highest to the lowest, are creatures of the law, and are bound to obey it"; Claiborne, 727 F.2d, 847, holding that "Article III protections, though deserving utmost fidelity, should not be expanded to insulate federal judges from punishment for their criminal wrongdoing."

98　Claiborne, 765 F.2d, 788.

99　Burbank, "Alternative Career Resolution," 671. *See also id*. at 671–72n.130 (citing authorities).

100　*Id*. at 671–72.

101　487 U.S. 654 (1988).

102　U.S. Code, vol. 28, §§ 591–98 (1988).

103　Brief of the United States as Amicus Curiae Supporting Appellees 47, quoted in Koukoutchos, "Constitutional Kinetics," 635, 710.

104　Morrison, 487 U.S., 714 (Justice Scalia dissenting).

105　The Judiciary Committee of the House or Senate, a majority of the majority party members of either House, or a majority of all party members of either such committee, may request, but not require, in writing that the attorney general apply for the appointment of an independent counsel. *See* U.S. Code, vol. 28, § 592 (g) (Supp. V 1987).

106　*Id*. at § 592 (b)(1).

107　Koukoutchos, "Constitutional Kinetics," 711 and nn.430–31 (noting prosecutions of two former attorneys general, federal judges, and the ABSCAM prosecutions of legislators); *see also* Logan, "Historical Uses of a Special Prosecution," discussing the St. Louis Whiskey Ring and Teapot Dome prosecutions and the scandal-induced prosecutions of various officers of the Reconstruction Finance Cooperation and the Internal Revenue Bureau.

108　Nixon v. Fitzgerald, 102 S.Ct. 2690, 2701 (1982).

109　*Id*. at 2701–04.

110　*Id*. at 2705.

111　Clinton v. Jones, 520 U.S. 681, 705–06.

112　*Id*.

113　Nixon v. Fitzgerald, 457 U.S. 731 (1982); U.S. v. Nixon, 418 U.S. 683 (1974).

114　"Watergate and the Constitution," National Archives, https://www.archives.gov/education/lessons/watergate-constitution.

115　Gerhardt, *The Federal Impeachment Process*, at 43; "The Impeachment Trial 1of Harry E. Claiborne (1986)," United States Senate (last visited Jan. 8, 2018), https://www.senate.gov/artandhistory/history/common/briefing/Impeachment_Claiborne.htm.

116　U.S. v. Nixon, 418 U.S. 683, 713 (1974).

117　*Id*. at 709–713.

118　"Articles of Impeachment Exhibited by the House of Representatives of the United States of America in the Name of Itself and of all of the People of the United States of America, Against Richard M. Nixon, President of the United States of America, in Maintenance and Supports of Its Impeachment Against Him for High Crimes and Misdemeanours." The American Presidency Project (last visited Jan. 8, 2018), http://www.presidency.ucsb.edu/ws/?pid=76082:

"In his conduct of the office of President of the United States, Richard M. Nixon, contrary to his oath faithfully to execute the office of President of the United States and, to the best of his ability, preserve, protect, and defend the Constitution of the United States, and in violation of his constitutional duty to take care that the laws be faithfully executed, has failed without lawful cause or excuse to produce papers and things as directed by duly authorized subpoenas issued by the Committee on the Judiciary of the House of Representatives on April 11, 1974, May 15, 1974, May 30, 1974, and June 24, 1974, and willfully disobeyed such subpoenas. The subpoenaed papers and things were deemed necessary by the Committee in order to resolve by direct evidence fundamental, factual questions relating to Presidential direction, knowledge or approval of actions demonstrated by other evidence to be substantial grounds for impeachment of the President. In refusing to produce these papers and things Richard M. Nixon, substituting his judgment as to what materials were necessary for the inquiry, interposed the powers of the Presidency against the lawful subpoenas of the House of Representatives, thereby assuming to himself functions and judgments necessary to the exercise of the sole power of impeachment vested by the Constitution in the House of Representatives."

119 *See* generally Congressional Research Service Reports & Analysis, "The Fifth Amendment in Congressional Investigations," May 26, 2017.

120 U.S. Constit. art. II, § 2, cl. 1.

Chapter 6

1 U.S. Constit. art. I, § 3, cl. 10.

2 "Role of the Senate in Judicial Impeachment Proceedings: Procedure, Practice, and Data," EVERYCRSREPORT.COM, Mar. 21, 2011, https://www.everycrsreport.com/reports/R41172.html#fn111.

3 *Id.*

4 *Id.*

5 Deschler's Precedents of the United States House of Representatives ch. 14 § 13.9.

6 U.S. Const. art. II, § 4.

7 *See*, e.g., Maria Simon, "Bribery and Other Not so 'Good Behavior': Criminal Prosecution as a Supplement to Impeachment of Federal Judges," 94 COLUMBIA L. REV. 1617, 1622 (1994).

8 Michael Gerhardt, "The Lessons of Impeachment History," THE GEORGE WASHINGTON L. REV. 603, 614 (1999); Precedents of the House of Representatives, "The Impeachment and Trial of West H. Humphreys," § 2387, 818; Jennifer Steinhauer, "Senate, for Just the 8th Time, Votes to Oust a Federal Judge," N.Y. TIMES, Dec. 8, 2010.

9 Michael Gerhardt and Michael Ashley Stein, "The Politics of Early Justice: Federal Judicial Selection, 1789–1861," 100 IOWA L. REV. 551, 600 (2015).

10 Precedents of the House of Representatives, "The Impeachment and Trial of West H. Humphreys," § 2387, 811.

11 *Id.* at 807.

12 *Id.* at 811.

13 Patrick J. McGinnis, "A Case of Judicial Misconduct: The Impeachment and Trial of Robert W. Archibald," 101 The Penn. Mag. of His. and Biography 506, 506 (1977).

14 *Id.* at 506–09.

15 *Id.* at 515.

16 *Id.* at 518–19.

17 H. Rept. 111–427, 111th Cong. (2010); Jennifer Steinhauer, "Senate, for Just the 8th Time, Votes to Oust a Federal Judge," N.Y. Times, Dec. 8, 2010.

18 Jennifer Steinhauer, "Senate, for Just the 8th Time, Votes to Oust a Federal Judge," N.Y. Times, Dec. 8, 2010.

19 *Id.*

20 In Judge Porteous's case, the vote was 94–2 in favor of disqualification.

21 "The Impeachment of Alcee Hastings," United States Senate (last visited Jan. 17, 2018), https://www.senate.gov/artandhistory/history/common/briefing/Impeachment_Hastings.htm.

22 *Id.*

23 *Id.*

24 *Id.*

25 *Id.*

26 *Id.*

27 *Id.*

28 *Id.*

29 *Id.*

30 *Id.*

31 *Id.*; "U.S. Congressman Alcee L. Hastings" (last visited Jan. 17, 2018), https://alceehastings.house.gov/biography/.

32 Articles of Impeachment against William Jefferson Clinton, H. Res. 105th Cong. (1998); Impeachment of Judge Samuel B. Kent, H. Rept. 111–59, 111th Cong. 2009.

33 Jennifer Steinhauer, "Senate, for Just the 8th Time, Votes to Oust a Federal Judge," N.Y. Times, Dec. 8, 2010.

34 "Senate Censures President," United States Senate (last visited Jan. 18, 2018), https://www.senate.gov/artandhistory/history/minute/Senate_Censures_President.htm.

35 *Id.*

36 Censure of the President by the Congress (Cong. Res. Serv. Dec. 8, 1998).

37 U.S. Constit. art. I, § 5, cl. 3.

38 *See,* e.g., ABC, *Good Morning America* (7:00 am ET), Dec. 22, 1998, transcript # 98122201-joi.

39 Tom Kuntz, "The Nation; Jackson: Censure Made No Sense," N.Y. Times, Dec. 13, 1998.

40 *Erwin Chemerinsky, Constitutional Law, Principles, and Policies,* Section 6.2.2 (Rev. Ed. 1999); Thomas B. Griffith, Note, *Beyond Process: A Substantive Rationale for the Bill of Attainder Clause,* 70 Va. L. Rev. 475, 476 (1984).

41 *See* Letter from Representative William D. Delahunt and Frederick C. Boucher to Members of the U.S. House of Representatives (Dec. 15, 1998) (indicating that 14 of 19 scholars testifying before the House regarded censure as constitutional).

42 "The Impeachment and Trial of John Pickering," Precedents of the House of Representatives, 709–10; Canon's Precedents, "The Impeachment and Trial of Robert W. Archbald," 1438; "The Impeachment and Trial of West H. Humphreys," Precedents of the House of Representatives, 818–20.

43 "The Impeachment and Trial of John Pickering," Precedents of the House of Representatives, 709.

44 "The Impeachment and Trial of West H. Humphreys," Precedents of the House of Representatives, 818–20.

45 Canon's Precedents, "The Impeachment and Trial of Robert W. Archbald," 1438.

46 Act of April 30, 1790, ch. 9, § 21, Stat. 1:112 (1845).

47 Bowsher v. Synar, 478 U.S. 714, 724n.3 (1986) (listing twenty members of the First Congress who were also delegates at the constitutional convention).

48 Ervin, "Separation of Powers," 108, 118 and n.43.

49 For a fuller discussion of the nature of the different viewpoints on the constitutionality of the Bribery Act of 1790, *see* Shane, "Who May Discipline or Remove Federal Judges?" 209, 228–29.

50 The necessary and proper clause provides that the Congress shall have the power "to make all laws which shall be necessary and proper for carrying into execution the foregoing powers, and all other powers vested by this Constitution in the Government of the United States, or any department or officer thereof," U.S. Const. art. I, § 8 (18).

51 *See,* e.g., U.S. Const. art. III, § 2, cl. 3.

52 For such protections, *see,* for example, 90, 105.

53 Constitutional Rountable Discussion before the National Commission on Judicial Discipline and Removal (December 18, 1992), Remarks of Professor Walter Dellinger, reprinted in *Hearings* 354–55.

54 Hamilton, The Federalist, no. 65, 427–28.

55 "Role of the Senate in Judicial Impeachment Proceedings: Procedure, Practice, and Data," EVERYCRSREPORT.COM, Mar. 21, 2011, https://www.everycrsreport.com/reports/R41172.html.

56 1st Cong., sess. II, ch. 9, 117.

57 U.S. Constit. amend. V.

Chapter 7

1 Kansas Constit. art. II, §§ 27–28.

2 Alaska Constit. art. II, § 20; art. IV, § 12.

3 *Id.* Commentary.

4 Calif. Constit. art. IV, § 18.

5 Arizona Constit. art VIII, part 2; Conn. Constit. art. IX; Mass. Constit. art. IV.

6 Mass. Constit. art. IV.

7 *Id.* art. VIII.

8 N.C. Constit. art. IV, § 4.

9 *Id.*

10 New York Constit. art. VI, § 24.

11 *Id.*

12 *Id.*

13 Arkansas Constit. art. XV, § 1.

14 Colorado Constit. art. XIII, § 2.

15 Calif. Constit. art. IV, § 18(b).

16 Conn. Constit. art. IX, § 4.

17 Florida Constit. § 17(a).

18 Mass. Constit. art. VIII.

19 N.Y. Constit. art. XIII, § 5.

20 N.C. Constit. § 17(1).

21 Ohio Constit. art. II, § 38.

22 Rhode Island Constit. art. I, § 3.

23 N.C. Constit. art. IV, § 17(2).

24 *Id.* at art. VI, § 8.

25 U.S. Constit. amend. I.

26 *See* Joseph Rogers Thysell, "The Impeachment and Removal of Governor Evan Mecham: A Case Study of Constitutional Crisis," Dissertation, 86.

27 "Arizona House Votes 46–14 to Impeach Mecham: Governor Must Step Down from Office Pending a Trial by the State Senate," L.A. TIMES, Feb. 7, 1988.

28 Thysell, at 11420.

29 *Id.* at 141–43, 153.

30 *Id.* at 125–29.

31 "Arizona House Votes 46–14 to Impeach Mecham: Governor Must Step Down from Office Pending a Trial by the State Senate," L.A. TIMES, Feb. 7, 1988.

32 "1988: Gov. Evan Mecham Impeached," TUCSON.COM, Feb. 8, 2016, http://tucson.com/gov-evan-mecham-impeached/article_c7c7d61a-ceab-11e5-9cb4-e36cafcf4cfc.html.

33 Thysell, at 220.

34 *Id.* at 230.

35 *Id.* at 122.

36 "Rob Blagojevich," CHIC. TRIBUNE, http://www.chicagotribune.com/topic/politics-government/government/rod-blagojevich-PEPLT007479-topic.html.

37 Ray Long and Rick Pearson, "Impeached Illinois Gov. Rod Blagojevich Has Been Removed from Office," CHIC. TRIBUNE, Jan. 30, 2009.

38 Susan Saulny, "Illinois House Impeaches Governor," N.Y. TIMES, Jan. 9, 2009.

39 *Id.*

40 Ray Long and Rick Pearson, "Impeached Illinois Gov. Rod Blagojevich Has Been Removed from Office," CHIC. TRIBUNE, Jan. 30, 2009.

41 Michael deCourcy Hinds, "Convicted Pennsylvania Justice Is Facing Impeachment," N.Y. TIMES, May 13, 1994.

42 Bill Moushey, "Larsen Aims His Defense at Accusers," PITTSBURGH POST-GAZETTE, Aug. 9, 1994.

43 Larsen v. Senate of Com. of Pa, 154 F.3d 82, 85 (1998).

44 Michael deCourcy Hinds, "Convicted Pennsylvania Justice Is Facing Impeachment," N.Y. TIMES, May 13, 1994.

45 *Id.*

46 *Id.*

47   Charles Gardner Geyh, "Highlighting a Low Point on a High Court: Some Thoughts on the Removal of Pennsylvania Supreme Court Justice Rolf Larsen and the Limits of Judicial Self-Regulation," 68 TEMP. L. REV. 1041, 1049 (1995).

48   Michael deCourcy Hinds, "Convicted Pennsylvania Justice Is Facing Impeachment," N.Y. TIMES, May 25, 1994.

49   Jennifer Latson, "The Strange Careeer of Assassinated Louisiana Politician Huey Long," TIME, Sep. 8, 2015.

50   Gerard N. Magliocca, "Huey P. Long and the Guarantee Clause," 83 TUL. L. REV, 1, 9 (2008).

51   *Id.* at 10.

52   *See* Freeman Klopott, "CRIME HISTORY: Lawmakers in Louisiana Impeach Gov. Huey Long," THE EXAMINER, Apr. 6, 2010, https://search-proquest-com.libproxy.lib.unc.edu/docview/442959193/BCEA50745CBC438CPQ/2?accountid=14244.

53   Ben Phelan, "Huey Long's Life and Legacy," ANTIQUES ROADSHOW, Feb. 24, 2014, http://www.pbs.org/wgbh/roadshow/fts/batonrouge_201306A24.html.

54   Magliocca at 35–36.

55   Norma Love, "N.H. Senate Clears Way for Justice's Impeachment," COLUMBIAN, Aug. 23, 2000.

56   Pamela Ferdin, "N.H. Chief Justice Faces Impeachment," WASH. POST, Jul. 6, 2000.

57   *Id.*

58   Carey Goldberg, "Clerk Challenges System, and Finds That It Works," N.Y. TIMES, Oct. 15, 2000.

59   Michele DeMary, "Legislative-Judicial Relations on Contested Issues: Taxes and Same-Sex Marriage," 89 JUDICATURE 202, 205 (2006).

60   *Id.*

61   Norma Love, "N.H. Judge Acquitted at Impeachment Trial," ABC NEWS, Oct. 10.

62   *Id.*

63   Hoffer and Hull at 87.

64   *Id.* at 87–89.

65   *Id.* at 89.

66   *Id.* at 89–90.

67   *Id.* at 91.

68   *Id.*

69   William L. Burnell, "Judicial Impeachment," 1 WESTERN STATE L. REV, 1, 10 (1972).

70   *Id.* at 10–12.

71   Jeffrey Frank, "Ike, Ford, and a Lost Voice in Supreme Court Nominations," THE NEW YORKER, Feb. 16, 2016.

72   William Arthur Wines, "Observations on Leadership: Moral and Otherwise," 43 J. MARSHALL L. REV. 159, 191 (2009).

73   *See* generally U.S. House Special Subcommittee on H.R. Res. 920 of the House Committee on the Judiciary, *Final Report on Associate Justice William O. Douglas*, 91st Cong., 2d sess., 1970.

74 Jess Bidgood, Richard Fausset, and Campbell Robertson, "For Roy Moore, a Long History of Combat and Controversy," N.Y. TIMES, Nov. 18, 2017.

75 *Id.*

76 Leada Gore, "Who Is Roy Moore? Former Alabama Chief Justice, '10 Commandements Judge,' Wins GOP Senate Runoff," AL.COM, Sep. 26, 2017.

77 Kent Faulk, "Roy Moore Timeline: Ten Commandments to Gay Marriage Stance," AL.COM, May 7, 2016, http://www.al.com/news/birmingham/ index.ssf/2016/05/roy_moore_timeline_ten_command.html.

78 Leada Gore, "Who Is Roy Moore? Former Alabama Chief Justice, '10 Commandements Judge,' Wins GOP Senate Runoff," AL.COM, Sep. 26, 2017.

79 In re Roy S. Moore, Court of the Judiciary Case No. 33, 4 (2003), available at https://www.splcenter.org/sites/default/files/d6_legacy_files/ glassrothvmoore_cojjudgment.pdf.

80 *Id.*

81 Kent Faulk, "Roy Moore Timeline: Ten Commandments to Gay Marriage Stance," AL.COM, May 7, 2016, http://www.al.com/news/birmingham/ index.ssf/2016/05/roy_moore_timeline_ten_command.html.

82 In re Roy S. Moore, Court of the Judiciary Case No. 33, 4 (2003), available at https://www.splcenter.org/sites/default/files/d6_legacy_files/ glassrothvmoore_cojjudgment.pdf.

83 *Id.* at 4–6.

84 "Ten Commandments Judge Removed from Office," CNN.COM, Nov. 14, 2003, http://www.cnn.com/2003/LAW/11/13/moore.tencommandments/ index.html.

85 *Id.*

86 Eric Velasco, "The Gospel According to Roy," POLITICO, Feb. 11, 2015, https://www.politico.com/magazine/story/2015/02/ roy-moore-alabama-gay-marriage-115128.

87 Kim Chandler, "Roy Moore Wins Chief Justice Race," AL.COM, Nov. 7, 2017, http://blog.al.com/spotnews/2012/11/roy_moore_bob_vance_chief_just. html.

88 Obergefell v. Hodges, 135 S.Ct. 2584 (2015).

89 Kent Faulk, "Alabama Supreme Court Dismisses Petitions Opposing Gay Marriage," AL.COM, Mar. 4, 2016, http://www.al.com/news/birmingham/ index.ssf/2016/03/alabama_supreme_court_dismisse.html.

90 "Judicial Ethics Complaint: Alabama Chief Justice Roy Moore and Same-Sex Marriage," SOUTHERN POVERTY LAW CENTER, Jan. 28, 2015, https://www.splcenter.org/seeking-justice/case-docket/ judicial-ethics-complaint-alabama-chief-justice-roy-moore-and-same-sex.

91 Kent Faulk, "Roy Moore Timeline: Ten Commandments to Gay Marriage Stance," AL.COM, May 7, 2016, http://www.al.com/news/birmingham/ index.ssf/2016/05/roy_moore_timeline_ten_command.html.

92 Memorandum by Roy S. Moore, *Re: Sanctity of Marriage ruling* (Feb. 3, 2015), http://media.al.com/news_impact/other/Chief%20Justice%20Moore's%20 memorandum.pdf [https://perma.cc/P7V4-F5D6] (invoking separation of

powers and federalism as reasons why the injunction did not apply to the probate judges).

93 Kent Faulk, "Roy Moore Timeline: Ten Commandments to Gay Marriage Stance," AL.com, May 7, 2016, http://www.al.com/news/birmingham/index.ssf/2016/05/roy_moore_timeline_ten_command.html.

94 Kyle Whitmire, "Roy Moore Suspended from Office: Alabama Chief Justice Faces Removal over Gay Marriage Stance," AL.com, May 6, 2016, http://www.al.com/news/index.ssf/2016/05/alabama_chief_justice_roy_moor_10.html.

95 *See* Kim Chandler and Jay Reeves, "Panels Sends Alabama Chief Justice's Ethics Case to Trial," Associated Press, Aug. 9, 2016, https://apnews.com/d2c2249d71e44d8fbfe95da0d8538e47.

96 Bill Chappell, "Ala. Chief Justice Roy Moore Suspended for Rest of Term over Gay Marriage Stance," NPR, Sep. 30, 2016, https://www.npr.org/sections/thetwo-way/2016/09/30/496089488/alabamas-chief-justice-roy-moore-loses-case-over-same-sex-marriage-stance.

97 Kent Faulk, "Roy Moore's Suspension Upheld by Alabama Supreme Court; Decision Next Week on Senate Race," AL.com, Apr. 20, 2017, http://www.al.com/news/birmingham/index.ssf/2017/04/suspended_alabama_supreme_cour.html.

98 *Id.*

99 Mike Cason, "Roy Moore Running for Senate, Resigns from Supreme Court to Challenge Luther Strange," AL.com, Apr. 26, 2017.

100 Stephanie McCrummen, Beth Reinhard and Alice Crites, "Woman Says Roy Moore Initiated Sexual Encounter When She Was 14, He Was 32," Wash. Post, Nov. 9, 2017; Chris Francescani, "Roy Moore Accuser: I Got Him Banned from the Mall," ABC News, Nov. 16, 2017.

101 Kim Chandler and Steve Peoples, "Democrat Doug Jones Wins Alabama Senate Race in Stunning Upset over Roy Moore," Chic. Tribune, Dec. 12, 2017.

102 Mike Cason, "Ethics Commission Finds Probable Cause against Gov. Robert Bentley," AL.com, Apr. 6, 2017, http://www.al.com/news/birmingham/index.ssf/2017/04/ethics_commission_finds_probab.html.

103 "Article VII Impeachments," Alabama Constit., http://ali.state.al.us/documents/CodeSectionsOnImpeachmentArticleVII.pdf.

104 Mike Cason, "Ethics Commission Finds Probable Cause Against Gov. Robert Bentley," AL.com, Apr. 6, 2017, http://www.al.com/news/birmingham/index.ssf/2017/04/ethics_commission_finds_probab.html.

105 *Id.*

106 "The Impeachment Investigation of Governor Robert Bentley," Pre-hearing Submission of Special Counsel, Apr. 7, 2017.

107 Kerry Sanders and Corky Siemaszko, "Alabama 'Love Gov' Robert Bentley Resigns to Avoid Impeachment," NBC News, Apr. 10, 2017.

108 Jess Bidgood, "Pennsylvania's Attorney General Is Convicted on All Counts," N.Y. Times, Aug. 15, 2016; Marc Levy, "Kane Resigns a Day After Conviction," Philadelphia Tribune, Aug. 16, 2016.

109 Angela Couloumbis and Craig R. McCoy, "Kane Shut Down Sting that Snared Phila. Officials," The Inquirer, Mar. 16, 2014, http://www.philly.

com/philly/news/20140316_Kane_shut_down_sting_that_snared_Phila__
officials.html.

110 Jess Bidgood, "Pennsylvania's Attorney General Is Convicted on All
Counts," N.Y. Times, Aug. 15, 2016; Marc Levy, "Kane Resigns a Day after
Conviction," Philadelphia Tribune, Aug. 16, 2016.

111 Jess Bidgood, "Pennsylvania's Attorney General Is Convicted on All
Counts," N.Y. Times, Aug. 15, 2016.

112 Id.

113 "Deputy Defends Promotion of Kathleen Kane's Sister," NBC
Philadelphia, Sep. 17, 2013, https://www.nbcphiladelphia.com/news/
local/Deputy-Defends-Promotion-of-Kathleen-Kanes-Sister-224168951.
html.

114 Jess Bidgood, "Pennsylvania's Attorney General Is Convicted on All
Counts," N.Y. Times, Aug. 15, 2016.

115 Angela Couloumbis and Craig R. McCoy, "Kane Shut Down Sting that
Snared Phila. Officials," Philadelphia Inquirer, Mar. 16, 2014.

116 Id.

117 Wallace McKelvey, "A Glimpse inside the Bribery Sting Case, and Kathleen
Kane's Claim It Was Tainted by Racism," Penn Live, Dec. 16, 2015, http://
www.pennlive.com/news/2015/12/kathleen_kane_legislative_inve.html.

118 In re The Thirty-Five Statewide Investigating Grand Jury, quo warranto
action, available at http://www.pacourts.us/assets/files/setting-4093/file-
4248.pdf?cb=069632.

119 Michael Wines and Jess Bidgood, "Pennsylvania Attorney General Quits on
Heels of Perjury Conviction," N.Y. Times, Aug. 16, 2016.

120 Id.

121 Daniel Kelly, "Pennsylvania Officials in Porn Email Scandal Named by
Attorney General," Reuters, Sep. 25, 2014, https://www.reuters.com/
article/us-usa-pennsylvania-emails/pennsylvania-officials-in-porn-email-
scandal-named-by-attorney-general-idUSKCN0HK2QY20140925.

122 Natalie Pompilio, "Pornographic Email Scandal Roils Pennsylvania
Politics," Wash. Post, Dec. 26, 2015.

123 Steve Esack, "Kathleen Kane Lets Public Judge J. Michael Eakin's Emails,"
Chic. Tribune, Oct. 23, 2015.

124 Angela Couloumbis and Craig R. McCoy, "Documents: Grand Jury
Recommended Multiple Charges against Kane," Philadelphia Inquirer,
Jan. 22, 2015, http://www.philly.com/philly/news/politics/20150122_
Documents__grand_jury_recommended_multiple_criminal_charges_
against_AG_Kane.html.

125 "Timeline: Kane's Troubled Tenure as Attorney General," Philadelphia
Inquirer (last updated Feb. 16, 2016), http://www.philly.com/philly/
news/politics/Timeline_Kanes_troubled_tenure_as_Attorney_General.
html.

126 Id.

127 Jon Hurdle and Erik Eckholm, "Kathleen Kane, Pennsylvania Attorney
General, Is Suspended from Practicing Law," N.Y. Times, Sep. 21, 2015.

128 Debra Cassens Weiss, "Pennsylvania AG Says Email Linked to Current State
Justice Had Racial and Misogynistic Jokes," ABA Journal, Oct. 2, 2015,

http://www.abajournal.com/news/article/pennsylvania_ag_says_email_linked_to_current_state_justice_had_racial_and_m/.

129   "Pennsylvania Attorney General Gets New Perjury Charge after Secrecy Oath Found," THE GUARDIAN, Oct. 1, 2015, https://www.theguardian.com/us-news/2015/oct/01/pennsylvania-attorney-general-kathleen-kane-new-perjury-charge.

130   "Timeline: Kane's Troubled Tenure as Attorney General," PHILADELPHIA INQUIRER (last updated Feb. 16, 2016), http://www.philly.com/philly/news/politics/Timeline_Kanes_troubled_tenure_as_Attorney_General.html.

131   Id.

132   Id.

133   Id.

134   Id.

135   Bill O'Boyle, "Pennsylvania Attorney General Kathleen Kane Announces She Will Not Run for Re-Election," TIMES-LEADER, Feb. 16, 2016, http://www.timesleader.com/news/513139/ag-kathleen-kane-announces-she-wont-run-for-re-election.

136   Id.

137   Dave Bohman, "UPDATE: Jury Selected in Kane's Trial," WNEP, Aug. 8, 2016, http://wnep.com/2016/08/08/jury-selection-underway-in-kanes-trial/.

138   Marc Levy, "Kane Resigns a Day after Conviction," PHILADELPHIA TRIBUNE, Aug. 16, 2016.

139   Id.

140   Jess Bidgood, "Pennsylvania's Attorney General Is Convicted on All Counts," N.Y. TIMES, Aug. 15, 2016.

141   Hoffer and Hull, 114–15.

142   Brian C. Kalt, "The Constitutional Case for the Impeachability of Former Federal Officials: An Analysis of the Law, History, and Practice of Late Impeachment," 6 TEX. REV. L. & POL. 13, 26–27 (2001).

143   "Impeachment," PARLIAMENT.UK (last visited Jan. 24, 2018), https://www.parliament.uk/site-information/foi/foi-and-eir/commons-foi-disclosures/other-house-matters/impeachment-2015/.

144   Hoffer and Hull, 310.

145   Krishnadev Calamur and Marina Koren, "The End of Dilma Rousseff's Presidency," THE ATLANTIC, Aug. 31, 2016, https://www.theatlantic.com/news/archive/2016/08/brazil-dilma-rousseff/498143/.

146   Vincent Bevins, "Brazil's President Dilma Rousseff Narrowly Reelected," L.A. TIMES, Oct. 26, 2014.

147   Id.

148   Bobby Ilich, "Brazil Presidential Election: Will Lucia or Maia Replace Temer in 2018?" INT'L BUS. TIMES, Aug. 8, 2017, http://www.ibtimes.com/brazil-presidential-election-will-lucia-or-maia-replace-temer-2018-2576000; Matt Sandy, "Dilma Rousseff's Impeachment Is the Start of Brazil's Crisis—Not the End," TIME, Sep. 1, 2016, http://time.com/4476011/brazil-dilma-rousseff-crisis-impeachment/.

149 Simon Romero, "Dilma Rousseff Is Ousted as Brazil's President in Impeachment Vote," N.Y. TIMES, Aug. 31, 2016.

150 Krishnadev Calamur and Marina Koren, "The End of Dilma Rousseff's Presidency," THE ATLANTIC, Aug. 31, 2016, https://www.theatlantic.com/news/archive/2016/08/brazil-dilma-rousseff/498143/.

151 Anthony Boadle and Ricardo Brito, "Brazil Electoral Court Dismisses Case That Could Have Ousted President," REUTERS, Jun. 9, 2017.

152 Id.

153 "Profile: South Korean President Park Guen-Hye," BBC NEWS, Mar. 10, 2017, http://www.bbc.com/news/world-asia-20787271.

154 Id.; "Choi-gate: South Korean President's Approval Rating Tanks at 4%," THE GUARDIAN, Nov. 24, 2016, https://www.theguardian.com/world/2016/nov/25/choi-gate-south-korean-presidents-approval-rating-tanks-at-4.

155 Ben Westcott, "South Koren President Park: 'All of This . . . Is My Fault,'" CNN.COM, Nov. 4, 2016, http://www.cnn.com/2016/11/03/asia/south-korea-president-park-apology/index.html.

156 Euan McKirdy, Paula Hancocks and K. J. Kwon, "South Korea's Parliament Votes to Impeach President Park Geun-hye," CNN.COM, Dec. 9, 2016, http://www.cnn.com/2016/12/09/asia/south-korea-park-geun-hye-impeachment-vote/index.html.

157 Id.

158 Id.

159 Matt Stiles, "South Korea's President Is Removed from Office as Court Upholds Her Impeachment," L.A. TIMES, Mar. 9, 2017, http://www.latimes.com/world/asia/la-fg-south-korea-park-impeach-2017-story.html.

160 Russian Constit. art. 93(3).

161 Richard Boudreaux, "Yeltsin Pleads for Time to Make Deal: Russia: In a Surprise Appearance before Lawmakers, He Asks for Talks with Chairman, Others. The Congress, after Rejecting Impeachment Bid, Reconvenes Today," L.A. TIMES, Mar. 28, 1993.

162 Michael A. Hiltzik, "Yeltsin Dissolves Parliament; Defiant Members Impeach Him in Showdown: Russia: President's Decree Plunges Nation into Deepest Crisis Since 1991 Coup Attempt. The Armed Forces Pledge Neutrality, and the Streets of Moscow Remain Calm," L.A. TIMES, Sep. 22, 1993.

163 Id.

164 Michael Wines, "Drive to Impeach Russian President Dies in Parliament," N.Y. TIMES, May 16, 1999.

165 Celestine Bohlen, "Yeltsin Resigns: The Overview; Yeltsin Resigns, Naming Putin as Acting President to Run in March Election," N.Y. TIMES, Jan. 1, 2000.

166 Id.

167 Id.

168 "Peru Launches Impeachment Proceedings against President Kuczynski," L.A. TIMES, Dec. 15, 2017.

169 Id.

170 Marco Aquino and Teresa Cespedes, "UPDATE 3—Peru's President Says He Won't Resign over Odebrecht Payments," CNBC, Dec. 15, 2017.

171   Simeon Tegel, "Peru's President Survives Impeachment Vote over Corruption Charges," WASH. POST, Dec. 22, 2017.

172   Andrea Zarate and Sewell Chan, "Peru's President Pardons Alberto Fujimori, Enraging Critics," N.Y. TIMES, Dec. 24, 2017.

Chapter 8

1   "Trump Elected to Shake Things Up," BALTIMORE SUN, Apr. 6, 2017, http://www.baltimoresun.com/bs-ed-trump-letter-20170405-story.html.

2   *See* generally, Stephen Skowronek, *The Politics Presidents Make: Leadership from John Adams to Bill Clinton* (1997).

3   U.S. Const., amend. XXV.

4   Alan Rappeport, "Trump's Unreleased Taxes Threaten yet Another Campaign Promise," N.Y. TIMES, Apr. 17, 2017, https://www.nytimes.com/2017/04/17/us/politics/tax-code-overhaul-trump.html.

5   "Donald Trump: A List of Potential Conflicts of Interest," BBC NEWS, Apr. 18, 2017, http://www.bbc.com/news/world-us-canada-38069298.

6   Ted Venetoulis and Thomas D'Alesandro, "Follow the Money: Demand Trump's Taxes," BALTIMORE SUN, Mar. 8, 2017.

7   Charlie Savage, "What Is Obstruction of Justice? An Often Murky Crime, Explained," N.Y. TIMES, May 16, 2017, https://www.nytimes.com/2017/05/16/us/politics/obstruction-of-justice-explained-russia-investigation.html.

8   Charlie Savage, "Trump, Comey and Obstruction of Justice: A Primer," N.Y. TIMES, June 8, 2017, https://www.nytimes.com/2017/06/08/us/politics/obstruction-of-justice-trump-comey.html.

9   Margaret Hartmann, "19 Times President Trump May Have Obstructed Justice," NEW YORK MAGAZINE, Dec. 5, 2017.

10   Jeremy Stahl, "Criminal Pardon," SLATE, July 21, 2017, http://www.slate.com/articles/news_and_politics/jurisprudence/2017/07/donald_trump_could_be_prosecuted_for_abusing_his_pardon_power.html.

11   Matt Viser, "Trump Has Been Sued 134 Times in Federal Court Since Inauguration," BOSTON GLOBE, May 5, 2017, https://www.bostonglobe.com/news/politics/2017/05/05/trump-has-been-sued-times-federal-court-since-inauguration-day/E4AqZBYaKYHtzwfQ3k9hdM/story.html.

12   Anna North, "How One Woman's Defamation Suit Could Shine a Light on Trump's Sexual Assault Allegations," Vox, Oct. 17, 2017, https://www.vox.com/identities/2017/10/17/16483946/summer-zervos-donald-trump-defamation-lawsuit-subpoena; Doug Stanglin, "Trump Settles Fraud Case against Trump University for $25M," USA TODAY, Nov. 18, 2016, https://www.usatoday.com/story/news/2016/11/18/reports-trump-nears-settlement-trump-u-fraud-case/94068946/.

13   Nick Penzenstadler et al., "Donald Trump: Three Decades, 4,095 Lawsuits," USA TODAY (last visited Jan. 30, 2018), https://www.usatoday.com/pages/interactives/trump-lawsuits/.

14   Nick Penzenstadler and John Kelly, "How 75 Pending Lawsuits Could Distract a Donald Trump Presidency," USA TODAY (last visited Jan. 30, 2018), https://www.usatoday.com/story/news/politics/elections/2016/10/25/pending-lawsuits-donald-trump-presidency/92666382/.

15   Matt Viser, "Trump Has Been Sued 134 Times in Federal Court since Inauguration," Boston Globe, May 5, 2017, https://www.bostonglobe.com/news/politics/2017/05/05/trump-has-been-sued-times-federal-court-since-inauguration-day/E4AqZBYaKYHtzwfQ3k9hdM/story.html.

16   Sheelah Kolhatkar, "Are the Emoluments Lawsuits Filed against President Trump Dead?," The New Yorker, Oct. 19, 2017, https://www.newyorker.com/news/news-desk/are-the-emoluments-lawsuits-filed-against-president-trump-dead.

17   Rebekah Entralgo, "Trump Sued for Allegedly Violating Presidential Records Act," NPR, June 22, 2017, https://www.npr.org/sections/thetwo-way/2017/06/22/533977417/trump-sued-for-allegedly-violating-presidential-records-act.

18   Charlie Savage, "Twitter Users Blocked by Trump File Lawsuit," N.Y. Times, July 11, 2017, https://www.nytimes.com/2017/07/11/us/politics/trump-twitter-users-lawsuit.html.

19   Josh Blackman and Seth Barrett Tillman, "The Emoluments Clauses Litigation, Part 4—An Emolument Is the 'Profit Derived from a Discharge of the Duties of the Office," Wash. Post (Opinion), Sep. 29, 2017, https://www.washingtonpost.com/news/volokh-conspiracy/wp/2017/09/29/the-emoluments-clauses-litigation-part-4-an-emolument-is-the-profit-derived-from-a-discharge-of-the-duties-of-the-office/?utm_term=.a4959cda846c.

20   Gary J. Edies, "Service on Federal Advisory Committees: A Case Study of OLC's Little-Known Emoluments Clause Jurisprudence," 58 Admin. L. Rev. 1 (2006); Seth Barrett Tillman, "The Original Public Meaning of the Foreign Emoluments Clause: A Reply to Professor Zephyr Teachout," 107 Nw. U. L. Rev. (Colloquy) 180 (2013).

21   U.S. Constit. art. II, § 1, cl. 7.

22   Id.

23   Michael Muskal, "Obama Wants FBI's Robert Mueller to Stay on 2 Extra Years," L.A. Times, May 12, 2011, http://articles.latimes.com/2011/may/12/news/la-pn-robert-mueller-fbi-director-20110512.

24   Matea Gold et al., "New Special Counsel Robert Mueller Has History of Standing Up to the White House," Wash. Post, May 17, 2017, https://www.washingtonpost.com/politics/new-special-counsel-robert-mueller-has-history-of-standing-up-to-the-white-house/2017/05/17/30ce58c4-3b4c-11e7-8854-21f359183e8c_story.html?utm_term=.60b66e05d0ff.

25   "James Comey" (last visited Jan. 31, 2018), https://georgewbush-whitehouse.archives.gov/government/comey-bio.html; Nicholas Schmidle, "James Comey's Intellectual History," The New Yorker, June 7, 2017, https://www.newyorker.com/news/news-desk/james-comeys-intellectual-history.

26   Mark Landler et al., "Loretta Lynch to Accept FBI Recommendations in Clinton Email Inquiry," N.Y. Times, July 1, 2016, https://www.nytimes.com/2016/07/02/us/politics/loretta-lynch-hillary-clinton-email-server.html.

27   Mark Lander and Eric Lichtblau, "FBI Director James Comey Recommends No Charges for Hillary Clinton on Email," N.Y. Times, Jul. 5, 2016, https://www.nytimes.com/2016/07/06/us/politics/hillary-clinton-fbi-email-comey.html.

28   Matthew Rosenberg and Matt Apuzzo, "Days before Firing, Comey Asked for More Resources for Russia Inquiry," N.Y. TIMES, May 10, 2017, https://www.nytimes.com/2017/05/10/us/politics/comey-russia-investigation-fbi.html.

29   Michael D. Shear and Matt Apuzzo, "FBI Director James Comey Is Fired by Trump," N.Y. TIMES, May 9, 2017, https://www.nytimes.com/2017/05/09/us/politics/james-comey-fired-fbi.html.

30   Candice Norwood and Elaine Godfrey, "Rosenstein's Case against Comey, Annotated," THE ATLANTIC, May 10, 2017, https://www.theatlantic.com/politics/archive/2017/05/rosenstein-letter-annotated/526116/.

31   Dan Merica, "How Trump Has Disparaged the Russia Investigation," CNN, Dec. 1, 2017, https://www.cnn.com/2017/12/01/politics/trump-russia-investigation/index.html.

32   "Full Text: James Comey Testimony Transcript on Trump and Russia," POLITICO, June 8, 2017, https://www.politico.com/story/2017/06/08/full-text-james-comey-trump-russia-testimony-239295.

33   Margaret Hartmann, "19 Times President Trump May Have Obstructed Justice," NEW YORK MAGAZINE, Dec. 5, 2017, http://nymag.com/daily/intelligencer/article/times-president-trump-obstructed-justice.html.

34   Jason Le Miere, "Trump Impeachment Articles Introduced by Six Democrats Calling for Hearings to Begin Immediately," NEWSWEEK, Nov. 15, 2017, http://www.newsweek.com/trump-impeachment-articles-democrats-president-711525.

35   Claire Allbright, "U.S. Rep. Al Green Push for Trump's Impeachment Dies in Lopsided 364–58 Vote," THE TEXAS TRIBUNE, Dec. 6, 2017, https://www.texastribune.org/2017/12/06/us-rep-al-green-begins-bid-force-impeachment-vote-us-house-floor/.

36   28 C.F.R § 600.7.

37   Erin Kelly and Kevin Johnson, "Rod Rosenstein, Deput Attorney General, Sees No Reason to Dismiss Robert Mueller," USA TODAY, Dec. 13, 2017, https://www.usatoday.com/story/news/politics/2017/12/13/deputy-ag-rod-rosenstein-face-hostile-house-panel-russia-investigation/945071001/.

38   *Id.; see also* Priscilla Alvarez, "Rod Rosenstein: I Have Not Seen 'Good Cause' to Fire Robert Mueller," THE ATLANTIC, Jun. 13, 2017, https://www.theatlantic.com/politics/archive/2017/06/rod-rosenstein-i-have-not-seen-good-cause-to-fire-robert-mueller/530142/.

39   *See*, e.g., Michael Gerhardt, "On Candor, Free Enterprise Fund, and the Theory of the Unitary Executive," 22 WM. & MARY BILL RTS. J. 337, 348 (2013).

40   Michael S. Schmidt and Maggie Haberman, "Trump Ordered Mueller Fired, but Backed Off When White House Counsel Threatened to Quit," N.Y. TIMES, Jan. 25, 2018, https://www.nytimes.com/2018/01/25/us/politics/trump-mueller-special-counsel-russia.html?rref=collection%2Fsectioncollection%2Fpolitics&action=click&contentCollection=politics&region=stream&module=stream_unit&version=latest&contentPlacement=14&pgtype=sectionfront.

41   *Id.*

42 *Id.*

43 *Id.*

44 Margot Hornblower, "Election '84: Massachusetts," Wash. Post, June 17, 1984.

45 Ray Locker, "Donald Trump, Richard Nixon, and Watergate: What's the same and What's Different," USA Today, May 10, 2017, https://www. usatoday.com/story/news/politics/onpolitics/2017/05/10/trump-nixon-and-watergate-same--different/101506662/.

46 *Id.*

47 "The Complete Watergate Timeline (It Took Longer than You Realize)," PBS Newshour, May 30, 2017, https://www.pbs.org/newshour/politics/complete-watergate-timeline-took-longer-realize.

48 Carroll Kilpatrick, "Nixon Forces Firing of Cox; Richardson, Ruckelshaus Quit," Wash. Post, Oct. 21, 1973.

49 *Id.*

50 *Id.*

51 *Id.*

52 Kenneth B. Nobile, "New Views Emerge of Bork's Role in Watergate Dismissals," N.Y. Times, July 26, 1987.

53 "Articles of Impeachment Adopted by the House of Representatives Committee on the Judiciary," The American Presidency Project (last visited Feb. 1, 2018), http://www.presidency.ucsb.edu/ws/?pid=76082.

54 Callum Borchers, "Special Prosecutors Are a Big Deal. Their Results Sometimes Aren't," Wash. Post, May 17, 2017, https://www.washingtonpost.com/news/the-fix/wp/2017/05/10/want-a-special-prosecutor-to-replace-james-comey-history-might-change-your-mind/?utm_term=.ee8a55faf251.

55 Marbury v. Madison, 5 U.S. 137, 164 (1803).

56 *Id.*

57 *Id.* at 167.

58 Brown v. Board of Education 347 U.S. 475 (1954).

59 United States v. Virginia 518 U.S. 515 (1996).

60 Andrew Prokop, "3 Potential Problems for an Obstruction of Justice Case against Trump," Vox, Jan. 25, 2018, https://www.vox.com/2018/1/25/16868268/trump-obstruction-of-justice-mueller.

61 Title VII of the Civil Rights Act of 1964.

62 *Id.*

63 "Facts about Sexual Harassment," EEOC (last visited Jan. 31, 2018), https://www.eeoc.gov/eeoc/publications/fs-sex.cfm.

64 10 USC § 920.

65 H. Rept. 111-159, 111th Cong. 2009.

66 *Id.*

67 "Transcript: Donald Trump's Taped Comments about Women," N.Y. Times, Oct. 8, 2016, https://www.nytimes.com/2016/10/08/us/donald-trump-tape-transcript.html.

68 Christine Hauser and Jonah Engel Bromwich, "From 'Locker Room Talk' to 'Muslims Report Stuff,' The Internet Strikes Back," N.Y. Times, Oct. 10, 2016,

https://www.nytimes.com/2016/10/11/us/politics/from-locker-room-talk-to-muslims-report-stuff-the-internet-strikes-back.html.

69   Matt Zapotosky, "Prominent Appeals Court Judge Alex Kozinski Accused of Sexual Misconduct," Wash. Post, Dec. 8, 2017, https://www.washingtonpost.com/world/national-security/prominent-appeals-court-judge-alex-kozinski-accused-of-sexual-misconduct/2017/12/08/1763e2b8-d913-11e7-a841-2066faf731ef_story.html?utm_term=.b647d06293f4.

70   Scott Glover, "9th Circuit's Chief Judge Posted Sexually Explicit Matter on His Website," L.A. Times, June 11, 2008, http://www.latimes.com/local/la-me-kozinski12-2008jun12-story.html.

71   Matt Zapotosky, "Prominent Appeals Court Judge Alex Kozinski Accused of Sexual Misconduct," Wash. Post, Dec. 8, 2017, https://www.washingtonpost.com/world/national-security/prominent-appeals-court-judge-alex-kozinski-accused-of-sexual-misconduct/2017/12/08/1763e2b8-d913-11e7-a841-2066faf731ef_story.html?utm_term=.b647d06293f4.

72   Jacey Fortin, "Federal Appeals Court Judge Is Accused of Sexual Harassment," N.Y. Times, Dec. 10, 2017, https://www.nytimes.com/2017/12/10/us/judge-alex-kozinski-harassment.html.

73   "Alex Kozinski's Full Statement Announcing His Immediate Retirement," Wash. Post (last visited Jan. 30, 2018).

74   Matt Zapotosky, "Nine More Women Say Judge Subjected Them to Inappropriate Behavior, including Four Who Say He Touched or Kissed Them," Wash. Post, Dec. 15, 2017, https://www.washingtonpost.com/world/national-security/nine-more-women-say-judge-subjected-them-to-inappropriate-behavior-including-four-who-say-he-touched-or-kissed-them/2017/12/15/8729b736-e105-11e7-8679-a9728984779c_story.html?utm_term=.3e53aaac7903.

75   Maura Dolan, "9th Circuit Judge Alex Kozinski Steps Down after Accusations of Sexual Misconduct," L.A. Times, Dec. 18, 2017, http://www.latimes.com/politics/la-pol-ca-judge-alex-kozinski-20171218-story.html.

76   Vivia Chen, "Can We Get Rid of Alex Kozinski?" The American Lawyer, Dec. 12, 2017, https://www.law.com/americanlawyer/sites/americanlawyer/2017/12/12/can-we-get-rid-of-alex-kozinski/; Cassandra Burke Robertson, "It's Time to Start Impeachment Proceedings of Judge Kozinski," PrawfsBlawg, Dec. 14, 2017, http://prawfsblawg.blogs.com/prawfsblawg/2017/12/its-time-to-start-impeachment-proceedings-of-judge-kozinski.html.

77   Deschler's Precedents, Ch. 14 § 18.

78   Ex parte Garland, 71 U.S. 333, 351 (1866).

79   *Id.* at 380.

80   *Id.*

81   *Id.*

82   Ex parte Grossman, 267 U.S. 87, 121 (1925).

83   *Id.*

84   *Id.*

85   *Id.*

86   *See,* e.g., Lauren Fox, "Ryan on Trump's Meetings with Comey: 'He's Just New to This,' " CNN.com, June 9, 2017, https://www.cnn.com/2017/06/08/politics/paul-ryan-donald-trump-new-to-this/index.html.

87 Sanford Levinson, "Impeachment: The Case Against," THE NATION, Feb. 12, 2017.

88 "Senate Prepares for Impeachment Trial," UNITED STATES SENATE (last visited Feb. 1, 2018), https://www.senate.gov/artandhistory/history/minute/Senate_Tries_Justice.htm.

89 "Vice President of the United States (President of the Senate)," UNITED STATES SENATE (last visited Feb. 1, 2018), https://www.senate.gov/artandhistory/history/common/briefing/Vice_President.htm.

90 U.S. Constit. amend. XXV, § 3.

91 U.S. Constit. amend. XXV, § 4.

92 John D. Freerick, "Presidential Succession and Inability: Before and After the Twenty-fifth Amendment," 79 FORDHAM L. REV. 907, 930–31 (2011).

93 Jeffrey Rosen, "The 25th Amendment Makes Presidential Disability a Political Question," THE ATLANTIC, May 23, 2017, https://www.theatlantic.com/politics/archive/2017/05/presidential-disability-is-a-political-question/527703/.

94 *Id.*

95 U.S. Constit. amend. XXV.

96 John D. Freerick, "Presidential Succession and Inability: Before and After the Twenty-fifth Amendment," 79 FORDHAM L. REV. 907, 911–12, 26 (2011).

97 *Id.* at 926–28.

98 Betsy Woodruff, "Justice Department 'Looking Into' Hillary Clinton's Emails—Again," DAILY BEAST, Jan. 4, 2018.

99 Erin Kelly and Kevin Johnson, "Senators Investigate Whether Loretta Lynch Tried to Stifle Clinton Email Probe," USA TODAY, June 23, 2017.

100 Michael M. Grynbaum, "Trump Calls the News Media the 'Enemy of the American People,'" N.Y. TIMES, Feb. 17, 2017, https://www.nytimes.com/2017/02/17/business/trump-calls-the-news-media-the-enemy-of-the-people.html.

101 Alex Ward, "Trump's Latest Tweetstorm Called Kim Jong Un 'Short and Fat,'" Vox, Nov. 12, 2017, https://www.vox.com/2017/11/12/16639462/trump-kim-north-korea-russia-twitter.

102 Warren S. Grimes, "Hundred-Ton-Gun Control: Preserving Impeachment as the Exclusive Removal Mechanism for Federal Judges," 38 UCLA L. REV. 1209, 1209 (1991).

103 *See* generally Richard A. Posner, *An Affair of State: The Investigation, Impeachment, and Trial of President Clinton* (1999).

104 Jennifer Steinhauer, "Bill Clinton Should Have Resigned over Lewinsky Affair, Kirsten Gillibrand Says," N.Y. TIMES, Nov. 16, 2017.

Conclusion

1 Jennifer Steinhauer, "Senate, for Just the 8th Time, Votes to Oust a Federal Judge," N.Y. TIMES, Dec. 8, 2010.

2 Michael Rothfeld and Joe Palazzolo, "Trump Lawyer Arranged $130,000 Payment for Adult-Film Star's Silence," WALL STREET JOURNAL, Jan. 12, 2018, https://www.wsj.com/articles/trump-lawyer-arranged-130-000-payment-for-adult-film-stars-silence-1515787678.

BIBLIOGRAPHY

Amar, Akhil Reed. *America's Constitution: A Biography*. New York: Random House, 2005.

Baker, Peter. *The Breach: Inside the Impeachment and Trial of William Jefferson Clinton*. New York: Scribner, 2000.

Benedict, Michael Les. *The Impeachment and Trial of Andrew Johnson*. New York: W. W. Norton, 1999.

Berger, Raoul. *Impeachment: The Constitutional Problems*. Cambridge, MA: Harvard University Press, 1999.

Black, Charles. *Impeachment: A Handbook*. New Haven, CT: Yale University Press, 1998.

Cerullo, John J., and David C. Steelman. *The Impeachment of Chief Justice David Brock: Judicial Independence and Civic Populism*. Lanham, MD: Lexington Books, 2018.

Chafetz, Josh. *Congress's Constitution: Legislative Authority and the Separation of Powers*. New Haven, CT: Yale University Press, 2017.

Currie, David P. *The Constitution in Congress: The Federalist Period 1789–1801*. Chicago: University of Chicago Press, 1999.

Currie, David P. *The Constitution in Congress: The Jeffersonians, 1801–1829*. Chicago: University of Chicago Press, 2001.

Currie, David P. *The Constitution in Congress: Descent into the Maelstrom, 1829–1861*. Chicago: University of Chicago Press, 2006.

Currie, David P. *The Constitution in Congress: Democrats and Whigs, 1829–1861*. Chicago: University of Chicago Press, 2013.

Gerhardt, Michael J. *The Federal Impeachment Process: A Constitutional and Historical Analysis*. Chicago: University of Chicago Press, 2000.

Gormley, Ken. *The Death of American Virtue*. New York: Crown, 2010.

Hoffer, Peter, and N. E. H. Hull. *Impeachment in America, 1635–1805*. New Haven, CT: Yale University Press, 1984.

Kriner, Douglas L., and Eric Schickler. *Investigating the President: Congressional Checks on Presidential Power*. Princeton, NJ: Princeton University Press, 2016.

Kyvig, David E. *The Age of Impeachment: American Constitutional Culture since 1960*. Lawrence, KS: University Press of Kansas, 2008.

Melton, Buckner F., Jr. *The First Impeachment: The Constitution's Framers and the Case of Senator William Blount.* Macon, GA: Mercer University Press, 1999.

Posner, Richard A. *An Affair of State: The Investigation, Impeachment, and Trial of President Clinton.* Cambridge, MA: Harvard University Press, 1999.

Rehnquist, William H. *Grand Inquests: The Historic Impeachment Trials of Justice Samuel Chase and President Andrew Johnson.* New York: Harper Perennial, 1999.

Rozell, Mark J., and Clyde Wilcox. *The Clinton Scandal and the Future of American Government.* Washington, DC: Georgetown University Press, 2000.

Stewart, David O. *Impeached: The Trial of President Andrew Johnson and the Fight for Lincoln's Legacy.* New York: Simon and Schuster, 2010.

Sunstein, Cass R. *Impeachment: A Citizen's Guide.* Cambridge, MA: Harvard University Press, 2018.

Toobin, Jeffrey. *A Vast Conspiracy: The Real Story of the Sex Scandal That Nearly Brought Down a President.* New York: Random House, 2000.

INDEX